"Doing It
the Hard Way"

"Doing It the Hard Way"

Investigations of Gender and Technology

Sally L. Hacker

EDITED BY

Dorothy E. Smith

and

Susan M. Turner

Boston
UNWIN HYMAN
London   Sydney   Wellington

Unwin Hyman, Inc.
8 Winchester Place, Winchester, Mass. 01890, USA

Published by the Academic Division of
Unwin Hyman Ltd
15/17 Broadwick Street, London W1V 1FP, UK

Allen & Unwin (Australia) Ltd,
8 Napier Street, North Sydney, NSW 2060, Australia

Allen & Unwin (New Zealand) Ltd in association with the
Port Nicholson Press Ltd,
Compusales Building, 75 Ghuznee Street, Wellington 1, New Zealand

First published in 1990.

Library of Congress Cataloging-in-Publication Data

Hacker, Sally, 1936-
  Doing it the hard way : investigations of gender and technology / Sally L. Hacker; edited by Dorothy E. Smith and Susan M. Turner.
    p.   cm.
  Includes bibliographical references.
  ISBN 0-04-445434-1. — ISBN 0-04-445435-X (pbk.)
  1. Women—Employment. 2. Sexual division of labor.—I. Smith, Dorothy E., 1926- .—II. Turner, Susan M.—III. Title.
HD6053.H16 1990
306.3'615—dc20
                                     89-16742
                                          CIP

British Library Cataloguing in Publication Data

Hacker, Sally L.
  "Doing it the hard way" - investigations of gender and technology.
1. Technology. Social aspects
I. Title—II. Smith, Dorothy E. (Dorothy Edith, 1926-)
III. Turner, Susan M.
306'.46
ISBN 0-04-445434-1

Typeset in 10/12 pt Palatino and printed in
Great Britain by The University Press, Cambridge

"I wanted to know what it *feels* like.
I called it 'doing it the hard way.' "
(Sally L. Hacker, describing her critical method)

Contents

Part IV

Acknowledgments ─────────────────────

Some special acknowledgments are called for in addition to those given to the people who have granted us permission to reprint previously published papers as chapters of this book. The Centre for the Study of Women and Society at the University of Oregon has been materially supportive more than once, and the existence of this book testifies to that. The concern of the Centre, of course, was for Sally and what she had done for women as a sociologist working in Oregon, but it remains for us to express the thanks that Sally cannot.

Our thanks too to Bart Hacker, who helped us in many ways, particularly with his hospitality to Dorothy when she visited Corvallis, with his support at stages of Sally's illness when it was difficult for her to address the kinds of editorial uncertainties we needed decisions on, and finally for providing us with references to the more obscure items in a literature that he and Sally knew in common as the background of their shared work on gender, technology, and militarism.

We want also to give special recognition to and acknowledgment of the work of Caralee Price in the creation of this book. Caralee was involved from early on in transcribing the interview material. In the final six months of putting together the manuscript, with all the contemporary technicalities of producing a word-processed typescript together with an index, Caralee has contributed very substantially and beyond what could be fully recompensed with the funds available to us. Though she never met Sally, she came to know her through transcribing the interviews. She shares our commitment to the kind of political and personal project that Sally's life and work represents, and has contributed her political sense and awareness of issues to our editorial work.

In the original papers that make up this book, Sally acknowledges the names of many who in various ways contributed to them. We recognize that this is probably a less inclusive list than she would have made and that names may be omitted that she would have wanted included. The following are those whose contributions are identified in the versions of her papers we have worked with: the women telephone workers; the *Social Problems* reviewers who reviewed her paper, "Sex Stratification, Technology and Organizational Change: A Longitudinal Case Study of AT&T"; and those who read and commented on her papers or otherwise worked with her in her research—Joan Acker, Catherine Conroy, Barbara and Ronald Dalton, Lynn Darcey, Delores Doninger, Jeanne Dost, Roz Feldberg, Mimi and Paul Goldman, Bart

Hacker, Roberta Hall, Wilma Heide, Louise Noun, Fred Pfeil, Joan Rothschild, Joe Schneider, Sheila Smith, Bruce Separd, Ed Starnes, and Irene Talbott.

We would also like to thank the following for permission to reproduce copyright material: The University of California Press on behalf of the Society for the Study of Social Problems, for "Sex Stratification, Technology and Organizational Change: A Longitudinal Case Study of AT&T" (Chapter 1), © 1979 by the Society for the Study of Social Problems, reprinted from *Social Problems*, Vol. 26, No. 5, June 1979: 539–557; Lynne C. Morris, editor of *Human Services in the Rural Environment*, for "Technological Change and Women's Role in Agribusiness: Methods of Research in Social Action" (Chapter 3), reprinted from *Human Services in the Rural Environment*, Vol. 5, No. 1, January-February 1980; Pergamon Press, Inc., for "The Culture of Engineering: Woman, Workplace and Machine" (Chapter 4), reprinted from *Women's Studies International Quarterly*, Vol. 4, No. 3, 1981: 341–353; Vivian Weil, Illinois Institute of Technology, for "Engineering the Shape of Work" (Chapter 5), reprinted from Vivian Weil, ed., *Beyond Whistleblowing: Defining Engineers' Responsibility*, 1984: 300–316; Pergamon Press PLC, for "The Mathematization of Engineering: Limits on Women and the Field" (Chapter 6), reprinted from Joan Rothschild, ed., *Machina Ex Dea: Feminist Perspectives on Technology*, 1983: 35–58; Charles E. Starnes, Oregon State University, for "Computers in the Workplace: Stratification and Labor Process among Engineers and Technicians" (Chapter 8), coauthored with Sally L. Hacker, 1983.

In addition, on Sally Hacker's behalf, we would like to acknowledge the support of a Ford Foundation Fellowship on Technological Change and Women's Role in Society and a Mellon postdoctoral fellowship, both of which contributed to her investigations of the culture of engineering.

—Dorothy E. Smith and
Susan M. Turner

Acronyms

AAAS	American Association for the Advancement of Science
AAP	Agribusiness Accountability Project
AFSC	American Friends Service Committee
AT&T	American Telephone and Telegraph Corporation
BET	Bachelor of Engineering Technology
CAD	computer-aided design
CADAM	computer-aided design and manufacture
CULA	Center for United Labor Action
ECPD	Engineering Council for Professional Development
EEOC	Equal Employment Opportunities Commission
ERA	Equal Rights Amendment
HEW	Department of Health, Education and Welfare
IEEE	Institute for Electrical and Electronic Engineers
MIT	Massachusetts Institute of Technology
NACLA	North American Council on Latin America
NEH	National Endowment for the Humanities
NORC	National Opinion Research Council
NOW	National Organization for Women
NSF	National Science Foundation
OEO	Office of Economic Opportunity [functions transferred to other federal agencies 1973–75]
OEO	Office of Equal Opportunity [NASA]
ROTC	Reserve Officers' Training Corps
SFTP	Science for the People
SNCC	Student Nonviolent Coordinating Committee
UCLA	University of California, Los Angeles
USDA	Department of Agriculture

Editor's Introduction ———————————————

On Sally L. Hacker's Method

Dorothy E. Smith

THE MAKING OF THE BOOK

*T*he form of this book needs introducing. It consists of a series of papers by Sally Hacker, introduced by edited materials from interviews I did with Sally in the summer of 1987. When I learned from Sally in April of that year that she had a terminal cancer, with possibly only four or five months to live, I thought of making a collection of her papers for publication. Her work represents a very distinctive and very valuable resource for feminist thinking in sociology. More than that, in discussion with her I had learned how deeply her papers were embedded in her life of social and political activity and in her relationships with the people around her.

We had talked once about how we had both been people who tended to research, think, write, publish, and then forget about it as we went on to the next thing. As I age, I've become more concerned to have my work known as the whole it is. I saw Sally's chances of doing the same being snatched from her, and I didn't want that to happen. Papers written years earlier, some published outside the regular sociological outlets, others presented at conferences but as yet unpublished—to lose these permanently would be a serious loss to feminist sociology.

She was already working on a book and putting a great deal of declining energy into finishing it.[1] She would not have time or energy to write the introductory material and do the editorial organizing that a collection of papers would need to make it into a book. So I thought of creating that material by interviewing Sally.

In the summer of 1987 I drove south from Vancouver, British Columbia (Canada), to Corvallis, Oregon, to spend four intense days with Sally. The mornings were spent interviewing her for as long as she was able to work. During the afternoons I listened to the morning tapes, reread the papers, and planned the next day's work. After some preliminary discussion, the work was organized first to provide general introductory material, then to "write" an introduction to each section. I devised the sections; Sally approved them.

1

Though I suggested the overall strategy for the book, Sally took it up joyfully as a form she was entirely at home with and found wholly congenial to her work and its intention. We had a great time together—I would question and listen; Sally would tell. We learned from each other; we laughed a lot.

The resulting material was transcribed by Caralee Price at the Ontario Institute for Studies in Education. Through Joan Acker's good offices, the Center for the Study of Women in Society of the University of Oregon made funds available for this (it wouldn't have been possible without their support). I put the transcribed material together to make coherent introductions, and then Susan Turner and I edited the papers and the introductory material. In early February 1988 I took it back to Sally in Corvallis to get her approval. She was quite ill and on morphine when I saw her, but, nonetheless, with Bart Hacker's help she was able to go through the introductory material and those papers that we had edited most. She asked for some changes and approved the rest. We also talked in short bursts to clarify and check certain points.

I visited her once more. She was then in constant pain and sedated. I could hold her hand and tell her that we had a publisher, that the book was going forward and I thought it an important and valuable work. I'm not sure it still mattered a lot at that point in her dying. She died a few weeks later.

HOW TO READ THIS BOOK

This book must not be read as an exercise in the sociology of knowledge. The material from the interviews is intended to locate the papers in Sally's political and organizational activities in the women's movement and on the Left. It is not intended to "explain." It is not intended to do a kind of sociological work itself. Perhaps Gouldner's (1970) notion of a "reflexive sociology" comes close, proposing that sociologists might properly enter their concerns and interests explicitly into their work. But bringing to the foreground the lived political and organizational contexts of the papers goes beyond reflexive sociology in showing the methodical relationship of the papers to a project of social action that was both personal and political. As Sally and I talked, we explored how her writing arose out of her political and social relationships and how it was intended to, and does, contribute to debate, knowledge, and ongoing organization in both organized and diffuse forms of social action. We explored how her work was situated as a "people's sociology," a sociology intended to empower through knowledge people without power and to support and to further organization among the grassroots.

The book as a whole puts together a work that is a whole. If we just look at the papers, we do not see it. The ground is integral to the figure. The book draws the ground into the text, making figure and ground inseparable. The papers are one part of a project and cannot be properly read in detachment from the whole.

THE SEPARATION OF SOCIOLOGY FROM LIFE

There is a struggle endemic to sociology between the world we put together in the texts of the discipline and the actualities of our and others' lives. Contemporary society has a special and distinctive organization specialized as management, administration, professional organization, cultural and scientific discourses, and mass media. These interlaced and intercoordinated relations I have called the *relations of ruling*, for two reasons: one is that they actually do the work of organizing and coordinating the overall societal process—they rule—and the second is that the mass of people play no part in how they operate other than as audience, consumer, marginally as voters, or as workers subordinated to their internal managerial or administrative processes.

Sociology is part of the relations of ruling; it services other institutional sites of ruling, such as health care, education, social welfare, and law, through the research and theorizing, and to some extent also in training their professionals; it researches and theorizes societal processes from the standpoint of its ruling, relying often upon the statistical data that government produces as part of its work of governing. The sociological discourse itself is based in the academic departments of universities and community colleges, though primarily the former. This means that those who are its members are for the most part dependent upon the acceptance they have within academic contexts. Sociological research funding is either from government or private foundations whose funding policies are highly influential in the general directions research takes. But it would be a mistake to view social science research as wholly subservient and conforming. It is by no means so. Sometimes sociology addresses contradictions; it is often critical. But exploring contradictions and writing critically operate within sociology as an established discourse that has already evolved its methods of theorizing. In the United States, it has largely excluded as bases for sociological thinking theories such as Marxism that represent oppositional understandings of society; it constitutes people as objects of investigation and study, as those whose behavior is to be explained, rather than, if we might imagine, explaining how the society works to the people who live it and live in it.

Sociology as a discipline looks at a world from a place that is outside our everyday experience of living in a society. Sociologists find various ways of creating leakage from what they care about in their lives into the discipline, but what they care about has to go through a conversion process to make it sociological. The contradiction for sociologists is living one way and writing another, separating, as Sally Hacker puts it, words from everyday life.

Sally Hacker's method of sociological investigation and thinking started from outside the relations of ruling and in the realities of people's lives. While she learned, loved, and was highly skilled in a sociology that was and is very much part of what I have called the relations of ruling, in her work she seeks to develop methods of investigation and analysis that make "words" and "daily life" "all of a piece" (p. 22).[2]

When you work as a sociologist, the pressures are to work within the relevances of the discipline. You start perhaps with a problem or question that comes out of some sociological theory, or with some concern you have, to formulate a theorized problem for research or thought that is made sociologically relevant. Sally Hacker's procedure is very different. What she calls "being with people" is central in organizing her research questions and problems.

> Being with people, you pick up what is really important, like the way in which the [telephone] operators would talk about—the curl of their lip when they talk about, a supervisor who treated them like a child. You can say that in so many words but you don't get the anger and the frustration. *It forces your attention away from going in with your questions, "I want to know the number of jobs now; I want to know the job structure at time 1; I want it noted at time 3 because I've got this hypothesis I want to test."* I was just hanging out with people: listening to the women's stories when they would come back from the union meeting—you know, getting put down; getting their issues put last, or ignored completely; talking to the union men and hearing their side of it, hearing the way they felt right there at the time. (pp. 23–24)

This passage contrasts methods of research aimed at testing sociologically designed hypotheses (emphasized in italics in the passage above) with a method grounded in "just hanging out with people," "listening to the women's stories," "hearing the way [the men] felt right there at the time."

"BEING WITH PEOPLE"
AS A METHOD FOR CRITICAL RESEARCH

When Hacker uses the word "hearing," she is not just talking about hearing what people said, but "hearing the way they felt." Evelyn Fox

Keller (1985), interpreting what she saw as distinctive about Barbara McClintock's method of investigating the genetic processes of plants, describes a distinctive approach that involved what McClintock called "hear[ing] what the material has to say to you" (Keller 1985, 198). In my own recent research I've radically altered my methods of interviewing and analysis, and I find myself, perhaps by no coincidence, describing what I'm doing now as "listening." "Listening" and, I take it, McClintock's practice of "hearing" don't have anything to do with mere sound, let alone, of course, with the surface features of talk as such (though my "material" is of course necessarily in words). In my own case it's an attentiveness to the shape or form or organization that the "material" is beginning to inform you about. The woodworking sculptor describes the "soul" of the tree coming to meet him as he cuts, carves, and polishes. Listening is that kind of practice—a tuning-in of a capacity to find, hear, and create a shape, an order, an organization, that releases from within the "material" shape, order, organization that is already there. It depends upon having learned (in my case) how to listen for social organization in what people say, because they are not, of course, going to tell you about what is in what they say but don't know how to talk about.

"Listening" or "hearing" in this sense cannot be described as gendered in an essentialist way, but we may see it as gendered in another way.[3] For if society has conceived of rationality and science as only one kind of knowledge and one kind of enterprise and has enforced these, then other methods of knowing are marginalized and suppressed. The enforced rationalities and knowledges have been identified with men, and men have dominated in their practice; women indeed have been silenced and excluded. We (women) have not been bound to the wheel of rationality as men have, so we have been and are in this time free to work with and free to put forward as systematic bases of inquiry, methods of knowing that have been repressed.

Sally talked about "listening" to people in a casual way to describe the place her work as a critical researcher would begin. But examining how she uses the term shows again that it is more than being attentive to what people have to say. When Sally talks about listening she means more than just hearing. For example, "listening to what is bothering people" (p. 27) tells the sociologist where to move next; it means taking up the relevances arising in the lives of people around you. It meant for Sally locating an opening into a larger problem, a space she could "hear" in what people were telling her that opened up problems and issues at the macrosocial level of analysis—what's happening in an industry, an economy, a political process.

Her project is more than a series of particular investigations responding to particular situations or organizational needs. Though she did not have an opportunity of systematizing her thinking in this respect, she was conscious of being part of building what she calls in one paper "critical research" (p. 90). Critical research goes beyond particular studies to build a systematic knowledge of society from the point of view of people. Its linkages with political organization are essential to it. The need for knowledge generated by the need to act has stimulated and stimulates new lines of thinking and inquiry and new methodologies. Military and corporate action have stimulated developments within established sociology. Critical action also needs research and a critical sociology needs linkages with critical action to develop its knowledge, theory, and methods of inquiry. It needs a people's methodology (p. 91). Without that linkage, Sally argued, both research and action suffer.

The sociological work begins with "hanging out with people" and "listening" to them. Here is where the first research questions are posed. Research is then developed to explore how macrosocial processes, the policies of large-scale corporations, the ongoing organization and reorganization of an industry in relation to its workers, and the like shape people's lives. The object is not to investigate their lives, but to find out how what is going on in the large-scale organization is consequential for them. For example, under the cover of corporate talk of the use of attrition as a gentle approach to labor-force reduction, women reported increasingly intensified and insulting surveillance of their work; under the guise of affirmative action, white men were laid off and black men or white women were brought in to do jobs that had been downgraded. Investigation picks up from the site of pain and goes after any sources that will yield a knowledge for people of what is going on, including the corporations themselves, but also what people know in their lives and what organizations working at the grassroots level know, through their membership, about what is going on.

Though the process begins with "being with people," it works toward becoming a knowledge, not merely impressions. Research is directed toward knowing what is going on among the powers of corporation and state that rules people's lives. The conclusion of the process is bringing this knowledge back to the people with whom it originated. As Sally described her experience of the process, it involved writing leaflets, organizing meetings, and so on; it meant sometimes beating the official experts out by using their kind of data in writing briefs, presenting cases, widening publicity; and it meant building toward a more general understanding of the powers and organization to provide a basis on which people might find a common cause against oppression and exploitation.

The papers in this volume represent this process. These materials are intended to bring together again the words and the living that the published texts make separate. The papers collected and connected back into Sally's life in this way are located differently in the political enterprises for which they were written, use different styles, and treat the data differently. The paper on sex stratification and technological change at AT&T was very much part of a political project, beginning with work in which Sally and Bart Hacker were involved in Houston with the National Organization for Women. It is a fully professional—and much respected—piece of work. Yet its professional character is part of the political enterprise in which it originated. Sally sought to mobilize the women's movement to address the issues raised for working-class people by what she had learned through her investigation of the company. She wrote a paper for *Ms.; Ms.* told her it wasn't professional enough, so she rewrote it as a professional paper, consulting the "literature" to find the appropriate "lead-in" (p. 37) that would legitimate it. Other papers were written with different audiences and political purposes in mind. The paper on women and agribusiness (Chapter 2) was written "for farm women and migrant women" and Sally's "fond hope was that it might be read more by farm women" (p. 39), but failing somewhere to publish it that would reach them, she published it in a feminist magazine, where she thought it might be picked up by women activists and reach farm women secondhand.

Sally did not, as some feminist sociologists have done, identify feminist sociology with a qualitative methodology. She found her exceptional skills as a quantitative sociologist very valuable. For her, the question of research modality was entirely functional. Talking with me about a later study she projected but did not complete, she said of the uses of quantitative data:

> You get that structural knowledge—you know I think "counting" is important. How many are there? How many are getting jobs as engineers? What race? What sex? What class-background? What education? How many have had calculus? So you can lay bare the system and people can *see*. You know, maybe parents will get off the backs of children who are trying to get their engineering degree and all of a sudden it's a little more difficult. Maybe the engineers will see enough to figure that maybe it's better to join with the technicians rather than put them off in their own paraprofessional society. Maybe even with women . . . I thought women need a larger view of how the world of work is changing so as not to fight merely for a place in things "as they are." (p. 157)

Sally worked all the time from what was available, what would do the job, what would be most effective in the contexts to which it would speak. When she found that numerical data were lacking in agribusiness, she sought other approaches, using the knowledge that grassroots organizations develop in their political and organizational practice, putting herself in contexts where she could learn through her own experience, as by taking courses at a community college in agribusiness (p. 38). But though she found sociological methods of investigation invaluable, she did not, as we might expect, find its concepts and theories of equal relevance.

I've often thought that her work and mine were complementary in this respect, because I have been interested in just what it is about how sociology is written that creates a standpoint in the relations of ruling and analyzes the world from that viewpoint. The analyses, the kinds of understandings conventional sociology creates, aren't those that will make sense of what is happening to people when we look at society from its grassroots. Sally was often dissatisfied with what sociological theory had to offer. When she was writing up the AT&T study for professional publication, she knew that what was needed to legitimize it was an appropriate sociological tag. She also hoped that the sociological theory of organizations that she used in this way would shed some light on what was going on in the corporations she was investigating. She was disappointed. The "organizational and *Administrative Science Quarterly* kinds of things" were not helpful. "I had the feeling that if I dug harder or had more patience . . . but it doesn't yield more than it shows" (p. 39).

I've argued that the problem she experienced results from how sociology is put together; it constructs a picture of the world looked at from the places from which it is ruled. It has to be put together differently if it is to expose the way things work for people. So I have made a project of figuring out how to write a sociology that would look at the world from the point of view of people's actual daily lives and experience (Smith 1987).

Sally, however, went out and did it and did it without, at least in the earlier stages of her work, being greatly concerned with the lack in sociology of useful analyses, understandings, even data. Yet it would be a mistake to see her work as unsophisticated conceptually. She adopted and used Marxist concepts as they opened up for her the organization of what she was investigating in relation to the people with whom she worked. Beyond that, however, she was never caught up, as many Marxists are, in forms of theorizing that equally adopt the standpoint of ruling and objectify people.

Fundamental to Sally's analytic strategies is an understanding of the world as put together by people. Her research always goes after the ways in which people are active and participate in the patterns and effects she displays and analyzes. Technology, for example, in her thinking, is never an autonomously driven and driving force.

It doesn't simply emerge. It is not operating on its own internal principles. It is carefully selected and its development directed by those men who own and manage. (p. 84)

Sally saw the progression of technological change and stratification at AT&T and in agribusiness not as some virtually natural process, but as an outcome of corporate strategies, planned and managed, and, in the case of AT&T, taking advantage of the leverage supplied by the legislation on employment equity. She did not see structures first; she saw people and wanted to understand how their lives, including the lives of those who apparently ruled over corporate processes of technological change, are themselves shaped, concerned, in the case of the corporate planners and managers, with understanding how they could indeed develop policies with such apparent indifference to those who would suffer from them.

I became curious about the apparent lack of interest or concern on the part of the engineer/managers about how their decisions affected others, or even the structure of their own profession. (p. 128)

"DOING IT THE HARD WAY"

A recurrent thread linking Sally's research practice and research enterprise is her reliance on her own experiencing of a situation as a place to start. Herself, her life, her being in the world, her relationships with people, are always already there determining the relevances of the inquiry.

You feel a part of them to begin with. Given my roots—much more similarity. My drinking companions, for example, are not likely to be academics, so it's not all for the sake of sociology or all for the sake of the movement. There's a lot of it that's fun. And I think that it makes for better sociology to know, identify with, walk in the steps of . . . (p. 43)

Her focus as she moved into a study of agribusiness was shaped by the relevances of her own life experience:

I grew up in a small town, and spent a lot of time on the farms of friends and relatives. Rural life, it seemed to me, offered a good blend of sensual pleasures, hard work, and whole tasks. As an adult, I've spent most of my life in the largest cities of the U.S. I am familiar, then, with rural and with urban living. But I wanted to know more about the transition from one to the other, and how it happened to so many of us so quickly. Especially, I wanted to know more about the changes in other women's lives in the shift from agriculture to agribusiness. (p. 69)

To explore questions that arise in the lives of working people is also to explore what had happened in her own life. Characteristically, too, when she encountered the kinds of blockages that corporations place in the path of investigation, she sought opportunities to enhance her own experience of contexts relevant to it. In Iowa, when she found that agribusiness did not maintain or would not make available the kinds of information she needed, she sought other kinds of access. Though she felt she understood the "agri" end of "agribusiness," the "business" end was unfamiliar, and she took courses in "Agribusiness Orientation" at a community college (p. 71). When she started at MIT she knew in general that she wanted to explore the "kind of blindness to people" she had discovered in her dealings with engineers and managers.

> I noticed that almost all of the managers with whom I spoke had a technical background, particularly in engineering. We spoke a different language. I would ask about numbers of people and jobs lost to automation; most were truly puzzled, and replied in terms of time and dollars. (p. 128)

But to begin with she did not know how. Characteristically, she relied on how she experienced the setting.

> I wasn't quite sure what I wanted to do or how I was going to do it. I just wanted to be there and kind of soak it up. Just get the sense of the place. (p. 106)

She was looking for a pattern, for something persistent. But how did she know what it was when she found it? Through her own response to the situation: "The jokes began to bother me" (p. 106).

When I try to describe how she worked, I want a verb like *feeling* or *felt* that is not reducible to impressionism or emotionality. The images that come to my mind are ones of bodily movement, touch and sensing rather than sight. Clearly "doing it the hard way" is an extension of the listening that Sally began with in the earlier stages of the project of making a critical sociology. She came to an exploration through experiencing. In her work, she never claims the position of observing, of standing outside what she is in the middle of. She relies on what she feels but feeling has in this context an acutely cognitive dimension, almost analytic in its prescience. The process of discovery is decisively a relation between herself as subject and a world to be known; it begins with her active engagement with it as a subject. Her experiencing is integral to the work that releases form from the "material" that is the object of her investigation. Thus, in problematizing what she describes as the peculiar blindness to people of those with technical or engineering training, she begins with racist and sexist jokes that "made my skin crawl" (p. 105). And she hears those jokes as someone who identifies with, walks in the steps of, those against whom they were made.

Her investigations go forward from the primary analytic moment of the experience of that separation, herself on one side and those who joke on the other; that analysis directs her systematic study of the cultural matrix of engineering, the kinds of personalities people who came to be engineers had, their feelings about sexuality and themselves. Investigation does not, of course, stop at the level of experience, but experience opens up a line of investigation. Investigation itself is systematic; it is important too to establish results objectively, and in her work Sally makes use of appropriate and established sociological methodologies to do so. She combines ethnographic study with a systematic series of in-depth interviews. She makes use also of content analysis to evaluate the patterns of jokes characteristic of MIT classrooms.

> I wanted some empirical data behind it, acceptable to the normal community of scholars. In a way it's like again fighting on their turf. There's danger in letting people define that. If that's all you do, I think you're down the tubes. But if you can do that *also* . . . (p. 107)

Her investigations of the historical work on engineering that came later are opened up in the same way. "I wanted to learn about the mathematics learning from the inside, from experience," she told me. So she took courses in mathematics in the engineering program at Oregon State University.

> I wanted to know *what it feels like*. I called it "doing it the hard way." I wanted to learn about the mathematization of engineering, where it comes from, what it does, how it's organized, how it is passed on, transmitted. It was after moving out here [to Corvallis, Oregon] and knowing what it felt like to be an engineering student, after I did the ethnographic experience that I then came to do the historical work. (p. 108)

I think the relation between eroticism and technology she was exploring in her later work arose also from her experiential analytic. The more formal analysis she was developing when she became ill was first illuminated by her sense that the energies of fusing with another person in the sexual relation and with the machine in the technological relation are the same. It's hard not to believe that this sense does not arise from her own experience—for she was that rare woman who was not barred by socialization from rejoicing both in her sexuality and in the technological extension of human powers (Hacker 1989, 3–4). The immediate political impetus to her investigations was the rancorous debates about sexuality, eroticism, and violence that deeply split the women's movement in the United States in the early 1980s. Her explorations sought a synthesis that she was not destined to achieve. Something was/is going on here, she knew; her acute sense of the opening up of a structuring of people's experience in contemporary capitalism proposes the multiple lines of investigation—structural, historical, experiential, ethnographic—that she knew so well how to exploit. The equation of eroticism with control over people is not just a matter of individual personality, it is a property of the culture of contemporary capitalism; it pervades sexual relationships, those among women as well as those among women and men. The organization of ruling in contemporary capitalism splits the erotic energies vested in technology from those vested in people; the former comes to substitute for the latter; the latter is denied, repressed; the personal fusion of those who rule with technology becomes an erotic of control; sexual eroticism is projected onto women, who are both desired and despised.

The movement from the analytic of experience to the exploration of properties of larger structures is characteristic of her method of investigation. It is caught, in her final paper, "The Eye of the Beholder," in the midst of a movement forward from the experiential grasp to the systematic treatment of the topic historically and theoretically. Characteristically again, her project is that of disclosing the common ground underlying divisions, divisions among women on issues of sexuality and violence, divisions between men and women of different classes on questions of sexual liberation.

KNOWLEDGE AND POWER

Sally Hacker's critical sociology confronts as a normal feature of its environment the denial of access by the established powers to information about the workings and effects of those powers. AT&T was legally required to maintain the kind of data she used in her AT&T study because it worked on federal contracts. Even so, the data were hard to get at because management avoided making them available if possible.

> You continue to be naive or whatever, but surprised when they lie. You know, some guy says, "We don't have the data" and then the data show up. That was what happened with AT&T. (p. 39)

In other settings, as in agribusiness, where there were no federal contracts, the data simply weren't available at all, or where data were available, they were denied.

> In the nearby land-grant university, a number of us researched the
> role of women and their participation in academic programs related to
> agribusinesses. We wanted the distribution by sex of faculty and students
> over these various programs and the per student budget for each of the
> several colleges. The data did exist and were public information by law.
> University officials, however, stated the cost of a computer run to organize
> the data in that fashion was prohibitive. (p. 94)

When there is information available from official sources, it must
be treated with care, even with suspicion. Information is developed in
the context of action, hence it conforms to the interests and needs of
those for whom it is developed. She quotes a farmer who pointed out
that government agricultural statistics serve agribusiness but don't give
farmers the kind of information they need about the prices of fertilizer
and fuel (p. 98). Special interests may also be at work in producing
inaccuracies, distortions, and simple absences.

Denial of information is reinforced by denial of funding to do critical
research. Her project to investigate how women and men engineers and
technicians made their living during a period of rapid technological
change (p. 159) was cut under the Reagan administration's withdrawal
of support for proposals to study race and sex discrimination. She
turned then to

> a large electronics association that funds research on education, technol-
> ogy, and employment. The guy I talked to asked a few questions, said
> yes, they did have about $6 million in a fund for research, but they tend
> to fund studies which would come to different conclusions than I seemed
> to be proposing. (p. 159)

Sally's investigations of corporate labor policies show the extent to
which the power of corporations in a democratic society depends upon
the control of knowledge and upon concealment of how their policies are
consequential for people. Information is denied, concealed, lied about.
Affirmative action policies provide the public rhetoric behind which
AT&T manages technological change and job displacement. "Backlash
myths" are spread by the mass media, presenting the AT&T settlement
as "a landmark victory for women's rights." She hears the white male
workers telling how "a white man can't get a job at AT&T these
days," blaming affirmative action for women and minorities for job
shortages created by the corporation's policies of technological change
(pp. 53–54). Similarly, corporations can represent their job displacement
practices publicly as being managed through the humane process of
attrition. Yet the actual picture that workers drew for her was of
attrition as an internal policy of increased work loads, supervisory
pressure, and other measures aimed at getting workers to leave. And

yet women were blaming themselves, rather than the corporation and
its policies.

A critical sociology (p. 89) confronts the systematic withholding of
information by corporations and professionals and the general problem
of "the social control of social research—in particular, the difficulty of
getting information about powerful organizations when those who run
them don't want you to have it" (p. 91). Because of these obstacles,
a people's methodology deploys innovative research strategies that
have been identified under various names: "muckraking sociology,"
"people's research," "insurgency research," "adversary research," and
so on (see Chapter 3).

In working around the resistances of the powerful to providing information that will enable people to know about the policies,
workings, and effects of the organization of power, Sally's method
assumes the multiple ways in which they appear in people's lives.
She conducted a kind of guerrilla warfare. There is knowledge there
somewhere. Sometimes it can be located even when it is officially
denied. But if information collected and stored by corporations or
by government is unavailable, there are other ways. Sally would
connect with networks of sources of all kinds, sampling at multiple
points the actual structures and effects of powers in which people's
lives are caught up and shaped. Denied official sources of information
about technological change and employment patterns in agribusiness,
she sought alternative resources. Given a tour of a poultry packing
plant, she heard the foreman talk about shifts to hiring women and
migrants because they will accept lower rates of pay. She spent time at
a bar near the plant where workers came after the second shift. A social
worker told her that women workers at the plant had been complaining
increasingly of bone and joint difficulties in their hands, suggesting that
"the tempo of meat stripping had increased lately." Through her political
work, she had connections with the local migrant health committee.
Through them she made contact with a "chatty" county official who
talked about mechanized harvesting; from them also she was able to get
the names of women working in the plant she was investigating and
hence to interview them (p. 97).

Sally's work is critical of the professional ethics of sociology; it
takes them as complicit in cutting people off from knowledge about the
workings of corporate and state power, as one-sided, and as failing to
take into account the ethics of the powers she sought to research. But,
for the critical sociologist, being unethical in research practice is not the
answer, because it does not address the problem of power—"Fighting
power with organization . . . work[s] better" (p. 42).

Grassroots political organizations are important sources of such
knowledge. During the period of Sally's work in Iowa, they were

important points of entry into the effects of technological change on people's lives and work. The local migrant committee connected her with workers in the plant; they had better data on the numbers of migrants in the area than government. A women's group on the campus of the land-grant university where she took courses had collected information on women's participation in agribusiness education.

Finally, of course, there were the ethnographic resources of her own experience. Along with other sources of information, she would select a site to work in connected to the focus of her interest where experience and observation would expand her knowledge of a given process. She is never just an observer. Even the phrase "participant observation" doesn't do justice to her strategy, because, as we've seen, she goes to work in a given setting not simply to observe but to find out what it is like to do that kind of work. She took courses in agribusiness; she went to MIT to study the engineers who made the decisions the effects of which she had studied in AT&T and agribusiness; she took mathematics courses for engineers at Oregon State University; and when she failed to get the funding she wanted to study women and men technicians and engineers during a period of technological change, she went to Los Angeles for a year to try to get a job as a technician in the aerospace industry.

KNOWLEDGE AND ORGANIZATION

For Sally, "being with people" as a site for sociological work means attention to the relevance of knowledge for empowering people. A critical sociology needs links to social action to develop; social action needs the critical research of a people's methodology. People need awareness of what is happening and how it is happening. Research into structures provides that. It can provide an understanding that shows common cause underlying the preexisting divisions that corporate strategies exacerbate and exploit. As a people's methodology challenges the spurious authority of the expert, people are empowered; they are empowered as the lies and concealments of those in power are stripped away and they are able to see the larger structures organizing their lives. Her sociology *is* a politics.

Consequently, her teaching was as much a political act as any other way in which knowledge might be brought into people's lives. But it would be a mistake to see her as a propagandist. In her work she seeks to know and to tell people about the actualities of powers and processes, and to give people understanding and means of reasoning about society. But this, of course, in the context of the contemporary concentrations of powers that withhold knowledge from people, is a highly political act.

DOROTHY: Do you view teaching, in some ways, as a sort of political process?

SALLY: Ohhh. Almost entirely! To take a bazooka to even the balance of power between me and what they are learning from everywhere else. So I don't feel very badly about coming on very strongly, politically. For one thing I tell them what I am doing. And I will tell them about alternatives. "So this is the way we study things like stratification. This is the way Marx studies" . . . he puts it together a little differently, a different way of looking at class. And symbolic interactionist and so on. I might give examples of each. And then I will tell them my own work, which might be a combination of methods that I think gets you . . . not closer to the truth, but gives you a fuller, richer picture/story to tell. Doing it that way, it doesn't hit them over the head—or their minds close. Yeah, it's an entire . . . it's a very political act. (p. 158)

Critical research as a politics means scrutiny of how political strategies, such as affirmative action, may be used to create division rather than build strength through uniting people in a common struggle. Unlike some of the dogmatic Marxists who were her contemporaries, Sally did not understand this problem as one that called for the burying of women's concerns with inequality in class and relegating "the woman question" to some future socialist utopia. Rather, the investigations reported in this book are highly tuned to how divisions among the people, whether among working people or among women, are put together and to how sociological work, by exploring the ground of those divisions, can help to build a common ground for struggle. In them she sees that women's ability to organize for themselves and in their own interests is hampered not only by management, but by male workers, husbands, and union officials. And though the ways in which male workers have used unions to keep women in their place need investigation, so do how the traditional family may inhibit men's ability to organize.

Her study of AT&T shows the uses of affirmative action policies against white male workers. But it also shows that these effects are not restricted to them. Corporate strategies of technological change, degradation of work, and displacement of a labor force involve women and members of minority groups down the line. White male craft workers are displaced by women or minorities; in their turn, men of minority groups striving to improve their position are displaced by women; in clerical work, women are displaced by men. Affirmative action legislation works for the minority of highly educated women and members of minority groups able to move into the new jobs new technologies are creating, but not for the mass of working people. In the investigations presented here, Sally develops research and analysis as a systematic exploration not only of corporate policies and practices,

but of the bases of divisions among people. Her research aims at a
knowledge that helps to build alliances, as, for example, linking the
women's movement, through NOW, with the union's resistance to job
displacement.

For Sally, the knowledge a people's methodology could produce
is always attentive to bridging divisions, to the search for potential
alliances, to enlarging the part a given social group might play in a
wider struggle. This is how she sees the uses of her project for a study
of the graduates of technical and craft schools in Oregon:

> Maybe the engineers will see enough to figure that it's better to join with
> the technicians rather than put them off in their own paraprofessional
> society. Maybe even with women . . . I thought women need a larger
> view of how the world of work is changing so as not to fight merely for
> a place in things "as they are." (p. 157)

Her political and personal commitments drew her into relationships
and organizations in which she found divisions and conflicts. She
understood these within the deeper division between the great corporate
powers and the powers of the state on the one hand and the people on
the other. A constant underlying theme in her research, and perhaps
more strikingly in her theorizing, is the search for the common ground,
the foundation of political organization underlying divisions. A critical
sociology relying on a people's methodology explores the structures
controlling and shaping people's lives, dividing and exploiting divisions.
It contributes to social action, depends on social action for its own
development, and, in these contexts, is itself a form of social action.

In Sally's absence, this book passes on to you, the reader, the project
of a people's method of creating a critical sociology that is both sociology
and politics.

NOTES

1. This has since been published as *Pleasure, Power, and Technology* by
Unwin Hyman.

2. Throughout this chapter, page numbers following quotes from Sally
Hacker refer to the locations of the quotes in the interview material in this
volume.

3. This way out of the problem of addressing gendered ways of knowing
without falling into the "essentialist" trap I owe to Terry Winant. I learned it
from her in conversation, so I'm not sure if I'm reproducing it exactly as
she formulates it. I look forward, of course, to being able to read it in
the future.

Introduction

DOROTHY: It's very clear that in your work you're looking at it from people's . . . from where people are. That you want to begin with people's everyday experience and that you've been trying to push the sociological and Marxist frameworks to get them to tell us . . . to tell people something about what's happening to them. Why their everyday lives have this character. But this wasn't just academic business. You had a political objective. That is, you saw this as part of a political process.

SALLY: Yes.

DOROTHY: So could you tell me a little bit about it? Because, I know you weren't taught [Sally: laughter] to do it this way, you know. So how did your sense of method and how you wanted to work as a sociologist shift from how you were taught to do it in graduate school?

SALLY: When I first came into sociology, I was so marginal. The whole thing was foreign. I was always feeling my way like a foreigner, not quite right off the farm, but out of the "boonies" of downstate Illinois.

DOROTHY: So where did you end up?

SALLY: The University of Chicago. I had never heard of it. It's interesting how you end up in the college you do. I had no idea. It was a series of accidents. There was a tool and die plant in Chicago, employing Italian workers. They were promised the world by the company should they move to southern Illinois and help set up the tool and die shop—they would have free houses, transportation, et cetera. They did that. Then they got fired one by one as the nonunion men in southern Illinois learned the skills. We had never seen the like of "ducktails" and leather jackets . . . . So Richard and I married.

Meantime all the workers had been urged back to Chicago. Richard was the son of one of these workers. He was a printer and there was simply more work in Chicago. So we went back there and I started school by television, because it was nonintrusive (this family did not believe in college for its men, let alone its women). Anyway the television blew out and I went to get my $5 back at the community college. At that community college most of the teachers were University of Chicago—getting their Ph.D.s, so there was some good "mentoring." They encouraged me to take night classes (that was, I think, the beginning of trouble in the first marriage). Daisy Taglicozza, a student of Peter Blau, was particularly helpful. So I would not feel out of place, she put me in her car and drove me through the University of Chicago campus to show me they "dressed in jeans" and so on. She said I would much prefer U. of C. to Northwestern, the other suggested option. Chicago offered one-half tuition and loans.

So I got there (the University of Chicago) and I was in sociology. I ignored the professors who would suggest that I was not really professional material. I ignored the people who said, "What you really want is a terminal master's." And I ignored the counseling, "Well, I did have a child—didn't I think I shouldn't . . ." because it sounded stupid.

What I learned in Chicago were "methods"—high-powered, sophisticated, numerical. I felt quite comfortable, because I had always loved math and physics. And so I was delighted with "methods." As an undergraduate I worked on small group research for Fred Strodtbeck. I did my M.A. with Mildred Schwartz and Peter Rossi, my Ph.D. with Alice and Pete Rossi at NORC [National Opinion Research Center]. Alice was just beginning her article on feminism. I didn't know about that then. It was methods, just learning the tools, that fascinated me. Jim Davis, I remember, said, "Each method you learn is like a tool in your tool kit." This analysis was intriguing to me. I loved approaching a problem from many different ways and using many different methods and getting the same answer. Or if someone with whom I disagreed and with whose politics I was uncomfortable said something rather pompously, I loved being able to do it better, using the same methods and finding a different answer, doing it right. I just felt good about the skills.

I had four years of graduate school and that was good liberal/progressive orientation that was new to me. One problem with little background in the literature is that so much of the political message was implicit. Small-town southern Illinois Republican was the background I came from. Mom and Dad were working class but they were Republican, and Republican meant "independence," and unions meant "bullies" and people who told you what to do. That was about the level of my awareness until I got to Chicago and had a neighbor, Helene Kolkowicz, who took me under her wing and explained that Nixon was not really a man of the people. I didn't know anything! Then there was some civil rights action on campus in 1961. There was a sit-in against Walgreens in sympathy for the action to integrate Walgreens dining counters in the South. I remember you got a choice of either going across the line and actually getting arrested or simply picketing on the other side of the street. Richard was a nice, good, fun-loving man, but he was upset with me even going to college. College and politics were just . . . you know, "Don't bring it home!" "Don't get involved!" So I was fearful that if I went home having been arrested or if I ended up in jail, there would be more hell to pay than if I were simply going to school. I remember feeling that I was betraying the cause for not stepping over that line, for not going the whole distance, because my feelings were there. So there was a little bit of civil rights education at Chicago, learning what things were about but not much. The campus was not "politicized" until much later, after I'd left. Then studying under Alice [Rossi] and looking at sex discrimination in the same way and getting those two general feelings of fairness, equality, equal opportunity for the individual going together with social structure—understanding for the first time why I had run into so many difficulties in what I wanted to do—seeing how the structure of things was related to my personal life, and how an "oppositional" politics, or politics of protest, was necessary and good.

Then I divorced—a disaster in the midst of graduate school. Then Bart [Hacker], historian and ace NORC volleyballer, and I married and moved to Houston in 1966. When I first got there I was working on my dissertation under Alice [Rossi].

DOROTHY: What did you do your dissertation on?

SALLY: I was working on Alice's panel study of all women who had graduated in 1962—high school graduates. I think it was a four-year panel study. It was very statistical. I was going to look at how work and leisure, how those clusters worked together, did leisure complement work? or whatever. Alice said to focus on one occupation and so I took "schoolteachers." So it's all about women schoolteachers who got their degrees in 1962. As it turned out, the people who had leisure interests that looked the most intellectual and who sounded like really neat people couldn't stand teaching because of the way it was organized, and they were getting out as fast as they could. So, that was the dissertation (as it happened, the group in the machine room played horses on the computer and used up all the students' time). We were faced with writing on what we had. My dissertation therefore is based on a "pattern" of differences in percents on the order of two or three (rather than on a few impressive whoppers).

DOROTHY: But the dissertation used kind of fairly traditional, sociological strategies. That is, that you were looking at variables . . .

SALLY: Yeah. Percentage tables. Building scales.

DOROTHY: Yes. So one of the things I would like to pursue is this issue of how you see the relationship between your work and your political activity. In your AT&T [American Telephone and Telegraph Corporation] work, for example, there's a way you work within a conventional sociological framework, a way you're using language that disappears in your later work. You're talking about organization as if organizations had properties recurring wherever there are organizations and at the same time you seem to be developing, within that framework, a sense of a historical process going on . . . that there's an irreversible process where you are getting real changes from one way of organizing capital to another way of organizing capital. I am interested in that kind of war going on within [Sally: laughter] your work in which you gradually break out of one kind of framework and into another. Does that make sense to you—in that way?

SALLY: It does. It does. And, I was, I think, trying to find out what was useful. Even writing the dissertation, there was a change. Halfway through the dissertation I began to shift away from worrying that I had the language right. I was writing in such a constipated fashion and when the sixties hit, I just thought, "Ffff, who cares about a dissertation?" So I started writing the way I wanted to and Alice wrote back a letter saying, "I'm amazed at the improvement in your writing style." So my values were already being expressed in the dissertation. When you stop being so uptight about "Is your dissertation going to be right?" that also lets you ask different questions. I think it frees your creativity—not to care. Pete [Rossi] began referring to me as a "data witch"—because you would see a pile of data and you would do a conventional analysis and you knew what it was going to tell you, using the upper-middle-class language analysis. I held Pete and Alice in the greatest respect. It was mutual. But people with different backgrounds, of course we are going to ask different questions.

Houston was a whole new experience of political action. The young people of Space City News were quite an education. A black guy, Lee Otis Johnson, who was a SNCC [Student Nonviolent Coordinating Committee] organizer, got busted for, allegedly, handing two marijuana cigarettes to an undercover agent. He didn't smoke to begin with and he knew the guy was an agent, but he got 30 years. So it took two years standing on the street corners and gathering signatures and visiting these fish-eyed prison officials to get any action on that case. At the same time, in Houston daily life was changing. You know, we were getting our house firebombed and our windows broken and our tires slashed; we were writing leaflets; we were working with many different people—you know, sandbagging at one guy's house—an elderly couple, "socialists," the guy was a railroad worker—because the rednecks would come and shoot his house up periodically—we'd pour sand in and seal these plastic bags and stack them up around their house. When you do things like that in daily life, I don't know how some people live one way and write another, how they separate words from daily life. For me, it was always a kind of a struggle; I wanted both to be of a piece. And then, too, perhaps more characteristic of women, you don't like those sharp separations between home and work and leisure so you are forever trying to pull them together.

So my work began to shift. I was working on a project wherein I was supposed to evaluate a mental health team in Houston who were taking care of the elderly suspected of mental illness. With all this going on in the rest of your life, the way people defined and used the concepts of health and illness was just funny. A real kick! And so my writing became a critique of "mental illness" and "mental health"—its definition, its political use. I would see something that would really tick me off, and I would want to say something—personally I was beginning to learn how to put that together in an analysis—but I would want to write also, and publish for other people in the field to share that anger and the amazement and amusement of "scientific" definitions. I would use a Goffmanlike framework on total institutions and write a kind of parallel theme for the elderly. This is back when people weren't thinking about the elderly. Try introducing the issues—class issues or at least economic issues—when it comes to the elderly! Because gerontology wasn't doing much of that either. So there is a knack to writing for professional journals without losing or ignoring your values. But then the leaflets, and the pamphlets, and the court reports would have to be written in another fashion if you wanted them to be effective.

With the sixties, I had to rethink how I was going to use all the stuff I'd learned in graduate school—sophisticated stuff for that time. It is also worthwhile; it helped in the court action cases and so on. It is good stuff; it does tell a story and you can call management on their own game because generally they had not even done their own analysis, for example, on the basis of no research, AT&T, and later, representatives of MIT [Massachusetts Institute of Technology] and the Office of Technology Assessment, still "predicted" new technology would create jobs rather than eliminate them. They didn't even play by their own rules. Nor had the organizational literature researchers—highly technical and positivist in orientation—done analysis of technological change by gender. I have nothing against using methods like that—I think it's dynamite. One more way to tell a story! You need to know the ways in which things work or what's going to be helpful. These methods, however, don't work well for investigating corporate executives—people with real power; how do you go about surveying the bank executives and people like that? All those methods turned out to be useful later, I'm not saying they weren't. But it doesn't do it all. The women of NACLA [North American Congress on Latin America] I met at an AFSC [American Friends Service Committee] conference showed me the NACLA research guide. That became my basis for researching power structures and for teaching how to do it for years.

In Houston, Bart's cousin from Chicago had talked with me at length and suggested I'd probably be interested in some left-wing or social anarchist literature.[1] He and the literature had a great amount to say. In Iowa the anarchocommunist collectives fit well with how I was beginning to see and prefer things [Hacker, 1989]. Decentralized and highly and radically political, sex and stuff were legitimate issues, at least enough for openers, along with class.

We got in the habit there in the sixties and seventies, as we learned some politics, of taking leadership from the people that were in motion—in action. When we moved to Iowa, we would hang around with the bank tellers and clerical workers, pass on the NACLA guide and our own local version, and find out what they wanted to do in this strike, or hang around with the people from the telephone company. And we would generally get in trouble with the women's husbands. I mean, they were not dummies, this *is* going to take time away from the family—it did. You know, the wife's not home to cook. Or the wife *is* there and so are all these other WOMEN, and not taking direction from the man. I was doing a lot of things like licking stamps and going bowling and getting to know the people and, I think, truly enjoying this because these are my roots as well. And it was really good to get away from campus.

Being with people, you pick up what is really important, like the way in which the operators would talk about, the curl of their lip when they talk about, a supervisor who treated them like a child. You can say that in so many words but you don't get the anger and the frustration. It forces your attention away from going in with your questions, "I want to know the number of jobs now; I want to know the job structure at time 1; I want it noted at time 3 because I've got this hypothesis I want to test." I was just hanging out with people, listening to the women's stories when they would come back from the union meeting—you know, getting put down; getting their issues put last, or ignored completely; talking to the union men and hearing their side of it, hearing the way they felt right there at the time—and some of them were getting "bumped" (the class action settlement meant that women could carry 18 years of seniority from an operator position into a craft position and bump a guy who had 10 years seniority); hearing people complain that a white man couldn't get a job those days.

So I worked by listening to the people, and going in the direction they wanted, and then trying to figure out how it was all put together. Sometimes your own analysis is better, more comprehensive, more progressive. I could see that we shouldn't just be working to get women into these jobs or into management jobs. I didn't want to work to have just a few "token" women get something. I could see that another kind of explanation was needed, would make sense—say, a Marxist interpretation—but that would set the teeth on edge with the women, both women in NOW [National Organization for Women] and telephone workers, with whom I was working.

DOROTHY: And when you say the Marxist [analysis] would set them on edge, why was that? What was it about Marxism that gave them trouble?

SALLY: We were clumsy then because we were learning the language ourselves, not having learned this in school. And sometimes we would use the word "capitalism"—you know, "This is a system and this is how it works, and there is a move to cheapen labor"—I think it was the language that we used that was the problem. They started to say, "I don't know about that, but I would just like conditions better" or, more sophisticated, a female union leader (there were very, very few) would say, "Well, that's not going to go over at the union meeting." So we tried to talk about a capitalist system without using certain kinds of words. But the more we did that, the further away we got also from their real concerns—at least what they wanted to talk about—trouble with their husband, trouble with their boss, trouble with their kids, an insult from a supervisor. There was a lot of irritation at insults or degradation of mild kinds. But there it was. Or when they were concerned with problems like who is going to take [time] off work if your kid's sick, we'd talk about equality—the boss would ask, "Since there's all this 'feminism,' why doesn't your husband take [time] off?" Now this is a couple who both work at the telephone company and the woman would have to say, "Well, I guess it is better for me to take [time] off because my husband earns twice what I do." We were concerned with those kinds of things that had much more to do with the personal lives of women. One woman who was a teller (this is in the article on AT&T) was telling what was happening to her on night shift. We were holding a meeting at another telephone worker's house and she was scared to be there. She was about 45 or maybe a little older because she was looking at early retirement. She would sit there and open mail all night—this was before AT&T had introduced automatic mail opening. At the end of the night, her supervisor (a woman) would show her this sheet with these little tally marks. She said, "What's this?" "Well that's how many times you yawned, that's how many times you scratched . . ." She felt she couldn't move. She got real paranoid. She thought they were trying to get rid of her so they wouldn't have to pay her pension. She was right. It was stuff like that that had them terrified and furious. Because you've got no alternatives. There was another woman I met after we moved to Des Moines—an older woman who lived in the country—and they gave her the option: "Well, it's women's lib. Do you want to learn how to climb telephone poles?" Well, you know what Iowa winter is like. Or, "You can keep your job, but you have to pick up stakes and move to Des Moines." So it was things like that they were concerned about.

Trying to get your analysis right *and* take direction from the women at the same time was very tricky but not impossible. We're still not doing a real bang-up job at connecting our understanding of the systemic, the macro-level processes with what happens with people in their everyday lives, though we did do a fair amount. One thing to do is just keep using examples—as many examples as possible per concept. So if you want to talk about the "degradation of work," you point out to the women you're talking to that Joan does *this* kind of work *this* year, but that *last* year it used to be organized *this* way and that what's-his-name did it at twice the pay.

DOROTHY: So after you moved to Des Moines you were more and more relating research to social action. Something like this: You'd talk to people and find out what was happening to them . . .

SALLY: Yeah, yes, yah.

DOROTHY: Then you'd do the research and then you would develop . . .

SALLY: Then look at the data.

DOROTHY: You would look at the data and have some kind of analysis. Then you'd tell what was happening and . . .

SALLY: Leaflets! Meetings!

DOROTHY: And how were the meetings organized?

SALLY: Differently in different cities, but in more or less this way—there would be a woman, or two, or three who would be kind of interested in this feminism stuff—women in the unions—these were all union women. They would contact us.

DOROTHY: They would contact you?

SALLY: Because, you know, we, the collective and NOW, would be in the news, doing one thing or another. It was the beginning of the women's movement. The media was always, forever looking. And we were always, forever saying things that they did not expect. You know it wasn't the media image. Whatever . . . people knew how to get in touch with us. They would want to talk about women's issues and they would say, "There are four or five others . . . can you come over Tuesday night?" So they would talk to us and we would talk to them. In other instances I would go out and meet with them. Women who were higher up in the union, for example, would not tend to operate that way . . . but I would make an appointment to talk with them and it was like . . . really, kind of . . . they would not want me to say too much or they would encourage me not to spread the word of what they were saying.

DOROTHY: So your collective in Des Moines would take up different issues?

SALLY: A number in the collective were working in hospitals—one guy was a cook and there were a couple of aides. So there was a hospital workers' newspaper and organizing. There was a grape and lettuce boycott and there were the anti-junior military. . . . "They" wanted to put an ROTC [Reserve Officers' Training Corps] program in from grades K through 12, which means kindergarten through high school. They had already put it into the junior high. So we had an action, which meant demonstrations, and literature review, and leaflets and all that sort of thing. There was a food co-op . . . organizing with the women in one of the banks, was one of the legitimate actions within the group. Those are the kinds of actions we were involved in.

[Sally was awarded a Ford Foundation grant to study women and technology in four industries, including AT&T.]

I shared the Ford Foundation money with a woman with an M.A. in economics. She worked with the Lighthouse for the Blind, which ran into financial difficulties and so she was without a job, not knowing whether she would have to move, or whatever. And to me, in a collective situation, $11,000 was too much to live on anyway—it was excess. So when she would try to bring her academic skills to bear on the data, it just . . . there's something about the way that traditional economics is organized . . . But she would try the curves and she would try the language—and she just couldn't do it. It's easier in sociology to get your message across but use the same language. . . . And she felt badly. You know, she wrote up a few things with a combination of some stories, which are good, and an analysis of wages and . . . it didn't . . . maybe it was my problem in interpreting the stuff, but she was not satisfied with it either. So she spent most of her time getting together with clerical workers that were starting to come together. She was trying to get people in to organize one of the banks in Des Moines and Des Moines is full of banks and insurance companies . . . but then the banks started to organize. She was trying to get people in from 9 to 5 but they were scattered too thin—I think they had just started and they couldn't send anybody out. And then she tried another union, but it seemed like nobody would come. And then finally, the Office and Employees Union I think, sent some turkey, that didn't know how to talk to women. That was some fiasco. He gave somebody cards to be signed and management started coming around and picking up the cards, so they knew everybody. And the women didn't expect it—nobody was ready for that—and didn't know *not* to give them the cards. So it was back to scratch. I don't think anybody lost their job, but we heard that people who tried to get hired after that were illegally questioned closely about whether their father had been a union member.

So, we shifted a little bit because people were complaining. And again, it's listening to what is bothering people. What the clerical women started complaining about was the United Way. You sign up and they take you in a room and twist your arm in a little way. You know . . . you want this job, you're going to sign up. They don't put it like that, but they ask them if they will sign up to have a certain proportion of their income donated to the United Way. And we had been having some general, liberal complaints about how much more the Boy Scouts got than the Girl Scouts. And I thought, "Jesus, I'm not too interested in either one." But we took it up as an issue and then we started looking again where the money came from and where it went. The town runs on clerical labor. Many of whom were earning under the poverty level. And they were still encouraged to give 1.9 percent . . . I forget what it was . . . which was more than the company was giving. So we did that kind of analysis. We had some public meetings with the media. I remember one woman saying, "Well, I'm a mother of four." And I said, "Well, I'm a grandmother." [laughter] So there we were playing "family status" with each other, which is not to be proud of. But that became an extremely well-publicized effort because most of the money was coming from clerical workers—many of whom were right off the farm . . . any job looked good. And it was going back, disproportionately, to racquetball clubs—middle-class male organizations. Or organizations for poor boys and not poor girls. And a very "hands-off" approach to birth-control clinics. So it shifted in that way, you know, without giving up the efforts to organizing. They had been sort of ineffective, maybe by our inexperience.

So we shifted to doing a lot of research and here is another decision too—whether to take what you are doing and publish. Oftentimes a publication does not seem like the best thing to do. So United Way never got written up. We wrote a musical, got it produced—with Charlie Chaplin characters.

DOROTHY: So you kept getting into the local newspapers.

SALLY: Yes, yes indeed. Taking from the poor and giving to the rich. Then, of course, we got into telling the Defense Department to bake their own cookies and we should take tax money for child care and stuff like that. It seemed easy to broaden those issues. . . . My God, you mention capitalism or socialism and you just lose 75 percent.

DOROTHY: So you're not just doing research that shows people how it works. You're also doing research for people to fight with. And you're not talking about studying working people, but about research that works for them and about research that works *with* social action. So you're not saying, "Use qualitative methods!" implying that quantitative methods aren't feminist. You're saying something more like, "Use anything you can! Anything that works!"

SALLY: Yeah. I don't put it together as quantitative versus qualitative. I went to a "theory" conference a couple of years ago in Seattle. There was a big discussion about whether or not one should use the quantitative methods—the methods of positivism. I don't care. I really don't care. If what it takes at that moment means using quantitative methods, then okay. I do think that you become what you do, and I do think there are dangers. But what it takes is what it matters. In court testimony, that's more effective—and we did this in Des Moines.[2] But if that's what it takes . . . and I find it fun to fiddle around with the quantitative stuff—it's so easy. And it immediately establishes a legitimacy. For example, I would still do that, if I were working with some of my friends in the lumber industry. If you know enough to find out that somebody has projected declining employment on the basis of how many board feet of lumber are going to be grown if you use herbicide spray and that it comes out to four decimal places, and then you find out what they entered into that equation is a guesstimate to begin with—a rule of thumb based on thin air . . . if you know enough to trace that back, you can use quantitative methods like guerrilla forces.

It's the organization of research with the context in which it's going to be used that makes the difference. You can use their own language almost in a sort of witty fashion. And you can say it straight so that anyone who is not "among the people" could read it and they are going to stop and think—unless they are totally cynical. In which case you have got power against power. So I think the humanist criticism that's been made of quantitative methods . . . there is this image of somebody on top of this mountain, rotating their factors . . . all that's true and it's hokum-pokum. Bart once commented, "If this were several centuries ago, we would be quoting chapter and verse, not levels of significance." If we were doing this several centuries ago, I would make sure that I knew Latin very well (I liked the study of Latin, anyway). And I would probably enjoy it. [laughter] You know, you grow up that way and you do tend, maybe more often than not, not to like the physical sciences and math. But every way of knowing seems valuable. To understand how it is done and to be able to do it. To be able to see through and demystify the misuse of a science—a way of knowing.

Especially if it works collectively or in a group. Because it's that process of people that I missed so much in last night's presentation [by Sonya Johnson, August 1987] where the response, the new action, and the reaction by women who spoke, was totally individualistic.

If you are doing an ethnography or a participant observation or whatever, you are going to be *with* some people. And doing things not only for the purpose of research, because you can't help identifying—hopefully that's one of the good things that happens. Having a bunch of people sitting around doing an analysis of farm worker magazines wouldn't be a bad idea, for example. And seeing what the white man's ways are.

Notes

1. He went on to get busted on a draft board sit-in, manhandled in court; his mother—brought up in a kibbutz—grabbed the guard doing the manhandling and got her teeth knocked out. Front-page stuff!

2. Except I had written the testimony and somebody else gave it and then they nailed her, "You cannot give somebody else's research as testimony." We were trying, for various reasons, to give other people a chance to do that.

Part I

WOMEN, TECHNOLOGY, AND THE CORPORATIONS

DOROTHY: If you'd been able to spend more time when you came to Toronto [February 1987], one of the things that Susan Turner and I had thought of getting you to talk about was your method. Not so much how to do the research but what is striking about your work is the way in which you located it in your experience of what's happening in the women's movement. So that your work is not a separate scholarly enterprise, but is, actually, part of a movement—your concerns with what was happening to women, and your concerns about divisions among women and between women and men workers or racial divisions. And I think that you could talk about that a little bit. You remember in Toronto you told us the story of how you had come to see what it was that the management people from AT&T who encouraged you to do the original study were after, and the way affirmative action became knitted into the corporate policy?

SALLY: So where shall I start?

DOROTHY: How did you get interested in AT&T?

SALLY: At that time [1972] the EEOC [Equal Employment Opportunities Commission] was trying to pick a city to hold its hearings in. Houston was the only one that sent a lobby to Washington to prevent this. So EEOC knew Houston would be a great city to hold hearings in. So they went down there. At first, even EEOC tended to hold meetings on women on one day and minorities on the other. So there was a divisiveness, there. Bart and I had done a really good job of getting people to testify, so we had a really good day at the hearings.

Bart and I had started a NOW [National Organization for Women] chapter in Houston and I got elected to the Board. Alice [Rossi] was one of the founders [of NOW], and she dropped a note to Bart and me a year after it was founded and said, "It's an organization you might want to join." And the more we looked at it, we decided to start a chapter. It became very large, very powerful. It started out concerned with economic issues and very left compared to others. I was the only Board member without a project and they said, "Why don't you do AT&T?" I didn't know anything about it, but they gave me this little book on AT&T—I think it was called *Monopoly*. It was quite interesting. It showed how bad they were on women, minorities, defense, and just in stratification. It tied them all together—it was beautifully efficient. You could bring them all together in working on one project. So that's what I did.

It was AT&T people who had suggested that this be a major project for NOW. There were two, a man and his wife, both of whom worked at the top levels of the corporation, not "executive officers," but on a top-level committee in business systems. They were active in NOW. They wanted us to protest; they wanted a straightforward affirmative action position, moving women into nontraditional jobs. They had some data laid out. They even had some posters made. They were real helpful. Our own friends were long-term NOW people from the working-class type rather than the professionals who came along somewhat later. We told them that the AT&T people were fine. We said, "Yeah, they're fine, they're dedicated, they're hard-working." So we would take the material [from them] and send it out, and we got the movement going.

When we began to look at their data, we could see that the affirmative action plans projected a decline in women after three years. Their data showed that more women were moving up, but we were looking at the marginals.[1] Women were becoming an increasing proportion of certain levels of management, but they were becoming a smaller proportion of the work force. Overall the numbers of women were decreasing, though they were increasing a little bit in management. So we showed this to this pair who were being so helpful and encouraging us to take this on as a major action. There were a couple more meetings after that, but they were not forthcoming. They were not interested in tackling the organization of technology, or what the implications of the shift from an electrical-mechanical system to an electronic switching system were, or in questions of the degradation of work at the craft level and whether the women who were going to work their asses off getting into those jobs would have any future in them because the jobs were already on their way out.

By that time we'd begun to become a little suspicious. As soon as we saw those marginals we'd started looking into it as much as we could. We couldn't figure out where those women were going. So we went to the company. The company stonewalled at first, and then they said I could come and visit the labs. They sent this gold-plated Cadillac to pick me up at my friend's in New York. They telephoned, "Your limousine is waiting." And I said, "What?" They said they would send a driver and I went down in my blue jeans and backpack and here's George the chauffeur. And there's this huge gold-colored Cadillac [laughter] . . . ohh, incredible!

So we drove out to Homedale and they said that they had not really studied the problem. I kept saying, "Give me your data. I mean, that's what I want—your data." They kept saying they hadn't studied the problem. And I almost believed them—except there was a dissertation in the Harvard Library where the guy had done work funded by the federal government with AT&T. It was on how you get people to quit ahead of time; how to manipulate their vacations and their work in order to increase turnover rate—it was all very abstract. So I knew better.

This one guy was showing me his slide show. He has this huge oval table that would hold 30–40 people. He's going on with his pointer and he's got these slides about technological change and so on and so forth. And his voice got louder and louder—I swear he didn't know I was there, he was so used to doing this for people—and this one slide comes up and it had the curves, the projections for what mix of skilled crafts, semiskilled, unskilled you would need in the work force given the current technological growth. It was an electrical-mechanical system, and then if you changed it to a full electronic switching system, what would be their projected mix? So I said, "Stop! that's the very data I need." And he sort of came back to himself. I never saw a slide disappear so fast in my life. He whipped it out of the machine and he put it under the table somewhere. And he said, "You know these are 'soft'; this is soft data. You know how projections are."

So they had been doing the work. It is true that their projections are "soft," but boy, they can predict . . . and they *had* the data.

DOROTHY: So all this, including the push for affirmative action with NOW, was all part of a managed process of change?

SALLY: Yes. And they had been doing it for 20 years. Some of the research was begun in the fifties in a lab in Illinois to see if women might, possibly, be capable of doing the repair work once it was transformed by this electronic switching system.

The research we did went into a national campaign. A lot of the AT&T action was nationwide, because it was one of NOW's national projects. I had to be a National Board member to be its director. And so we had a newsletter and each [NOW] chapter . . . You know, you send out a kit of materials in the form of a newsletter and it says, "This is a new action." And "Here's the data—women are thus and so percent." You know the "inequality" stuff. And then by the next newsletter we say, "There's something strange going on with the data, and we think thus and so," and then the next newsletter would say, "You know, we just discovered this is the fifth-largest defense contract." And then some people would say, "Hold it, wait a minute, this is not a feminist issue." So we were forever trying to keep the picture in mind that was developing without losing touch with the people you most wanted to talk to. Many of the working women were *not* interested in the antiwar movement. You know . . . a bunch of college kids, long-hair hippies, that were against the working people. We would say, "Yeah, but if you would take a look at what's happening to the tax money and AT&T." I think they were the major contractor for the Nike [air and missile defense] system. But trying to explain cost overruns and tax dollars and three-tiered contracting and how you can rip off people that way . . . It wasn't until David Noble's work (he was my officemate when I got to MIT) that you could see how they were affected more directly and how that would affect somebody keeping a tally sheet on a woman's yawns and scratches. You could make that connection pretty clear.

This was when AT&T stopped giving any kind of support at all (though I understand that the people who were on the committee responsible for dealing with the settlement were delighted with the results and were promoted and lived happily ever after). But that didn't stop us. We ferreted old unpublished dissertations in Harvard's Widener Library with the help of a friend who had a card; we got data from peace groups such as the American Friends Service Committee, interested in AT&T as a defense contractor. We met with and helped form networks and a newsletter among groups of women across the country who worked at AT&T, were members of NOW, or both. We learned from their experiences at work, at home (sometimes a husband also worked for the phone company), in and out of unions. We learned that the company had had such and such a proportion of craft work and that within a year, [the proportion] had been reversed to clerical work with very little craft.

Jesus, I get pissed just thinking about it. Management were slick but they were not all that conscious. The middle management in a company like AT&T would be the head of the state telephone company—which is a big business in itself. Sometimes they just wouldn't know. You would talk to them and they would say, "Automation creates jobs." It was a litany. We would say, "Do you have data?" And of course they didn't and it was an impudent question, and we knew they wouldn't give it, but it was a gentle way of "calling" them on it. They would splutter and so we would show them the data for their very own company. You just cannot keep them focused in on data that shakes their view of reality. Other people would look at it and really feel badly. But *they'd* say, "You know we were beginning to try—you know, we were *really* beginning to try." And then they would just shake their head and then they'd point out and would say, "Well, you see we are moving some women up. And we're moving some black women up." And it was true. And we would say, "But the overall . . . "

Those meetings were . . . oh, God . . . just fighting over the construction of reality. When you have what is ordinarily, commonly accepted as data and the people with power don't have it. They've got the power and you've got the data—the accepted data, the legitimized data . . . Whew! You can describe scenes like that to working women and they get a little better sense of . . . I mean nobody's dumb—*they* know there's a bigger picture and that things are moving in a certain way. But how do you deal with your husband at the same time? And deal with the union at the same time?

Writing the AT&T paper was part of trying to get this story out. After I'd gone to Iowa and was living in collectives, *Ms.* magazine wrote to me. They were going to do an article on the AT&T settlement (that was in '72, '73, somewhere around there). I wrote a story that they didn't like. They told me it wasn't quite professional. Well, at that time I wasn't going to write professional literature; I wasn't going to take the time to write for professional grant money. I'd heard all this analysis, that it's all dishonest money and this and that and the other. Well . . . along came the Ford Foundation and said that they were going to do something about women and technology. So Bart encouraged me to apply because it was $11,000 for one year. And I said, "Naw, you know Ford money, nobody wants to take it." He said they had never funded something the way I'd want to do it, and he said, "Give it a try."

The practice in writing to get access helped. It helped to write it in such a way that you don't lose your integrity, which you are not willing to do. But you are also not lying about what you want to do. So the funding came through. (I shared that with unemployed in the collectives. Because I lived cheap and still live that way.) And *Ms.* magazine wanted a piece. So I thought that it would be good to get out that story.

When I sent *Ms.* the analysis of AT&T, it was written in the style of the times, the sixties. I got a note back from somebody saying, "Well, if you publish this in a professional style . . ." So I decided that I would write a professional article. So that's what the article I published on AT&T is all about. So I sent it to them. But by that time the cast of characters had changed and I got back a note saying, "This is a little professional for our style." [laughter]

So I wrote it originally for a professional journal in order to get it in *Ms*. I thought that's what they meant by "Well, it's not quite 'professional.'" I thought they meant it hadn't been "legitimized." So I went to the library and in three or four days looked for the various kinds of organizational and *Administrative Science Quarterly* kinds of things to see what the language was at the moment, and to see what kind of insight it would give, you know, knowing what we did about how the company worked. It wasn't really helpful, but that's a good lead-in to a professional paper—that I have covered the literature. And I found some good lines there from the union, too—you know, "Those are women's jobs, who cares."

I did that for legitimating purposes, but it didn't work because *Ms*. wouldn't do anything with it after it was done. They wanted a story that told that women can get money if they protest; that women can break into nontraditional jobs; that women can move up the corporate ladder. They said that times are kind of difficult and we need success stories. For me, I think we need the truth; the stories aren't going to do you any good. But it was in that period that people were moving for more membership—you know, how do you get more women in? So they wrote the story without any attention, as I recall—maybe a line or two—about the use of women as a reserve force. They wrote it without any attention to AT&T being the fifth-largest defense contractor.

I wrote back a fiery letter to the editor—it must have gone on for three pages—never saw a word of it in print. In a way it was the same reaction as a guy at the *Des Moines Register and Tribune* when we were doing our analysis of changes in printing. He said, "Your stories are just too complicated. The public can't assimilate that." That's what most of the reporters from around the country said. They wanted a short story about AT&T and the success of women. I would say, "Don't look at it as a success" and they would get very impatient because they'd got their line already.

You know, there were women in Boston who were hired by AT&T. For example, there was one sociologist, who was doing really good work analyzing the sexist construction of the crafts in AT&T. She was action oriented, so she was working with the company to set up these centers where you would train women in the new skills. She came over one night and we talked at length about this. Because to me that would have . . . ah . . . how could you do it knowing what's happening? And she would say to me, "What are you going to do in the meantime?" She said, "Here are these women working as operators, secretaries and with five, six weeks training they can be working as a line man or switch man." And I'd say, "Yeah, but you know five years down the road they are going to automate framework and 80 percent of switch work—can't we do both at once?" So it was a difficult conversation. Her publications would look like normal, standard sociology with a feminist thrust to it. But without looking at the organization of technology or the organization of labor or divisions within the labor force that get used by folks in management, you just can't get at the true picture.

DOROTHY: So this Ford Foundation grant you applied for was to study the automation in other industries as well as AT&T? So you had actually mostly done the AT&T research?

SALLY: More or less.

DOROTHY: So then you started out to look at others.

SALLY: Yeah. But agribusiness, you couldn't get the damn numbers . . . and then the numbers wouldn't agree with each other and it was so sloppy. So there was no way to do what we wanted to do.

DOROTHY: You had wanted to do a study comparable with the AT&T one?

SALLY: Yes, and see how much variation there was by industry. *And* work with the grape and lettuce boycott people at the same time. But I didn't know anything, didn't feel I knew enough, about agribusiness—which is funny, you know, being closer to the farm generation (my parents were farmers). So I was first generation off the farm. But agri*business . . . business!* So that one summer I sat in, five, six, seven, hours a day, every day, taking courses in agribusiness. What I wanted was to do the research and then be able to go to people and say, "Look, this is what's going on." Or that "there is sure an awful lot more going on here than 'hours' and 'wages' and if we don't know that we're going to get screwed. If we don't argue, argue, bargain for controls . . . some control over technological change, we're going to be screwed."

The paper on women and agribusiness, "Farming Out the Home," came out of our organizing. We were trying in the grape and lettuce boycott to work between the small farmers in Iowa and the migrant workers. Because there was tension. It wasn't like the tension in California, you know, where you confronted the bigger growers. There the differences are just obvious. In Iowa there would be *the* big agribusiness company. In this case it was Heinz—the Heinz tomato plant for catsup and stuff. Then there would be a bunch of small farmers contracted by the big company and each would maybe have 20 migrant workers. The company could run all over the farmers. One winter, for example, the company said it was getting out of the migrant business. This meant that the farmers had to upkeep and maintain the migrants' homes—I mean their shacks—all through the winter. So anyway there was a lot of tension, but a good strong migrant-action-workers group. What we were doing was working with them to the extent we could. We could put bodies in front of the liquor stores and boycott Gallo and that sort of thing. But it also seemed a good idea to write something that might draw farm women and migrant women closer together—and that's the purpose of that paper. But there was no place to publish that would reach them.

So if it was written for farm women and migrant women, what was the wisdom of putting it in *Second Wave*? *Second Wave* is one of the first of the women's magazines, journals, whatever. It comes out of Boston. And has a nice social anarchist or anarchofeminist cast about it. It seemed to me that *Second Wave* was . . . I thought that published there it would likely get picked up by women activists who would be in that particular area—working between issues of race, and class, and gender. Oh . . . my fond hope was that it might be read more by farm women, but there is no place . . . there wasn't at that time . . . where that would be acceptable. So I figured, sort of second-tiered, you know, to get it into the hands of women who would be activists connected to farm women. Now I think that was totally unrealistic. I don't think . . . the farm . . .

DOROTHY: You don't actually know, do you?

SALLY: I don't know. I don't know. I ran into a priest at a meeting five years ago who said they were beginning to organize again along those factions and they were using the article. But that's the only word I've heard. [Chapter 3, "Technological Change and Women's Role in Agribusiness: Methods of Research in Social Action."]

I also wanted to tell people that if you start working in this fashion, they're going to resist you strongly. Now at AT&T we had the government on our side, prying information loose that's not loose in private industry. There are a number of ways in which they can try to mess up the works. And so again, to make this professional—it was aiming towards a professional type publication . . . and I should have done more of the reading on how organizations are analyzed but I just couldn't stand it 'cause I thought it was so useless. I had the feeling that if I dug harder or had more patience . . . but it doesn't yield more than it shows. I have always thought, "Well, I should have done more with the methodology paper on agribusiness," in terms of really nailing the literature down and showing, even using their own models, how to analyze the crookedness of corporations—how they lie—*that* they lie and they cheat. Because I was dumbfounded and by that time, I was many years into the movement. There was maybe that half-generational gap; you continue to be naive or whatever, but surprised when they lie. You know, some guy says, "We don't have the data" and then the data show up. That was what happened with AT&T. Or the other one who circulated the memo and said, "Ms. Hacker wants to study technological change and women. We had better give her names of companies only where women have improved their employment." A secretary leaked that memo to me. Reuther had the same problems, apparently, back in the fifties, trying to show the effects of automation.

So I thought that word should get out to people *along* with some hints on how to get around it. You know, you can lie and cheat and be as mean and rotten as they are, but they're much bigger. There's just no way that you can "out," be a bigger "baddie," because they've got too much power. It's hard. It's a lot of fun to beat them at their own game—to be as unethical as they are. Now, one time my friend, Louise

Noun, from Iowa and I were having a United Way meeting and she got up to go to the bathroom and came back and . . . pssstt! And so I went out and went to the bathroom, didn't know why . . . and here are these books lying open on the table and there was the data they *would not* give us—the amount the corporation had donated to the fund as compared to the amount the clerical workers had been "encouraged" to give. And so we each took a turn going to the bathroom, copying down as much as we could and leaving a little marker on how far we'd got. And that is what?—stealing data, getting data that we weren't supposed to have, one way or another. That's the gray area. And I don't care because to me private property in "knowledge" makes you sick. *Knowledge* of all things! So I didn't have compunctions about that. Lying is something else. Or dissembling or being deceitful. In one way it's a lot of trouble and you have to remember. And then in another way . . . you know I'm not good at that. I don't remember what stories . . . But it's hard to keep it all together and it doesn't feel real good.

But the paper for activists about methods of investigating agribusiness isn't just about how companies lie and cheat. In my experience with these four different companies the closer you worked with real movement groups, the better the data, the more comprehensive the understanding. In other words, action-oriented research gets around the problem of getting data directly from the companies themselves.

DOROTHY: Because you are drawing on people's collective experiences and they have accumulated data or knowledge?

SALLY: Yes, yes, yes. Like the guy who was telling me, "There aren't any farmers in town. You can't interview those people. You know those old farmers, they don't want to talk to you, they don't want their names being public." He was lying through his teeth. He was a manager at the Heinz tomato factory in southern Iowa. And I was trying to figure out how in the world I would find out . . . here's a bunch of farms, how would you know where and how many people are working? Given you are operating on limited time and money? But the farm workers knew where everybody was working. They knew who was hiring and so on. So that helps. And feminist groups are usually particularly well organized with information, data, contacts—can tell you who to go to interview, for example. They might know a social worker who's working up in the poultry plant up at Estherville. So then you can play the information back and forth.

DOROTHY: But it's clear in what you propose here that there is a major barrier to the . . . well, to the reality of democracy in society if there is control of information of this kind. And that the kinds of approaches you are proposing are ones that go against institutions protecting that control of information and hence limiting the effectiveness of the democratic process.

SALLY: Yes, yeah. Well put! The model I was using was a guy who was studying West Point [Spencer 1973] [see Chapter 3]. Now there are ways in which West Point can deal with its own. That kind of problem we didn't have because we weren't outsiders. One of the companies isn't named by name because the migrant woman we were getting the information from didn't want it named by name because they would have suspected that it was she. So you know that kind of ethical issue, that's fine. Nobody's got any problems with that. There's more of a problem when you're sitting in class and developing a personal relationship—Arlene [Daniels] did a nice job on this when she was interviewing military people (Daniels 1972)—and you develop what seems to be close, warm, sympathetic rapport and then you are going to write things where you clearly do not like many of the values this person holds, or systems which he supports and stands for. That's a problem but there you are. You know there are loyalties and then there are loyalties. Trying not to lie—but a half-truth, I'm not sure how better that is. You know, "Why are you in this class?" "Because I am interested in how the field is organized." I think it would be unreasonable to say, "Well, I am doing radical feminist research on men's domination and exploitation of women." I could have done that. I don't think it would have done any good or any harm. I don't think he would have cared. Because we are so small and scattered—you know, powerless, compared to the institutions that this fellow was representing.

DOROTHY: Yeah, but on the subject of gender, class, and race in agribusiness like you were addressing here, there would be concern to conceal because the companies wouldn't want the sort of thing you were able to do with AT&T.

SALLY: Well, yeah. That was another location altogether. Tied to the major point in the paper, by looking at these different case studies, I was trying to bring out—though I couldn't show this systematically—that the more sophisticated the management, the more professionally degreed people in management, people who'd been to school or business school, the more crooked you come out at the other end. The guy I sort of buddied with, he taught a community college course which was not embedded in a whole framework of sophisticated administrative apparatus, he was kind of okay. So was the guy who ran his own poultry plant up in Estherville. There again, there wasn't much in the way of administrative apparatus. The other two places were the university and the large Heinz plant. One a part of a multinational, and this other this large, large Iowa State University. It was at Iowa State where people hid the information "let's only give her the names of the companies where women have advanced." That was a consulting group of engineers at the university. AT&T, of course, was just in another world by itself—the biggest corporation in the world . . . or was. The lousy ways they control knowledge. I had one conversation with a guy who was in middle management, up toward the top of one management company. I was asking him the same old questions. You know, "Given this particular change in technology—towards the electronic switching system—how is the work structure going to be affected? What proportion of crafts, clerical, etc. will there be?" He was truly puzzled . . . he wasn't . . . you can sort of tell when you've been doing this long enough—he was truly puzzled, and was trying to be helpful—he was a nice guy.

He was in favor of affirmative action. And he said, "I don't know. I can't tell you. We've got the economist doing that." He said, "But you know, we've got the data in terms of dollars and time, we don't know about people and jobs." And that was such a mind-boggler—just how you can conceptualize people out of existence.

So I think it has to do with the use of knowledge as a tool, as a weapon, as a piece of private property to enhance your own status, strength, position. Yeah, I would say it varies by management. And it is very difficult for me to think about ethical problems with these folks.

DOROTHY: Yeah. I would like to bring that out, because it raises problems of professional ethics as a kind of censorship.

SALLY: It's a highly political issue.

DOROTHY: Yes, it is a highly political issue.

SALLY: And it is important because, like I say, it's becoming a big business and it's stifling one kind of research but not the other. You know, ethics in manufacturing napalm? [laughter] Ethics in missile production? It's just ludicrous. But still, if you think the solution is to fight fire with fire, "I can be just as unethical as they can"—that doesn't work because of the concentration of power. So it's fighting power with *organization* that in these cases worked better.

DOROTHY: But the politics of professional ethics are also part of that institutional process . . . that cuts people off from knowledge. You know, we were talking how you hoped that this paper published in the *Second Wave* would get to farm women, at least indirectly through the reaching out to activists. It's the building of those connections that seem particularly problematic.

SALLY: Yes. The "methods" paper ["Technological Change and Women's Role in Agribusiness"—Chapter 3] . . . Some people in Tennessee put out a journal of social work. A woman from there called and asked if I would give a talk at this social work conference in Tennessee. It was the Knoxville School of Social Work. And I had some second thoughts. Having reservations about the ideology of social work. But I went down. And here were people who were going out into the hills of Appalachia on muleback teaching literacy programs, particularly to women. I've forgotten what the illiteracy rate was. This was in '79 or '80 and it was tremendous. And they were doing it uphill. Sometimes teaching the woman over the wishes of the guy. Sometimes birth control . . . up there in the hills. There was a group of activists in the mine . . . in mining. There were people doing work in the cotton mills. It was a group of social workers and academic people, but you could tell where their heart was, you know it was in helping out—to see what they could do. So that was the journal that came out in. That could have been a mistake, also, because folks like that know everything that I would have to tell them. But they might be able to pass it on, you know, to people who are trying to do the right thing—to do research the right way and follow the laws and all that and work through the courts, and that kind of stuff. Which I think you can do usefully from time to time but if that's all you are going to do, you're going to be hung.

DOROTHY: So it's not just, "Here are these cases or instances of different organizational situations," which is very much the sociological way of viewing things, but, instead, seeing them in the context of the political work you were doing.

SALLY: That's the process of looking at these three articles in terms of the process of the political times and doings of the day and it has to do with our tools of trade—conceptualization, ideas, analysis, critique. Now hopefully we've been given money by the state somehow or another—it's the people's money. And hopefully what we are going to do is help, use the free time we've got. We'd be doing this whether we'd have to be waiting tables ten hours a day, we'd still be doing sociology. So you want to do something with that because you "owe." Now what can you best do? The origin, it seems, for what you can best do is to really keep listening to working people—working women particularly, whose voice has been so stifled. For one thing you will do better research. The ideas have got to be fresher. You know everybody else has got more voice. So that's the starting place of the knowledge itself. You know where you can put yourself to work with the skills you have been trained in. You know, for the people, with the people. It's listening, being with people, helping out—working women, unemployed women. Listening and being with people, you will get more of a sense of what's important. And for academics, it takes that to jar yourself out of that set mind.

DOROTHY: But you're not "studying" them, are you? You are not looking *at* working women?

SALLY: Yeah. You feel a part of them to begin with. Given my roots—much more similarity. My drinking companions, for example, are not likely to be academics, so it's not all for the sake of sociology or all for the sake of the movement. There's a lot of it that's fun. And I think that it makes for better sociology to know, identify with, walk in the steps of . . . . And then the women's movement, too.

You can use sociological tools sometimes against the powers that be that are trying to squash you and your friends or the working-class woman in general. And sometimes you can do that by using their own language against them. You see really "schlock" publications by the government; you hear presentations by the Office of Technology Assessment where they are twenty years out of date. And they don't know they are talking off the top of their head. They have no data gathered and you can come back, in their same terms, and wipe them out. And that gives people courage. You know the expert has been "DE-experted" and it seems to release energy everywhere.

NOTE

1. Marginals, in a frequency table, are the row totals and column totals that reflect the univariable distribution of each variable separately.

————————————————————————

Chapter 1

Sex Stratification, Technology, and Organizational Change: A Longitudinal Case Study of AT&T

——

*M*ainstream sociological research on stratification has generally ignored women (Acker 1973), but research on women—especially as related to employment—is deeply concerned with sex as a variable of stratification. Here I focus on yet another aspect of employment—technological displacement, or the loss of jobs to machines. The questions are (1) How are women workers affected by technological change? and (2) What are the implications for sociological theory and research?

In the course of NOW's civil rights action for equal employment at AT&T, we discovered that planned technological change would eliminate more jobs for women than affirmative action would provide. This led me to search sociological literature for explanations of the impact of technological change on women's employment. Conventional literature slights the concept of sex stratification—a hierarchical division of tasks and rewards based on sex—and so explains less than it might. More helpful are new approaches that suggest that the impact of technological change on women's work varies by the political and economic framework of particular technologies, by the stage of development within such frameworks, and by linkages between family and work.

In this paper I present a case study of technological change in one corporation and the impact of the process on workers. The research arose in response to a stalemate in legislative paths to equal employment opportunity.

BACKGROUND:
CIVIL RIGHTS ACTION FOR EQUAL OPPORTUNITY

AT&T, or the Bell System, is the largest private employer in the United States. It comprises headquarters, 23 operating companies (such as Pacific Northwest Telephone, Illinois Bell, New York Telephone), Long Lines, Bell Laboratories, and Western Electric. (AT&T also manages Sandia, the New Mexico center for nuclear weapons systems research and development.) This research deals with the operating companies and Long Lines, employing some 800,000 people, half of them women.[1]

In 1971, the Equal Employment Opportunities Commission (EEOC), urged by civil rights groups, investigated the many claims of sex and race discrimination at AT&T. It found women and minorities, clustered at the lowest levels of both management and nonmanagement categories, the victims of significant discrimination in hiring, promotion, and pay. EEOC (1971) called the corporation "the largest discriminator against women in the U.S." and filed suit under Title VII of the Civil Rights Act.

Judith Long Laws (1976) testified before the Federal Communications Commission in 1971 that, within AT&T, "sex discrimination was the primary organizational arrangement: upon this, racial, ethnic and age discrimination were imposed." The two largest departments in each operating company were heavily sex segregated: Traffic (operators and their supervisors) was 96 percent female; Plant (crafts and some clericals) was 84 percent male. Upper-level jobs often required working one's way up through Plant or through an all-male management program.

In 1972, the government required AT&T to produce affirmative action plans, with a three-year timetable of goals for employment of women and minorities at each occupational level. Management programs were to be opened to women; women and minorities were to be hired for positions previously held by white men. The marginals, however, revealed a rather surprising pattern: the plans showed an overall decline in the proportion of women working anywhere in the system after three years of affirmative action. While some women moved up, more moved out. And we discovered, however belatedly, the process of technological displacement. Affirmative action concerns the equitable distribution of workers among existing jobs. It does not touch the number of jobs available, or the specific problem of job loss to machines. The plans were legal, despite the projected decrease in percentage of women workers.

SOCIOLOGICAL LITERATURE

I explored the sociological literature on technology and workers for information concerning women's work. Here, I review three segments of that literature on the effects of technological change on workers.

Literature on Organizational Change

Until the work of Acker and Van Houten (1974) and Kanter (1975), writings on organizational change ignored sex as an important analytic variable. Current research addresses significant issues of coordination and control in complex systems (for example, relationships between size and differentiation, particularly of the management component). It has a sophisticated methodology, refined measures, and a concern for precision in prediction and explanation. Kimberly's (1976) critique summarizes nearly 80 such studies. Nevertheless, it is very difficult to discern what happens to women workers during times of organizational change. Clerical workers, for example, are sometimes included in the management component, sometimes not. One might say it is not the purpose of organizational research to tell us about women workers, but I suggest that a focus on sex and race would help clarify important aspects of the research.

First, women are not randomly distributed throughout management and nonmanagement occupations; rather, they hold the lowest-paid positions in both. Variations in the proportion of women during periods of organizational change may reveal as much about these processes as do variations in the proportion who are in management or in administration.

Second, some of this literature gives serious attention to the impact of technological change on organizational structure. For example, the most sophisticated technology produces greater differentiation in the work force (Gibbs and Browning 1966; Blau et al. 1976) and a larger management component (Woodward 1965; Harvey 1968), and most research finds that a relative increase in management corresponds to a decrease in overall organizational size (for example, see Pondy 1969; Kasarda 1974). Some studies report an increase in skill among workers as industry moves from mass- to process-production technologies (Blau et al. 1976). Here we need to ask whether women's work is most differentially affected during technological change, and whether or not an increase in the skill level of workers merely reflects the elimination of women's work from the occupational structure.

Third, in most of this research on technology, the concept takes on a life of its own as an independent variable, which may or may not cause structural change. (There are exceptions; for example, see Zald and Hair 1972; Perrow 1978.) Rarely do researchers explore the selection of technology and structure, and when they do they tend toward a management point of view. Pondy (1969), for example, argues that organizational theory ought to be able to predict optimum administrative intensity to maximize profit. An alternative orientation may provide us with a different understanding of the dynamics of technological change. I found such an approach primarily outside the conventional literature on organizations (Braverman 1974; Glenn and Feldberg 1976; Greenbaum 1976; B. Hacker 1977b; Marglin 1974; Noble 1977, 1978). These, then, are several of the intersections between the fields of sex stratification and organizational research—potentially useful to both.

Literature on Technological Displacement

Traditional research on technological displacement treats job loss, but neglects sex as an important variable (see Owen and Belzung 1967; Brunhild and Burton 1967; Harrison and Bluestone 1975). Researchers have examined the importance of mechanization of farm work (Hightower 1973; Rony 1971), but paid little attention to rural women (Hacker 1977). In the 1950s and 1960s displacement research centered on automation as it threatened craft and production work. Many authors deliberately excluded women workers. A union official reported the loss of 80,000 jobs in the telephone company, but saw no problem because "frankly . . . technological innovation affected telephone operators and clerical operatives where turnover was high" (Beirne 1965). Union-sponsored research began when male craft jobs were threatened.

Other researchers explained:

> We do not know what happened to the women displaced as clerks. . . . [Those] displaced by computers in one firm or industry may well have found jobs in other firms. (Weiss et al. 1971)

Another believed that:

> large groups of teenagers and women in the white collar occupations have much less need for jobs than do the adult men . . . [who predominate in] the blue collar workforce. (Ryscavage 1967)

Still another noted that automation, necessary for national defense, was promoted by turnover rates in clerical work, stemming from "the employment of women, who marry, have children or resign for other reasons" (Shils 1963, 305). This chapter concludes with suggestions for reducing "the chances for unionism among white collar workers" (p. 319).

An important exception was research focused directly on displacement of office workers, for example, Ida Hoos's (1960) studies in the 1950s.[2] In insurance, banking, and government agencies, computers multiplied jobs for executives, designers, and installers, but displaced low-skilled clerical workers (Killingsworth and Steiber 1966). In retail employment, Arner (1966) projected declines in the proportion of lower and middle management, but even more in clerical work. Silverman's (1966) summary of 55 empirical studies concluded that automation of physical work and paperwork would most likely reduce employment. In general, these authors show office automation boosting employment in some areas, but slowing growth rates in clerical work and in low and middle management positions. Increased employment or heightened skill level of workers, however, often masked a marked decline in female employment (Helfgott 1966).

Interest in these issues, waning since the sixties, has picked up again (see U.S. Department of Labor 1973, 1977; Goldman 1978, on retail trade). Perhaps interest flagged since displacement affected both management and nonmanagement positions alike. Again, it is possible that female jobs in management and nonmanagement were those to be most seriously affected.

Research on displacement in these highly sex-segregated industries and occupations—especially on automation of office work—was carefully done, generally longitudinal, often based on firms rather than industries. But, with some exceptions, it explained too little. By failing to recognize technology as an intervening variable it missed the key questions: Why were certain technologies selected, by whom, or for what purpose?

Converging Feminist and Marxist Literature on Technological Change

Traditional feminist theory and research on employment does note the importance of sex stratification in employment, such as the causes and consequences of occupational segregation (*Signs* 1976). Women function as a flexible source of labor or as a reserve labor army (Ferber and Lowry 1976). Institutional linkages, especially those between home and workplace, must be analyzed if women's economic condition is to be understood fully (Safilios-Rothschild 1976; Boulding 1976). But Gordon (1976) notes that this literature also tends to ignore the role of those who select technology and who organize work. Policy suggestions stemming from even the best of this research rarely deal with the occupational structure of the jobs available. Without attention to these problems, affirmative action penalizes white male workers to provide equal opportunity for women and minorities. (We shall see here that this criticism is more myth than reality.)

Marxist literature does deal with who benefits by technological change, and who pays. It explains that profit-oriented firms require a reserve labor army in order to change technologies or move quickly to capture new markets (Baran and Sweezy 1966), and that women provide this reserve (Christoffel and Kaufer 1970). Technological change may draw women in when work is being simplified or push them out when simplified work is being automated (Braverman 1974).

Roemer (1978) shows that a Marxist theory of exploitation is valid for a differentially exploited labor force, such as one segregated by sex. Feldberg (1978, personal communication), among others, suggests that since women and minorities have been treated differently within the working class, they may be differently affected by capitalist development. Sex or race may have better predictive value than class during certain periods of development within capitalism. A marxist framework offers explanations for technological displacement—explanations of a high order of abstraction that can be empirically examined—but it subordinates sex to class as an explanatory concept. Sex is important as a divisive factor among the working class, at the workplace.

Feminist and radical literatures converge in seeking the material base for patriarchal systems (sex-stratified systems in which men are dominant) of which capitalism is merely a special case. Hartmann (1977) finds capitalism to be only one form of sex/gender-based domination. Her historical analysis of home and work tasks shows how male workers and managers alike derive economic and other benefits from a patriarchal system. Lazonick (1978) notes how the development of capitalism builds on hierarchies of existing patriarchal systems.

Baxandall et al. (1976) and others criticize Braverman's analysis of technology for centering on the workplace alone. It is in the family where the consciousness of the worker emerges and is reinforced, where women's unpaid services benefit both management and male workers, and where technological change reshapes homemaking as well (Weinbaum and Bridges 1976; Bose 1978).

Articles in a recent issue of *Signs* (1977) address the impact of political/technological development on women in the Third World. Some stress sex and culture, while others stress class and economic systems, but all point to complex patterns of hierarchies, or stratification based on sex, class, and race. One may be more dominant than another, as conditions vary. For example, agricultural mechanization sometimes affects the poor, men and women alike, but more often works the greatest hardship on women (see also Boserup 1970; Leghorn and Rodkowsky 1977).

Scholars address the sources of variation. These are emerging formulations with no claim to sure answers, but clear indications of the need to address interrelationships of work and family and the political and economic systems in which new technologies emerge.

The problem of technological displacement of women workers does not appear to be addressed adequately in any of the areas of sociology that should be most relevant. Organizational research pays too little heed to the sex and race of workers. Studies of technological displacement, even when dealing with women's work, too readily accept technology as a given. Feminist studies likewise tend to ignore key questions about who chooses technology. Marxist scholars avoid this pitfall but stumble into another trap by slighting the importance of women's general social role under patriarchal systems of all kinds, and especially the links between family and work. The emergent synthesis of feminist and radical thought promises a more productive approach to the question of women's technological displacement and other problems as well.

Within this framework I will discuss employment patterns in a large corporation undergoing rapid technological change. I present data and interpretations in five major sections, each organized around a central question: (1) What was the movement of workers (by sex and race) into and out of various occupations during a time of rapid technological change within AT&T, and how was this movement related to affirmative action legislation? (2) What were the structural relationships among class, race, sex, and organization change? Specifically, what were the best predictors of occupation decline in this period? (3) What is the evidence that corporate planners used women as a temporary and cheaper source of labor in simplified craft work, as this work was readied for automation? (4) What political and economic factors affected AT&T choices and made technology an intervening rather than an independent variable? (5) How did the experiences of women workers—specifically the interrelationship between their

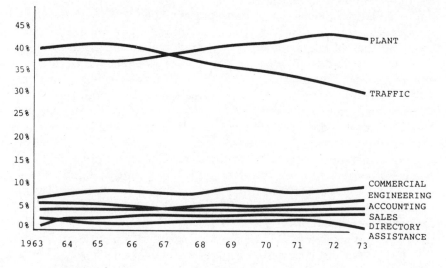

FIGURE 1.1
Percent of Total Iowa Area Employees by Department by Year.

roles of worker and woman—allow AT&T to make the choices it did?

FINDINGS AND INTERPRETATIONS: OVERALL GAINS AND LOSSES BY SEX, RACE, AND CLASS, AND EFFECT OF AFFIRMATIVE ACTION

Loewenberg (1962) showed the telephone company's shift from female to male labor: from 69.5 percent female in 1946 to 57.9 percent in 1960. He discussed the increasing skill level of workers during this crucial period of postwar technological change:

> While there may have been increased skill requirements in individual jobs, a large part of the overall increase in skill has come from the reduction of people at the lower end of the skill scale. . . . In operating companies, the upward shift has been the result of decreases in lower-rated operating and clerical groups and increases in the generally higher-rated plant crafts, professional workers, and business and sales employees. (chap. V, 44–45, 47)

Loewenberg's care in phrasing his findings should serve as a model for organizational research addressed to the effects of new technology at the skill level of workers. By showing lesser-skilled work being eliminated, and noting the characteristics of those doing the work, he avoids leaving the impression that the process is merely a benign improvement in the skill level of existing workers.

A 1964 study sponsored by the Communications Workers of America noted that all telephone company employment had declined since 1958; women had held most of the 80,000 jobs eliminated in that six-year period (Beirne 1965). The 1972 affirmative action plans for AT&T and Long Lines showed a continuation of this trend, projecting a three-year decline of women workers, from 52.4 percent to 52.0 percent by 1975. This was a conservative estimate; in December 1975, women's participation stood at 50.1 percent.

Data from the Iowa Area of Northwestern Bell for the period 1963–73 parallel Loewenberg's historical account, indicating a fairly steady reduction of the share of the employment by the female-intensive Traffic Department (see Figure 1.1). Of 38 job titles eliminated from the work force of this area office over the same period, 31 (primarily clerical) were traditionally female jobs.[3] Company and technical literature indicated that this recent decline in the proportion of female workers is due to new methods of handling and recording calls and of doing clerical work. A Bell Labs engineer reported, for example, that Customer Records and

Billing has at times made for "people savings" of up to 50 percent (see Thayer, 1968).[4]

TABLE 1.1
Occupational Distribution, All Operating Companies Plus Long Lines: 1972 and 1975

Job Category	Number of Jobs 1972	Number of Jobs 1975	Percentage Change	Numerical Change
1 Third-level management and above	15,780	16,610	+ 5.2	+ 830
2 Second level	43,168	48,297	+11.9	+ 5,129
3 First level	95,492	102,867	+ 7.7	+ 7,375
4 Administrative positions	32,716	31,181	− 4.7	− 1,535
5 Sales	5,813	6,541	+12.5	+ 728
6 Skilled craft, outside	65,107	65,553	+ .7	+ 446
7 Skilled craft, inside	76,542	78,047	+ 2.0	+ 1,505
8 General services	11,347	13,304	+17.2	+ 1,957
9 Semiskilled craft, outside	66,104	63,549	− 3.9	− 2,555
10 Semiskilled craft, inside	18,011	18,012	+ .0	+ 1
11 Clerical, skilled	82,392	97,336	+18.1	+14,944
12 Clerical, semiskilled	74,689	70,006	− 6.3	− 4,683
13 Clerical, entry level	45,140	37,674	−16.5	− 7,466
14 Operators	148,622	124,431	−16.3	−24,191
15 Service workers	12,365	11,374	− 8.0	− 991
Totals	793,288	784,752		

Source: EEOC data, 1976.

These systems reduced the need for operators and lower-level clericals. As these jobs were cut back—a job loss of over 36,000 at AT&T between 1972 and 1975—so were those of lower-level supervisors (level 4). Over 1,500 such positions were eliminated in this time period (Table 1.1). Women's positions, management and nonmanagement, were being displaced by new technologies.

Table 1.2 shows that men as a group gained 13,767 jobs over their 1972 level, while women lost over 22,000 during the same time. Affirmative action might have been expected to moderate the impact of technological change on women in this case. This was true in middle management. For nonmanagement workers, however, although some women did achieve nontraditional positions, affirmative action placed thousands more men in traditionally women's work than it placed women in traditionally men's work.

These data should counter backlash myths. At AT&T, most white male workers with whom I've talked tell me, "A white man can't get a job at AT&T these days," directing job shortage anxiety not toward economic and technological processes, but toward affirmative action for women and minorities. The facts are that 16,300 men gained formerly women's work; only 9,400 women gained formerly men's work during these three years of affirmative action (AT&T 1976). This parallels Carol Jusenius's (1976) reexamination of Fuch's data, showing that where decreasing sex segregation in employment occurs, it is primarily due to men performing traditionally women's work (for example, public school teaching, nursing, social work) and not to women performing traditionally men's work.

Men taking jobs as operators or clerical workers represent all races. They may form a new underclass, or, as female operators have described them, they may be "young college kids on their way up" or looking for temporary employment. Most likely they needed to work and AT&T could no longer bar them from traditionally women's jobs. This may be a relatively new phenomenon. Milkman (1976) suggests that men did not move into women's work during the Great Depression when the men's own jobs disappeared because of sex stereotyping by male workers. Perhaps management resistance best explains that lack of movement. According to David Copus (1976 personal communication), EEOC's attorney for the AT&T case, all management had to do to get men into operator and clerical work was lift the proscription and hire them. AT&T management has traditionally preferred women in jobs scheduled for reduction, because women had a higher turnover rate than men (Loewenberg 1962). In the early 1970s, management still strongly opposed men working as operators. The law insisted; management yielded. Management opposition appears to be fading, as experience reveals that men working as operators have turnover rates three times higher than those of the women operators.[5]

The proportion of white women was adversely affected more than any other sex/race category during these three years, decreasing by 8 percent, or 28,000 positions held. The proportion of minority women increased 8 percent (with black women showing the lowest increase, at 1 percent). Gains for minority women in skilled clerical and lower-level management, however, may be subject to the next round of automation.[6] Despite some losses, the overall share of minority women's employment has increased during this phase of affirmative action.

White men gained 2 percent over their 1972 level; minority men gained 25 percent. The overall share of employment by minority men, however, is still below their percentage in the labor force. (In 1975, the AT&T work force comprised white men, 45.0 percent; minority men, 4.9 percent; white women 39.3 percent; minority women, 10.8 percent.) While men moved into management and into women's jobs at the bottom of the structure—as operators and clericals—minority men gained at almost all levels.

TABLE 1.2
AT&T Employment Shifts: Operating Companies and Long Lines, 1972 versus 1975 Profile Data

Classification	Grand Total	Total Men	White Men	Minority Men[a] Black	SSA	AI	A/O	Total Women	White Women	Minority Women[a] Black	SSA	AI	A/O
1 Management 1	+ 830	+ 423	+ 282	+ 77	+ 55	+ 22	+ 7	+ 407	+ 383	+ 16	+ 5	+ 0	+ 3
2 Management 2	+ 5129	+ 2395	+1812	+ 302	+ 186	+ 50	+ 45	+ 2734	+ 2386	+ 246	+ 66	+ 14	+ 22
3 Management 3	+ 7375	+ 3547	+1982	+ 847	+ 534	+ 86	+ 98	+ 3828	+ 2229	+1089	+ 335	+ 60	+ 115
4 Supervisors	− 1535	+ 818	+ 607	+ 111	+ 82	+ 9	+ 9	− 2353	− 3105	+ 480	+ 202	+ 35	+ 35
5 Sales	+ 728	− 161	− 360	+ 133	+ 49	+ 10	+ 7	+ 889	+ 628	+ 207	+ 49	+ 8	− 3
Skilled craft													
6 Outside	+ 446	− 84	−1830	+ 832	+ 780	+ 65	+ 69	+ 530	+ 441	+ 45	+ 35	+ 8	+ 1
7 Inside	+ 1505	− 2409	−3486	+ 537	+ 478	+ 85	− 23	+ 3914	+ 3246	+ 467	+ 151	+ 34	+ 16
8 General services	+ 1957	+ 360	+ 193	+ 50	+ 82	+ 6	+ 29	+ 1597	+ 1149	+ 347	+ 86	+ 6	+ 9
Semiskilled craft													
9 Outside	− 2555	− 3735	−3672	− 482	+ 282	+ 93	+ 44	+ 1180	+ 969	+ 136	+ 55	+ 12	+ 8
10 Inside	+ 1	− 2185	−1143	− 722	− 269	− 11	− 40	+ 2186	+ 1575	+ 394	+ 163	+ 17	+ 37
Clerical													
11 Skilled	+14944	+ 4220	+3164	+ 494	+ 427	+ 35	+ 100	+10724	+ 4514	+4049	+1580	+ 199	+ 382
12 Semiskilled	− 4683	+ 3953	+2967	+ 570	+ 304	+ 8	+ 104	− 8636	−11068	+1611	+ 466	+ 65	+ 290
13 Entry	− 7466	+ 2536	+2119	+ 181	+ 188	+ 9	+ 57	−10002	− 8282	−1623	− 162	+ 11	+ 54
14 Operators	−24191	+ 4867	+3696	+ 529	+ 539	+ 43	+ 60	−29058	−23058	−6550	+ 306	+121	+ 123
15 Service workers	− 991	− 778	− 103	− 705	+ 22	+ 3	+ 5	− 213	− 204	− 101	+ 79	+ 2	+ 11
Grand total	− 8506	+13767	+6228	+2754	+3719	+495	+571	−22273	−28197	+ 813	+3416	+592	+1103
Percentage change	−	+ 1.8	+ 1.8		+ 24.6					− 8.4		+ 7.5		

Source: EEOC data, 1976.
[a] SSA = Spanish American; AI = American Indian; A/O = American Oriental.

In terms of numbers of jobs, men benefited more than women by technological change and by affirmative action. But it is clear that some suffered. Many traditionally male jobs were eliminated, especially at the semiskilled craft levels. At skilled craft levels, there are thousands fewer white male workers than there were, and thousands more minority males in these positions. There are also far fewer men (minority and white, but especially fewer blacks and Chicanos) in semiskilled jobs. Many of these positions are now filled by women.

Men who had aspired to craft jobs cannot be expected to view affirmative action with pleasure, despite gains for their group as a whole in higher-level management or lower-level "women's work." The stage is set for sharp antagonisms among classes, races, and sexes. White male blue-collar workers are pushed by women and minority men; minority men who might have attained semiskilled craft positions are bumped by women; poor women find even lowest-level phone company jobs now filling with men; white women see skilled clerical work and low-level management—formerly their preserves—taken by minority women and by men. A very small proportion of women and minority men with higher levels of education or technical skills are advantaged by the new legislation, which tends to open middle-management positions to them, and some are no doubt advantaged by openings due to newer technologies. But their poorer counterparts—the large majority of each group—have fewer entry-level jobs available to them.

PREDICTING STRUCTURAL CHANGE: CLASS, RACE, AND SEX

Various segments of AT&T occupational structure appear to be in different phases of technological change at the same time. One can see the automation of women's work and the disappearance of women workers. Simultaneously, one can see the degradation or simplification of men's craft work and the appearance of women clerical workers. Even so, it may be possible to discern some general patterning. Table 1.1 shows the changes in occupational distribution from 1972 to 1975. I wanted more systematic information about social characteristics of occupations (rather than of individual workers) that predict declining employment opportunity during periods of technological change. Specifically, I wanted to see how variables such as race, sex, and class predicted changes in opportunity.

Table 1.3 presents correlations among class, race, and sex characteristics of occupations in 1972 and the planned (first and second columns) and actual (third and fourth columns) changes in employment at each occupational level. For example, the numbers and percentages of females and minorities at each level are correlated with the change—proportional and numerical—in job opportunities at each level.

TABLE 1.3
Predicting Occupational Displacement from Sex, Race, and Class: Sex, Race, and Class Characteristics of Occupations, 1972, by Predicted and Actual Occupational Change (Numerical and Percentage) 1972–1975 (Product = Moment Correlations)

Characteristics of Occupational Levels	1972 Predicted Change by 1975		Actual Change by 1975	
	r with Percentage Change in Jobs Available at Each Level	*r with Numerical Change in Jobs Available at Each Level*	*r, Percentage Change*	*r, Numerical Change*
Sex characteristics				
Number of females	−59**	−22	−40	−53*
Percentage of females	−44*	−19	−44*	−34
Race characteristics				
Number of minorities	−56*	−24	−57**	−72**
Percentage of minorities	−01	−37	−46*	−38
Class/status characteristics				
Class (management = 0; nonmanagement = 1; point biserial r)	37	08	−21	−26
Status (15 levels, from top management = 1 to service workers = 15)	−10	−13	−56*	−45*

* Significant at the .05 level.
** Significant at the .01 level.

In 1972 (first and second columns), the best predictor of planned decline in jobs at an occupational level was not class, status,[7] or occupational segregation by sex or race (percentage female; percentage minority),[8] but the number of female (r = .59) and minority (r = .56) employees at any level.

By 1975 (third and fourth columns), actual decline (both proportional and numerical) in an occupational level was most strongly

TABLE 1.4
Predicting Occupational Decline from Sex/Race Characteristics of Occupations
(Product = Moment Correlations)

Characteristics of Occupational Levels	1972 Predicted Change by 1975		Actual Change by 1975	
	r with Percentage Change in Jobs Available at Each Level	r with Numerical Change in Jobs Available at Each Level	r, Percentage Change	r, Numerical Change
White males				
Number	04	71**	16	28
Percentage	37	25	46*	35
Minority males				
Number	22	45*	−08	06
Percentage	41	−18	07	07
White females				
Number	−59**	−18	−36	−48*
Percentage	−42	−16	−38	−28
Minority females				
Number	−58**	−33	−51*	−69**
Percentage	−44*	−28	−64**	−55*

* Significant at the .05 level.   ** Significant at the .01 level.

related to the 1972 numbers of minorities at the occupational level.

We need to attend also to the interaction of sex and race. Minority men, white men, minority women, and white women all have different sets of social experiences, and, within AT&T, different sets of occupational experiences. Table 1.4 examines the ability of these four race/sex categories (numbers and percentages of each within an occupational level) to predict growth or decline during this three-year period of technological change. As before, it appears to be the number, rather than the percentage, that is the better predictor.

The corporation planned to hold growth or cut back on jobs at occupational levels employing large numbers of females, and to increase jobs at levels employing large numbers of white males. In actuality, however, the best predictor of slow growth or decline was both a high number and a high proportion of minority women employed at that level. Structurally, in this case study, technological displacement is best predicted by a combination of race and sex. Displacement struck most sharply where minority women worked.[9]

How does one reconcile this finding with the fact that white women as a category were most seriously displaced during this time (Table 1.2)? Occupations such as operator and lower-level clerical worker suffered most displacement. It is here where minority female employment is greatest (19 percent to 25 percent). Those levels showing greatest increase were skilled clerical, general services (for example delivery), sales, and upper-level management. Some occupations formerly employing large numbers of white women, such as skilled clerical (81 percent white female) increased, but these are positions into which AT&T moved more minority women than (and as many white men as) white women. Thus, although at this time white women's employment suffered most, traditionally minority women's occupations were most disparately affected.

Finally, as technological sophistication increased during this three-year period, there was, as predicted by research, greater differentiation in the work force (more even distribution over occupational levels, adjusted Gibbs and Martin's D: 1972 = .63; 1975 = .66). Despite corporate projections, but according to organizational research, there was an increase in the proportion of management (level 4 and above; 23.6 percent to 25.4 percent) and a corresponding decrease in size (number of employees). But there was an even greater decline in the proportion of female employees (52.4 to 50.1 percent) than in the proportion of management and nonmanagement during this time. Further, organizational research needs finer analysis than is offered by the category "clerical." If clerical workers are taken as a whole, there is only minimal change in their proportion of total employment (.5 percent change). We would overlook important transformations taking place—a sharp (18 percent) increase in skilled, but a 6 to 16 percent decrease in lesser-skilled clerical workers.

PLANNED TECHNOLOGICAL CHANGE AND DIVISIONS IN THE LABOR FORCE

A more thought-provoking discovery in the mid-1970s, from Bell journals and reports, was that significant technological changes were also under way in the very "male" jobs into which women were being encouraged. As women learned to climb poles, AT&T was shifting to microwave and laser (fiber-optic) transmission systems. As women learned to install telephones, "clip and take" customer installation and phone stores were markedly reducing the need for installers. Framework is a semiskilled craft job (level 10) where women have made strongest inroads into craft work (from 20 percent in 1972 to 32 percent in 1975), often replacing minority men. Framework is slated for total automation. A Bell engineer reports that the electronic switching system (ESS), first installed on the East Coast in the mid-sixties, can virtually eliminate most switchwork and all framework formerly necessary to change telephone connections. (There are no more wires to disconnect and connect, and computer-stored information can be easily changed.) For example, a

manager in the Roxbury plant in Boston, employing many minority
men, expected a 60 to 80 percent reduction in the work force when
they changed to ESS in 1976.[10] Furthermore, microwave and laser
transmission foretells severe restriction for construction and repair
work as well (Reed 1971; *Laser Focus* January 1978). An international
representative for a phone worker's union estimates a 10 percent (80,000)
work-force reduction due to technological change in the near future,
particularly in craft and construction.

AT&T tries to avoid layoffs, letting the humane path of attrition
take its toll. Yet attrition is also manipulated by the corporation. A
Bureau of Labor Statistics bulletin (U.S. Department of Labor 1973)
shows that in four Bell Companies, AT&T increased the work load
and reduced flexibility on the job to help maximize attrition during
and after a shift to less labor-intensive telephone technology. These
efforts, aided by hiring temporary help, minimized the necessity for
layoffs and severance pay. New York City telephone operators provide
earthier descriptions of these processes than "humane attrition" (Center
for United Labor Action [CULA] 1972). More often, however, women
tend toward individual explanations, blaming themselves for the lack
of advancement.

The question of AT&T's intentional manipulation of social divisions
must be addressed directly. In my experience, most people in management were sincere about affirmative action. Those in local offices
and operating companies were unaware of the overall displacement
of women. Most of them vaguely believed that technological change
created more jobs than it eliminated, or at best they reverted to the
attrition argument.

At AT&T Headquarters and at Bell Labs there was less surprise
and an unwillingness to share future plans and projections.[11] These
incidents and impressions are very soft data. However, Loewenberg's
thesis documents intentional displacement of men by women in AT&T's
recent past, in readiness for the newer technologies now sweeping
through the system.

As early as the 1950s the company considered moving women into
maintenance work in the computerized central offices, as Loewenberg
(1962) noted. In the case of line assignment:

> Since turnover of males is much lower than that of females, turnover could
> not play the same part in alleviating displacement following introduction of
> computers. Management therefore wanted to reduce the number of male
> assignors before programming their work for computers. (p. III-30)

Data from New York Telephone Company indicated a planned shift
from 69 percent male craft workers and 30 percent female clericals in

line assignment in 1957 to 79 percent female clericals in 1965. Similar transformations are reported at New Jersey Telephone Company for example (Loewenberg 1962, V-21). Loewenberg commented prophetically on this reassignment of men's to women's jobs:

> Although women are not used elsewhere in craft work at this time [late fifties], many in the industry believe that the prospective simple skill requirements for regular maintenance in the electronic central office may open the way for more use of women in the plant crafts. It is an open secret that women have been used for general maintenance in the Morris, Illinois trial of the electronic office. These women, with no previous mechanical experience or special aptitudes, were placed on the job after two weeks' training. If AT&T has assessed the work of these women, it has not made the results of the assessment public; nor has it revealed its plans about staffing other electronic central offices. It is not unlikely, however, that the question of women replacing men in the central office will be one of the future work reassignment problems of implementing change. (p. III-33)

Loewenberg foresaw little difficulty in this transition; skilled workers would not care for "highly repetitive 'idiot maintenance' work" (p. IV-14). He concluded:

> There are three reasons why work may be reassigned between the sexes, particularly from male to female: 1) preparation for displacement by computer or other mechanized process; 2) simplification of work; and 3) savings in wages. (p. V-28)

At this point, women's employment has not yet turned upward in the corporation. But, with the help of affirmative action, women are moving into the very craft work Loewenberg described. AT&T top managers quite intentionally used social divisions such as sex to enhance profit and to ease transitions to a new technological base. Whether or not a few actually planned to use affirmative action in this way—aiding the shift from male to female labor, defusing worker hostility toward race and sex issues and toward civil rights legislation—must remain an open question.

CHOOSING TECHNOLOGY

The picture in the late seventies is that of a vast corporation shifting rapidly to a higher level of process technology. One executive calls it a "giant nationwide computer" (Sutton 1977). The motive for recent changes derives more from AT&T's desire to compete in the lucrative data transmission market than to improve telephone service. AT&T

is not a protected monopoly in data as it is in voice transmission. That data market (for example, governmental/military, business, and information) demands more precise digital transmission than does voice, for which analogue transmission would suffice. Rate structures are also dependent on the amount of capital investment. The more money tied up in equipment, buildings, and computers, the higher the phone bill can be (Goulden 1970). The data market is one of the fastest growing in the industry. Its military content may be obscured by new phrases such as "business information processing" (*Fortune* 1978) and its connection to business and military may be obscured by AT&T advertising emphasis on small consumer services such as "conference calling," "call forwarding," and "call waiting" (*Wall Street Journal* December 26, 1978).

An exploration of AT&T's interorganizational relations suggests that military and economic concerns are paramount in its selection and development of machine technologies such as microwave, satellite, and fiber-optic transmission and computerized switching systems (Lambeth 1967; Silberman 1967; Cordtz 1970; Goulden 1970, 1972; Shepherd 1971).[12]

HOME AND WORKPLACE

Recent criticism of Marxist literature requires that we expand our analysis beyond the narrow economic focus on the workplace, particularly to women's general social role and to the interrelationship of home and work. In this research/action project, I observed these relationships exerting a pervasive influence on the ability of women to organize in their own interests. Their efforts were often thwarted by male workers, husbands, and union officials, as well as by management. A few examples may suffice. One set of meetings of women workers ended when the organizer's husband, an AT&T craft worker, felt that his wife took too much time away from the family for these efforts. Another union woman had been active before her marriage, and again after her divorce, for similar reasons. In a union local meeting, women's issues on the agenda were postponed for a film on hunting and fishing. In another local, a union representative had worked first for the company, and then for the union. She reported more sexism in the union. Women labor officials from three states recalled women workers' difficulties with husbands, and with male co-workers and their wives. All of these women are strongly prounion.

Analysis and practice require attention to ways in which male workers have used unions and the law to keep women in their place (Hartmann 1977; Feldberg 1978b), and especially to the fact that child care is still women's work in socialist as well as capitalist societies (Weinbaum and Bridges 1976). That the institution of the family has also inhibited men's ability to organize (Christoffel and Kaufer 1970) clearly speaks to the need for analysis of these interrelationships.

SUMMARY

Taking sex stratification as a major conceptual focus, this case study provides insight potentially useful in several areas of sociological research:

1. Technological displacement was seen to cut across management and nonmanagement categories, affecting most severely white women's employment and traditionally minority women's occupations. Sex and race were better predictors of structural change and of technological displacement than were traditional categories of management/nonmanagement.
2. Higher levels of skill and responsibility due to technological change reflected the elimination of traditionally women's work.
3. Under affirmative action, men gained more traditionally women's positions than the reverse.
4. Women do serve as a reserve labor army. Here, we can see the conscious manipulation of the push and pull factors, operating at the same time, that affect women workers.
5. Corporations select their technologies. In this case, military and economic interests appear to predominate, with sex and race divisions in the labor force facilitating the change to a more sophisticated telecommunications technology. The corporation was able to shift a large part of its organizational uncertainty to the most disadvantaged groups in society (see Noll 1976).
6. Finally, working men are advantaged to some degree by sex stratification, as Hartmann (1977) suggests. They can and do use unions and the law to keep things that way, and they are directly advantaged by women's subordination in their private as well as public lives. This subordination helps maintain the processes summarized above.

POLICY AND SOCIAL ACTION IMPLICATIONS[13]

(1) Civil rights groups should become aware of the pitfalls of legal measures to achieve equality in opportunity, but there are creative

ways to use affirmative action as it stands. Court decisions such as *Griggs v. Duke Power* declare any process illegal that disparately affects disadvantaged groups. Technological change that has such a disparate impact is clearly illegal (Krantz 1977). However, as Hashimoto's (1974) analysis of two major settlements—AT&T and U.S. Steel—shows, legislation means only paper equality unless there is continual and strongly organized public action ensuring enforcement. Otherwise, government agencies such as EEOC are caught between a rock and a hard place. Action and scholarly research can be mutually beneficial. Research can inform efforts to organize into unions or caucuses and efforts to win representation in these groups; action tends to provide richer insight and data than are usually the case.

(2) Backlash myths are fed by the media, which present the AT&T settlement as a landmark victory for women's rights. This is an apt description, perhaps, only for women in middle management. The press could provide the public with deeper awareness of the effects of technological change, and of the realities of affirmative action.[14]

(3) In the short run, unions might strengthen requirements for automation clauses, assigning decision making on technology to both management and workers. At present, less than .5 percent of the organized U.S. work force is covered by such clauses (National Center for Productivity and Quality of Working Life 1977). Loewenberg (1962) remarked that

> perhaps the most notable feature arising from an investigation of contract issues that have occupied the parties since 1946, or almost from the beginning of large scale bargaining, is the general absence of issues that directly concern (technological) change. (p. VIII-1)

He saw a major problem in the ability of management to dictate change to the unions. When the company does give information to the union, time is usually too short for the union to explore its implications. The Communication Workers of America did consider an automation clause in its most recent contract, requiring six months' notice of new technologies with disemployment implications. Even this modest clause failed to make the contract. In the long run, we should explore models of technological change that do not cause the poorest groups in society to pay for such changes (Rothschild-Whitt 1974; Nygaard 1977).

(4) Newer models of change that focus only on democratic participation in the workplace, and do not include attention to work performed in the family and the community, should remain highly suspect. Analysis and practice directed against patriarchal domination and capitalist exploitation appear the most fruitful for dealing with issues discussed in this research.

NOTES

1. The action was brought before the Federal Communications Commission, the regulating body for the operating companies, and Long Lines, which includes about four-fifths of all employees. Most other AT&T components are regulated by the Department of Defense. Hence, data are available only for the operating companies and Long Lines. EEOC lawyers note that all operating companies are organized so similarly that format and much of the text of affirmative action plans were identical from company to company, with blank spaces for the name of a particular company. A finer analysis on a company-by-company basis should, however, reveal some variations in the structure due to different levels of modernization. AT&T began this most recent wave of technological change in highly urban areas, and primarily on the East Coast, some 15 years ago. Data from more rural areas will not reflect the full impact of new technologies; areas of new construction, such as the South, may reflect greater impact.

2. See also Elizabeth Faulkner Baker (1964), who described historic shifts in the sex composition of the industrial labor force of various industries during times of technological change. Whether the industry was textiles, silk, shoe binding, printing, watchmaking, electric lamps, or office work, women moved in when work became less sophisticated, more tedious, and routinized, required less judgment, and was more narrowly defined. Men were employed to tend, supervise, repair, and adjust more machines per worker, larger machines, faster machines. Smuts (1971) also traces the shift from female to male labor accompanying technological change in the textile industry in the nineteenth century. This process interacts with ethnic divisions in the labor force (Dublin 1975), or can affect minorities primarily (Allen 1977).

3. Personal interview with personnel director, 1973.

4. Personal interview, Bell Telephone Laboratories, 1974.

5. Personal interviews with personnel director, engineer, and president, Iowa area, Northwestern Bell, 1973.

6. Table 1.2 indicates that thousands of black and brown women did lose lower-level jobs; it is unlikely that they were the same women as those gaining jobs at lower levels of management. AT&T prefers women in supervisory positions to have college degrees, according to Loewenberg (1962), to "lessen supervisory aspirations of ordinary operators" (p. VI-8).

7. Some agree that level 4, lowest-level supervisors, should be included in "management" on objective grounds (such as exclusion from the bargaining unit and supervisory duties) and on subjective grounds (such as title and identification). Traditional research would also place level 4 with management. Others disagree, given objective factors such as relationship to the means of production and wages. These objections, however, refer to all but the top-level executives. In my experience, traditional socialist groups in practice tended to ignore the difficulties of women at this level, some referring to them as "class enemies." In a discussion among socialist sociologists in the early seventies, telephone operators were described as "white collar" or "bourgeoisie," and were excluded from the definition of proletariat. Engineers and unemployed (declassed) college professors were not.

Since these issues are far from settled conceptually, I use the measure of class closest to that in traditional sociological research to indicate the need for attention to sex stratification (management = levels 1–4; nonmanagement = levels 5–15). But given these difficulties, I also use a continuous measure of status, all 15 occupational levels.

8. Ferber and Lowery (1976) show that men in traditionally women's work fare worse than women, for example, in turnover rate and unemployment. Perhaps this is why the relatively large numbers, rather than the traditional indices of segregation (percentages), is the better predictor. One must note also the particular phase of change at AT&T. Skilled clerical, a highly sex-segregated occupation, is expanding as it replaces degraded craft work. However, many thousands of women already work at simplified crafts (for example, level 10), although their proportion is still relatively small (20 percent in 1972). Relatively large numbers of women, then, work at the least technologically sophisticated, most labor-intensive occupations, both traditional and nontraditional. This will not be reflected in indices of sex segregation (percentages), but will when one uses the number of women employed at any level.

9. Second-order partials in the class, race, and sex correlations, above, show that except for management's plan to reduce its own share of employment, neither class nor status predicts occupational change, controlling for sex and race. Sex and race, controlling for class or status, still predict change. Multiple regression of the four sex/race categories and status shows again that, controlling for all other variables, only the percentage and number of minority women significantly predict decline. This analysis, however, is clouded by severe problems of multicollinearity, given that the number of minority women and the number of white women across all levels are correlated at $r = .95$.

10. MIT Telephone class tour, 1975.

11. As I became more interested in AT&T technology, the two NOW members who first suggested this action to the organization, and who provided much information on employment patterns of women and minorities in the early seventies (and who are highly placed in AT&T's corporate structure), were not as helpful in the mid-seventies in providing information on the planned technological changes under way in the corporation.

12. See Galloway (1972) for the deforming impact of military needs on telecommunications technology. For an analysis of the effects of such needs and technologies on social relations, see B. Hacker (1977a). For an account of similar origins—military and economic—of AT&T's social technologies (for example, job description, personality and aptitude testing, education and training), which then found their way into industry and public schooling, see Noble (1977).

13. The information on displacement has been disseminated to women's, minority, and workers' groups and organizations in different ways: through the NOW AT&T newsletter and correspondence with members of this action committee composed largely of AT&T workers; through informal and formal meetings with union representatives and other labor organizations; through reports and interviews to women's and workers' newspapers and magazines; through speeches to national meetings of affirmative action

officers; and to other civil rights organizations such as the civil liberties union.

In the early seventies, both NOW and traditional unions were slow to respond to the problem of technological displacement of women. NOW and other civil rights groups were geared heavily toward legal and legislative action. Challenging displacement under the law was and is unpopular because it has such a low probability of success. The movement needed a "success story," such as the millions of dollars in back pay awarded through the 1973 consent decree or "settlement" (largely a few hundred dollars apiece to some women and minorities). Also important to long-range goals, NOW began to focus heavily on passage of the Equal Rights Amendment (ERA).

Unions provided little information and accepted technological displacement "as a parameter within which we work," in the words of one. Women workers were largely unaware of the overall picture (an exception being the New York-based Center for United Labor Action, whose newsletter provided insight into working conditions during periods of technological change). As women move into union management, and as male craft work is simplified, these tendencies are changing.

14. In practice this has been a tricky process, as management in the newspaper industry faces similar issues of technological displacement. In some cities, for example, Des Moines, NOW members resorted to leafletting as an alternative medium, but one of limited power.

Chapter 2

Farming Out the Home: Women and Agribusiness

I grew up in a small town, and spent a lot of time on the farms of friends and relatives. Rural life, it seemed to me, offered a good blend of sensual pleasures, hard work, and whole tasks. As an adult, I've spent most of my life in the largest cities of the United States. I am familiar, then, with rural and with urban living. But I wanted to know more about the transition from one to the other, and how it happened to so many of us so quickly. Especially, I wanted to know more about the changes in other women's lives in the shift from agriculture to agribusiness. I found that this shift usually means a change from rural to urban homemaker; from farmer to clerical worker or factory hand. For migrant women it may mean further degradation in living and working conditions, or no job at all. This interest in women and agribusiness is both personal and political. It forms part of an exploratory research project on technological change and women's work in several industries.[1] Iowa is an appropriate setting for this research. A green and lovely place, it contains the largest farming population in the country (544,000) and the third largest percentage of farmers (19.2 percent of the population) (Iowa Farm Bureau 1977, 27).

It takes a lot of money to farm these days. The average Iowa family farm represents almost half a million dollars tied up in land, buildings, and machinery. Yet the annual net income of this family is only $10,000 (Iowa Farm Bureau 1977, 6, 12).

The family farm is a farm where people who live on the land also work it and make decisions about it. It is losing out to agribusiness. Agribusiness is the system of large corporations that control food production and supply industries, packaging, marketing, distribution, and sales. The key ingredient in agribusiness is new technology—machines, processes, and social relations that have radically transformed the work of food production (DeMarco and Sechler 1975).

Family farms don't lose out because they're less efficient. In fact, if one reckons efficiency in terms of energy consumption or environmental costs rather than in terms of people displaced, smaller-scale farming outperforms agribusiness corporations handily (Perlman 1976). The large corporation "farmer"[2] wins out in the uneven battle of land speculation, stock market manipulation, and increasing control over significant industries (Perlman 1976).

The U.S. farm population has dwindled from 23 percent of the total to less than 4 percent in the last 35 years. Smaller farms go first. For example, the size of the average farm in Iowa has increased from 190 to 261 acres since 1960 (Iowa Farm Bureau 1977, 1). Concern is usually cast in terms of the displaced farmer and his son. Yet census data indicate that women are pushed or pulled off the land at an even greater rate than are rural men; except for the 30–40 age group, the ratio of men to women is larger in rural than in urban areas of the United States (U.S. Department of Commerce, Social and Economic Statistics Administration, Bureau of Census 1970).[3]

Rural life was none too romantic, particularly for the poor. Their farms, like that of my grandparents, didn't stand a chance. Aunt Louise left the farm for the shoe factory, where she spent her working life. As she put it, "If we planted corn, wheat prices were up; if we planted wheat, it was a corn year." Mother was a farming woman who left to work in a film-processing shop in town. When I'd tell her I'd like to try farming, she'd say, "Oh no, the work is hard and it never ends." Women's lot was the worst—hard labor often coupled with endless rounds of childbirth. Cash income for hard work would have provided some autonomy from the family unit, but there was little if any of that to be had on the farm.

Still, many of us feel we've lost a lot in the transition to urban living. We would like a life closer to the soil, where physical, social, and mental work again form an integrated, organic whole. Farm life can also blend work and leisure—living in the basement until the house is finished, working outside, cleaning out the barn, spreading manure, milking, listening to the fine country music on the barn radio, feeding chickens and gathering eggs, cooking and eating what you've grown. Although some women are regaining this kind of life,[4] many more are still in the process of losing what they have.

The practical skills required by farming give many women and their daughters a sense of resilience, competence, and self-esteem. In farm communities there is little in the way of a highly visible upper class after whom one's daughters might be styled; daintiness in dress and manner are inappropriate for most rural work. But rural sons and daughters learn a wide range of crafts as well as the agricultural skills directly related to food production. On the farm, homemaking entails useful and highly respected skills. As one Iowa farming woman explained:

> There's always something different. There's no other occupation like it, where you can spend that much time doing things with your family.

In spring, you start planting. Everybody participates. Then there's the hoeing, then grain to be harvested, bailing straw, then the cantaloupes start coming on. Then there's irrigation through all this. My daughters work—they can all plow and disc. They do the same as my sons. Now, sometimes, I take care of the kids while my daughter rides the picker. I love the sweet potatoes. The kids ravel [knock off the dirt] in the morning. My husband and one son snap during the day.

Farming women are often baffled by the (urban) feminist analysis of the degradation of the homemaker's role: "Equal pay for equal work is OK, but I want to be a wife and mother, the role God gave me. I don't want to compete, I only want to be a loved person."

A Wisconsin farming woman noted: "Most of the farm women I know declare fiercely that they are not feminists as they tramp out to the barn to mind forty-one cows and shovel manure twice a day" (quoted in Knaak 1977, 4).

In turn, adherence to traditional roles of wife and mother often baffles an urban feminist, for whom homemaking has become much less rewarding. However, many farming women realize that their way of life is threatened by the same forces that oppress women elsewhere. I spoke with a young farmer in her roadside vegetable stand. As we talked, her small daughter hammered away repairing a crate.

If my husband died, I'd like to stay on the farm or rent the land. But for a woman alone in this day and age, it's impossible. She wouldn't be listened to as much as in earlier days: you really have to be strong-minded [Noun 1969]. Corporate farming is coming in. You can't stop it. It's just the way society is going. Just like the grain market is controlled by the government. Bigger everything.

Bigger everything will indeed affect the lives of women. As Elizabeth Faulkner Baker points out in *Technology and Women's Work* (1964), labor in a variety of industries shifts from female to male as machines become larger and faster. Agribusiness technology affects women's participation similarly.

Traditionally, farm children have learned most of the technical and social skills of food production and preparation through observation and practice in the home. To learn the skills associated with the agribusiness systems, young people may attend formal educational institutions where these newer skills are taught.

To observe this training firsthand, I audited a series of vocational courses on "agribusiness orientation" at a central Iowa community college. The curriculum included agribusiness sales and marketing, animal science, soils, crops, fertilizers, and petroleum and petroleum products. One of the first lessons of agribusiness is that this is men's work—I was the only female.

The more fortunate go to the land-grant university; the poor usually don't go at all. This session, part of a two-year program, was directed toward the sons of lower- to middle-income farming families. These young men learn the skills necessary for middle-level occupations such as sales and marketing but are rarely encouraged to think about the more prestigious roles of corporate executive or scientist.

The ideology of agribusiness was most obvious in the class on sales and marketing—the only class taught by men with an urban background. They preached the virtues and benefits of profit and expansion in guest lectures by representatives from industry, the Farm Bureau, and the State Development Commission, and in texts, class discussion, tapes, and films produced by the industry itself. We learned we should create and stimulate consumer needs, directly (for example, for pork and beef) and indirectly (for example, for microwave ovens, which increase the purchase of meat). Our teachers portrayed the ability to stimulate and create new needs as the manly art of salesmanship, as opposed to the womanly role of salesclerk, or "order taker," who merely supplied what a customer wanted.

Agribusiness, like any hierarchical system, is based on this rigid gendering of knowledge and experience that tells young men which occupations, attitudes, and behaviors to respect and which to ridicule and avoid. This applies even to specific classes. For example, the students in horticulture class, including one female and a few long-haired male students, were referred to as the "flower sellers" by the agribusiness faculty. Students were encouraged to think masculine, think aggressive, and think business (more than farming) management.

The message was clear in the sales and marketing class. Question: "How does a salesman contribute to the high level of living in this country?" Correct answer: "He creates a high demand for luxuries." Question: "Why is the United States the richest nation in the world?" Correct answer: "Because luxury items have created new needs." The microwave oven is one such luxury item, which cooks a turkey in one hour instead of seven. One "problem" the supersalesman must overcome is the housewife who prefers the longer cooking time, with savory aromas filling the house. The instructor was philosophical: "How do you sell against tradition like that? It would take four hours of class time to discuss it."

This experience was obviously alienating to me; I listened often in cold anger. It appeared to affect the young men as well, who could be seen playing with pieces of paper or Ping-Pong balls, and chucking pebbles at each other.

Some students did challenge faculty statements. For example, a faculty member blamed farmers in a nearby state for overfertilizing the land. A student suggested that the fertilizer firms that sponsor grain yield contests, and the salesmen who represent these firms, were responsible for damage to the land. To this the instructor replied, "No, the farmers just wanted to get their names in the paper." Another student questioned the turn from dairy to beef cattle production. He was told, "Beef makes more money, and the name of the game is profit." A third asked if the instructor thought destroying food, or cutting back on its production, was wasteful or immoral. His response:

Waste is everywhere. I wasted gas driving in this morning. Could've walked. Waste is the name of it here in this country. Military men waste. I saw fifty gas masks thrown away, eggs thrown away at breakfast every morning. Some things are moral, some are immoral. Some are legal, some illegal, but let's face it—that's just the way things work in this economy. That's just the good ol' U.S. of A.

Most students were practical; job placement could, of course, depend on apparent acceptance of consumerist dogma. From conversation and observation, those who appeared most successful on tests and class reports seemed to resist the ideology least.

Instructors acknowledged the degradation of the farmer's work. Thanks to agribusiness development, the farmer has been robbed of many craft skills. However, instructors had an explanation for this: "Farmers used to get information from their neighbors. Now they can get it from the dealer."

Further, small farmers who lose out in competition with larger operations are blamed for their own condition. As a representative of the Beef Improvement Council stated: "The name of the game is profit. How do you have a successful beef operation? Like any other business, a few inefficient operations will fall by the wayside." He, like other industry speakers, ignored any other possible causes of this development—such as the onset of technology that only a few farm families can afford. Attrition, he would have us believe, is simply inevitable.

This community college program represents an effort to ease the transition of these young men from farmers to agribusiness salesmen, merchandisers, and dealers. But the role of women is not ignored. Today's farm woman should become a volunteer and provide free labor for agribusiness.

Often women are expected to provide ideological support and promotional activities. The local Cattlemen's Association publication contains a section for the women's auxiliary, the Cowbelles, that informs women of their duties. They suggest that farm women "be knowledgeable about arguments refuting the high cost of meat and meat boycotts" (Iowa Cattlemen's Association 1973a) and "organize to help fight legislation negative to meat prices" (Iowa Cattlemen's Association 1973b).

Moreover, the woman's role is explicitly defined as a moral obligation rather than an occupation:

> Lots of women are already helping their husbands in promotion of our beef industry, but we feel that belonging to our Cowbelles would make them consciously aware of their responsibility to the beef industry, and they would work a little harder on PR and beef education as well as promoting beef. (Iowa Cattlemen's Association 1973c)

The report on the accomplishment of Farm Bureau women in *Nation's Agriculture* (1972, 13) includes promoting products, meeting with legislators, and objecting to a high school text that portrays Cesar Chavez as a hero. These ideological support services, free to the industry, come from women who believe their best interests are identified with those industries and their power.

The public relations campaign directed at farm women extends to attempts to alienate them from other women. Faculty contrasted the hardy, no-nonsense farm woman to the frivolous know-nothing city woman, who might, for instance, side with environmentalists "who give blanket opposition to any chemical on the farm . . . then the New Jersey housewife is afraid of getting Iowa chemicals in her drinking water!" The urban homemaker can dangerously exercise her right of choice as a consumer. She may choose meat analogues (vegetable additives), which, according to a representative from the Beef Industry Council, are "a cloud on the industry." The urban homemaker might boycott high-priced products, even though she "doesn't want to get her white boots dirty in the barnyard." In class the beef boycott effort was derided, but in the *Iowa Farm Bureau Spokesman*, the boycott was elevated to a serious menace similar to labor and government controls:

> We think Mr. Meany's folks should pay for what they eat. . . . Neither he [Uncle Sam] nor the boycott gals can force us to raise meat at a loss. (Murphy 1973)

As the boycott demonstrated, the homemaker still exercises decision-making power at the supermarket. However, agribusiness representatives suggest stripping even this level of skill from women, transforming it into a paid occupation for young men:

> That the housewife sets the pace is the biggest fallacy yet. She doesn't know the difference [between cuts of meat]. The housewife can't tell by

looking . . . she's not educated enough to know. (representative, Beef Improvement Corporation)

Most housewives don't know beans from apple butter. They need meat specialists to tell them what the cuts are. Meat merchandising could be a job of anyone in the room. (representative and editorial writer, *Farm Bureau Spokesman*)

Catching my eye, he added, "Incidentally, you gals can do this too!"

In regard to women, the contradiction between agribusiness ideology and action is striking. Clearly, agribusiness representatives both fear and ridicule the urban homemaker, whom they perceive as troublesome and unpredictable. On the other hand, although they venerate the woman on the farm, agribusiness itself hastens the transition from the rural to the urban homemaker.

In industry, more sophisticated technologies lead to increasing hierarchy on the job: the number of levels between the top and the bottom increases.[5] Management makes decisions; those at the bottom of the occupational structure are limited to routine, detail, and maintenance operations. The future agribusiness middlemen in the classroom were advised explicitly:

Don't spend dollars doing penny tasks. . . . The most productive type of labor for a manager is thought . . . plan, direct, analyze, control. If you want to be a manager, you've got to keep your head above the details. Hire somebody else to wallow in it. . . . Industry needs men who think. . . . Wars aren't won by men with small ideas! (tape: "A Challenge for Tomorrow's Managers")

Naturally, this division of labor allocates the penny tasks to women. In another session, they learned from an ace insurance salesman that he "had no secretary at first. Then somebody said go out and get a secretary and you'll double your business. I did, and sure enough, my business doubled. She takes care of all the details, every detail." Sexism is the first form of social hierarchy. Valuable tasks are taken by the men; detail work is left to the women. As one manager put it, "My wife takes care of everything at home. I don't have to do any of it. Sees the lawn's mowed, takes kids to the dentist, the doctor. I don't do any babysitting."

Even more than classroom instruction, I gained insight into the future role of women by observing the experiences of women in agribusiness. To illustrate the number and variety of jobs available in agribusiness, the college invites young men on field trips to agribusiness corporations and cooperatives[6] around the state. I went along, persisting in the face of a faculty suggestion that "women might be in the way."

We visited a turkey plant that employs 600 people. According to our guide, 80 percent of the workers are women. The plant was cold, smelly, noisy, and wet. Some women wore galoshes as they stood in place on the assembly line. The first in line chopped off the feet. Others performed limited disemboweling operations on the carcass, as it passed along an overhanging track winding through the plant. A woman I spoke with reported her wages as $2.50 an hour. She said they had been organized by the Teamsters.

At a warehouse that employed some 60 people, men loaded, unloaded, and moved crates and cartons of tires by forklift truck. Our guide gave their starting wages at $3.50 to $3.60 an hour. A few women worked in the office, but he did not know their wages.

A highly automated dairy again showed no evidence of women; the guide reported that a few worked in the office, but again he was unsure of their wages. He gave the average wage for the men as $5.50 an hour.

A similar situation existed at a large grain-loading port (see Hamilton 1972).[7] Here, mechanization and automation had reduced the labor force to about 27 men. Craneloading operators earned $9.60 an hour; once more the guide didn't know what the "few women working in the office" made.

At a grain exchange we visited, male industry representatives, traders, and brokers on the floor earned starting salaries of $20,000 per year. Female chalkers, who stood at blackboards around the balcony changing the information as new statistics arrived, were reported to earn $2.50 an hour.

The more varied and better-paying occupations available in agribusiness are almost exclusively a male domain. A few women work in research kitchens, but most are limited to positions as factory hands and clerical workers. When I asked about the role of these women in agribusiness, an instructor replied, "The gals on the line? They are not considered a part of agribusiness. They do no decision-making at all."

The alternatives for most women leaving the farm are bleak. Many are on welfare. Women occupy the lowest-paid, most tedious jobs in packing and canning plants around the state. Since automation and other factors seriously affect these jobs, the unemployment rate among these women is much higher than for women in other occupations, and higher than that of male operatives (Iowa Security Commission 1975, Tables 3, 3A, 4, 4A).

Many rural women turn to clerical labor, which is also notoriously underpaid. Des Moines, Iowa, is dominated by insurance companies and other financial institutions and has the lowest clerical wages and the slowest rates of growth in clerical wages among cities in the entire north central region (U.S. Department of Labor, 1976, Table 87, 163–176). In fact, the State Development Commission invites other insurance companies to locate in the state and take advantage of low labor costs. The following advertisement appeared in *Fortune* magazine:

> Iowa workers add 15 percent more value to the products they produce than the average American worker. That's 69 minutes productivity for an hour's pay, 46 hours productivity for 40 hours pay, or 59 weeks of productivity for a year's salary. But no matter how you look at it, the fact is, Iowa workers work better.
>
> It's one reason why 165 of America's top 500 companies now operate 455 plants in Iowa. For more information, write: The Iowa Development Commission "A Place to Grow." (May 1976, 167)

According to the manager of another poultry processing plant I visited—which, incidentally, received a major share of its business from the Department of Defense—rural women make the best workers because they're used to hard work. This particular plant employed some 400 workers, primarily Anglo women on the day shift, migrant Chicanas at night. Most women worked standing in the heat and the wet and the smell, stripping cooked meat from the bones of chicken carcasses piled in the bins before them. Recently bone and joint difficulties have increased, particularly among older women, as the tempo of work has increased. The women wanted higher pay. The night foreman, the company president's nephew, wasn't sure if company response would be mechanization (e.g., a deboning machine) or a move further west to capitalize on American Indian labor. Several months later a newspaper reported the work force had been cut to 225, then the plant closed "for renovation" (*Des Moines Register and Tribune* 1974, incomplete reference). It never reopened, but moved out of state.

Migrant workers are located at the bottom rung of the agribusiness ladder. Some 2,000 Chicana/o migrant workers are employed in Iowa each year.[8] They harvest the crops and work peak seasons in caning and meat-packing plants around the state. As in the Anglo community, men tend to work in beef packing and women in poultry. Some "settle out" of the migrant stream to become permanent Iowa residents.

Two Chicana nurses, Sister Irene and Sister Molly, described their reactions to migrant living and working conditions:

> When I came here and saw what my people, the Chicano people, were really going through . . . I became a different person. . . . I was really shy and timid before. . . . We're not like the nice Chicana [laughter]. We used to be on a lot of boards, you know, like the token Chicanas. But now they're catchin' on to that. And they're not going to ask us on too many boards because we're not going to be their little tokens, huh-uh. There's the Chicana woman behind all the trouble. We no

more get the police to arrest some of 'em, than she's down there way ahead of the police gettin' to the station, gettin' 'em out. And not only that, she's a sister. And she's got a sister who's a sister. They're both troublemakers.

Sisters Irene and Molly spend most of their time helping the migrant field workers and their children, and those who've "settled out" get mind and soul and body together.

They have low back pain, any time they have anything wrong with the whole spinal column or a disc, from all that lugging and back-bending kind of work. Pesticides. There's pesticide poisoning, and we know there is. But it's never really been documented. And I think physicians sometimes miss it too. They're not really trained as far as pesticides are concerned. But we've had incidents every summer. . . . Somebody will come in all swollen all over, difficult respiration, the whole thing, and says "It was right after I was out there picking tomatoes for an hour or so." So what do you do? You document it. I think you can send it in to HEW [Department of Health, Education and Welfare], but there's no real follow-up on it. And there are no warning signs that this field has been sprayed. None of that . . . nothing like that. Nothing. People don't even know what the pesticides are. Sometimes the grower doesn't even know the pesticides being used because [the company] is sometimes afraid to give away that information.

Farm work is nearly three times as deadly as the national average, according to an Assistant U.S. Secretary of Labor (*Des Moines Register and Tribune* 1974, incomplete reference). And of all farm workers, the migrants are the least protected.

Conditions in the migrant camps contribute to poor health. According to the sisters:

They had high incidence of diarrhea—they didn't like us coming in and checking the water. This was when we didn't even have a migrant health and housing law, so we had a young man employed as a sanitarian and he had to go out and check the water or I'd check the water. And then they had occasions when they had accidents—the lady was there getting water out of the faucet, and the cement was not really fixed there for her to step on, and she fell. And [the company] had to follow through and pay for all her health coverage. I made a point of it.

In the face of continuing public pressure, the company recently got out of the migrant business. They sold the housing to the farmers and told them to take future responsibility for contracting and housing. The farm women I talked with employed about 20–30 migrant workers. The large cannery in their small Iowa city was a subdivision of an agribusiness giant. The cannery contracted the farmers to grow produce, hence the term *grower* applied to these farmers. Until very recently, this company also contracted and housed the migrant field workers.

The farmers find it too expensive to improve the quality of housing: "They [migrants] are only here six weeks, and it would cost us $20,000 to build new." Another reports:

> [The company] used to own the houses. They saw it coming, sold the houses—and gave the responsibility to the farmers. The houses are used only two months, but we have to maintain them during the winter. We got no increase from [the company] for this responsibility.

Placing the responsibility—and the expense—of migrant housing on the farmers led to mechanization of the field work, for example, through the use of the mechanical tomato picker (Hightower 1973).[9] Under conditions of mechanized farming, there is a more profound division of labor. For example, one farm woman reported that a migrant woman drove a truck and loaded, but this was unusual. Generally, the job of loading and driving was held by the migrant men. Almost exclusively, women and children performed stoop labor. A western Teamster official indicates that as technology becomes more sophisticated, Anglo men will take over the operation of large farming equipment (Bernstein 1973, 20).

As social and economic pressures continue to affect the farmer, it is likely that those who can afford it will move toward further mechanization. In 1973, the number of migrant workers coming through this area decreased by 15 percent because of mechanization (Muscatine Migrant Committee 1973, Section I-D).

The farming women I talked with did not express hostility toward the migrant workers. They could identify with certain aspects of the migrant women's lives—the double work of homemaker and field worker—but also knew their own lot was easier. They'd say, for example: "I have another place here [the home]. Migrant women don't."

They opposed the general community feeling that poor housing conditions were the migrant women's fault. "The women said they didn't come here to keep house. They came to work in the fields, earn money, and go. They want livable housing."

These farmers directed their sharpest criticism against the media picture of the horrors of working in the fields. They had experienced a lifetime of field work, although under obviously better conditions, and judged the horror overdrawn. They also resented "outsiders running through the backyard speaking for the migrants." Before the local migrant health committee had formed, church groups had provided minimal services to migrants as an act of charity. The new era of conflict and confrontation was unsettling.

Given economic conditions, and the fact that the company does not compensate the farmers for the added responsibility of migrant housing, migrant living conditions are unlikely to improve significantly. As Sister Irene says:

> We had that big run-in with the grower and the inspector. I said [to the inspector], " . . . when you tested that water, didn't you see that hose attached to it?" "Yes I did, but that's not my job to tell them to take the hose off." [Water may test well at its source, but be contaminated by running through the hose; this practice is illegal.] So we had a little round right there. OK. Then there was a lot of diarrhea in that camp, and that's where, possibly, the contamination was coming from. They were filling their buckets and everything.
>
> You see a lot of staph infections, and that's just from the conditions they're living in. We had a lady that was bitten by a brown recluse spider. We wanted her to document that. Oh, she had, she was a mess. She was prevented from working, the whole thing, taking care of her children. We had to dress it every day. We went out to check on the house, to document it, maybe file a suit. [The grower] burned the house that same night, or the next day.

Maternal and infant mortality rates—a key index of overall health care[10]—are reported to be more than 100 percent higher among migrants than the national average. The conditions producing these rates are immediately apparent:

> Sometimes families come in large semi trucks—carries two or three families all squashed in there. And sometimes he doesn't make an effort to provide sufficient stops along the way, so consequently the people are really sick, and the babies arrive with vomiting and diarrhea. The mother was breast-feeding her child during the trip but her milk went dry. She didn't produce enough milk for the child and the child had diarrhea. He didn't make enough stops along the way. A lady arrived with a gall bladder attack after the long, hard trip. We had another arrive in labor—we had to deliver the baby ourselves.
>
> When you're pregnant, I don't care if you're pregnant, or what you are, a diabetic or whatever condition you have, you're out there pickin'. I mean you're here to earn some money and if you're physically ill, that's really too bad. You're still out there doing it. They don't complain, they're just out there. And you say, you know, you really got to be home and elevate your legs, if it's varicose veins, or whatever, but they feel like they have to go out there. Provisions for pregnant women? No. Nothing. We say, I think you should go, you have this kidney infection, and the grower sometimes accuses us of taking his workers away from the field.

We had a maternal death here about two years ago. This was just because of a lack, a lack of prenatal care. She just didn't have any money. They said they just didn't have the money to go and see the doctor. She arrived here in her eighth month of pregnancy. We got her to the doctor right away, and she had a history of weight loss and anemia. At about the same week she went to see the doctor she went into labor on the weekend, and she delivered a premie, and she died of postpartum hemorrhage. The doctor from our clinic said it was a lack of prenatal care, and she wasn't followed, and they just didn't have the money.

Conditions for the children who survive are also perilous:

When you get a family history, invariably you always find at least two or three children that died. Died at 2 years old, died at 8 months. And then you ask, and they said, "Well," they said, "I thought, well, I never really knew, they never really told us." And that just kills me when they say that. "We think it was pneumonia, but we're not really sure." You always get a history of somebody dying: the children.

Last summer we had a child, he was just, he had parasites; he had amoebas. He was just, he looked pregnant, like two or three months, right along, a little tummy. He was just full of them. He was just full of parasites, amoebas, the whole thing. They had to take him to Iowa City. And that's another thing. He left the area before the treatments were finally done. Treatment had to be gradual. You didn't want to irritate the worms too badly, because when you did they'd start coming out of his nose, his mouth, other cavities—ultimately they would choke him. But the whole family had them. They were living in some of the most atrocious conditions over there. You know the grower doesn't understand that. They say, "It's their fault, and they're not clean."

Migrant women also provide useful, unpaid work, stabilizing the community. Some growers formerly hired only single men, but no more, according to a member of the migrant health committee.

Single men? Growers don't want single men. They have more prob-lems—more drinking, they bring girls, women there from the community. There's not one camp left with single men, and this guy will never have them again. Not because they want to keep the families together, but just, economically, it's better for the growers.

This same health committee member, a priest, comments on the role of the migrant woman:

It's really true, the migrant woman does suffer the most. It's harder for the husband in his dignity, and income and all that (compared to the nonmigrant), but the woman—not only because she works right next to the husband full-time, but she still does have to take care of the kids, the cooking. There's no doubt about it. She's the child bearer, and again, with the pride issue, the maleness, and all that, the migrant, not because he's Chicano, but because of the migrant situation, and the subculture, and the economic situation, children are still important. I hope they're always important; but they need more children.

Sister Irene tells of some community response blaming the victims, the migrant women, for their own conditions:

"Why don't those women take care of their kids?" they'll ask. You know, "The kids are dirty," or this type of thing. "If they have enough time to go on to meetings and fight for this and that, how come they don't take care of the kids?" Or when they see the children running around all the time. Or they say, "Why don't the women take care of their homes?" And I'll say, "Well, have you thought about working your tail off for ten hours in the fields, and then come home and clean up a house, or shack, and make the food?" Who's going to worry about the house being clean? My God. Housekeeping.

A young migrant woman spoke briefly about her experience during her hurried visit to the migrant health clinic—the migrants had only recently won the privilege of time off from the fields for clinic visits. The young woman was married, with two small babies. She had not come from a migrant family. Her mother was a homemaker, her father a school janitor. Because her husband couldn't find work in Texas they joined the migrant stream. She often felt unwelcome there, in Anglo motels, stores, and coffee shops. She said she wouldn't mind working in the fields so much if the pay were better, but thought she would like to train to be a nurse's aide instead. "Application after application was turned down," however.

The worst part of field work was "when it's cold and rainy or muddy, or when all eighteen women I work with line up outside the single toilet facility. Sometimes you have to wait." She doesn't let her babies use this toilet but uses a clean can instead, for their safety. Usually she works alongside her husband, picking four rows of vegetables each. But at home, "I do it all myself. [My husband] rests while I'm bathing the babies, making tortillas, cooking, cleaning. It makes me mad, but it's just easier to do it. Maybe things will change. If sons and daughters are raised the same, maybe there will be some change."

Irene and Molly have seen many changes. The migrant health committee is beginning to work more closely with the farmers, whom they can see as allies in their struggle with the company:

Growers are really up a creek, and they know it. They don't know from year to year, from season to season, how many workers they're going to need. Because [the company] waits until the last moment to say. They say "We want every grower to cut back . . . from 100 acres to 70 acres of tomatoes." Even the growers don't know how much the other growers get paid for a ton. It kind of sets the growers against each other too. They don't know until the very last moment, when [the company] is ready to give out its plans, how many acres they will have, if they will be contracted . . . or not. That's their concern, and they've been voicing that with us very seriously. Very openly.

For the most part, however, Sister Irene and Sister Molly work with the migrants—rapping in Spanish with older Chicanas about folk medicine; helping a woman whose husband's immigration papers weren't properly processed; dealing with workers' difficulties at the cannery; rushing a woman and her daughter, whose arm had been caught in a wringer, to the clinic after a local doctor put them off; printing cards with instructions in Spanish and English about rights when arrested.

A rigid, divisive organizational structure—rural divided from urban, Chicana/o from Anglo, men from women, decision-making from labor—is brought to us by "agribusiness and the companies it keeps."

Most people are convinced that the spread of agribusiness is inevitable. One farmer, describing the company's policy of secrecy about pesticide contents used under contract, was very concerned with effects on the local environment. But, she said, "There's no way to go back. I know we're taking some chances, but there's no other way to feed people here and abroad." This ideology of necessity, of course, is exactly what agribusinessmen have told her.

Neither the farming women nor the students in the agribusiness classroom had encountered workable alternatives to agribusiness as we know it.[11] They were unaware that, in many ways, agribusiness has a detrimental, rather than a positive, effect on the poor in the Third World countries. Susan DeMarco and Susan Sechler in their book *The Fields Have Turned Brown* (1975), document increased unemployment and decreased protein in the diet of the poor, as Third World countries adopt Western agribusiness technology. Advocates of the new technology encourage the production of luxury crops or herds grown for export to wealthy nations. Meanwhile, land allotted to grains and other staples has decreased. The distance—in wealth and protein consumption—between the rich and the poor increases.

In auditing classes, taking trips, talking to people, and looking at data, I learned a little about the transformation in women's lives when agribusiness replaces the family farm.[12] Women's work on the farm is often directed by the needs of the man. To some extent it differs from the work of that man. But compared to the way agribusinessmen organize work, farming women and men more often shared skills, tasks, responsibilities, and power.[13]

The organization of work under large corporate agribusiness diminishes the autonomy of most farmers considerably and all but eliminates it for women and migrants. It creates alienating work for many Anglo men as well, but keeps many of them content with minor power over others—for example, the secretary, wife, and factory hand. Hierarchy holds it all together. You're relieved not to be at the bottom, or unemployed, but scared you will be if you're not careful. Hierarchy, with its related fear and uneasy relief, is a very effective source of control and characterizes most, but not all, forms of social organization.[14] Agribusiness, compared with agriculture, exaggerates hierarchy in social relations.

Profit and expansion are powerful engines in this industry that has such low regard for people in general, and for women and minorities in particular. Accompanying these economic factors are older tendencies of political domination—concentrating power and decision-making among the men at the top.

Agribusiness didn't create, but certainly increases, the subordination of women, people of color, and the poor. It is not unreasonable to think that liberation from these conditions is intricately related to the problem of technology—who controls and directs it, and what kind of technology we get.

Technology—the way we organize energy and materials to get work done—can be, and often is, selectively developed to ensure social hierarchy. Technology is not simply a collection of machines. It also includes social relations in the way that work is organized. Technology, then, is both social and technical. It doesn't simply emerge. It is not operating on its own internal principles. It is carefully selected and its development directed by those men who own and manage. And their choices are made in their own interests (Glenn and Feldberg 1976, 11ff.; Marglin 1974; Noble 1977; Braverman 1974).[15]

Migrant workers have organized a response to agribusiness (Matthiessen 1969). Farm women now also discern the outlines of this industry that destroys the way of life they value for themselves and their children. Few can afford the mechanization now in process. Along with migrant workers, they are increasingly excluded from the skills to use it, anyway. The land is more easily rented and bought from the farming woman, who, as one said, "isn't listened to as much these days."

One farm woman wrote recently to Roxanne Conlin, a vigorous feminist and Iowa's assistant state's attorney at the time:

At the present time, if a farm husband and wife own property jointly and something happens, the entire property is thrown into the husband's

estate and taxed. A farm wife is not considered to do a thing toward the
family income. This is a very bitter pill and has caused the selling of the
farm in some cases to pay the tax and [the farm] was the very lifeblood
for the widow. This is very ironical when many, many farm wives spend
every bit of their energy and 10 to 12 hours a day beside their husbands
assisting with milking, farrowing baby pigs in −20 degree temperature
when you have to be with them 24 hours a day, driving tractors 12 to
16 hours a day in 100 degree temperature, endless chores 7 days a week,
cooking for hired help, chasing, sorting, loading hogs and cattle, and on
and on and on. There is no time for us to go to town and get a job as
we're desperately needed right here and town people resent us coming
in and taking jobs they want. Yet, the way the law is now, only personal
money that the wife earns from an outside job that she can prove was
away from home will apply to give her any little share of that property
at his death as tax exempt even though she had to sign all the notes to
borrow the money and has done without numerous things in the house,
which other women regard as absolute necessities, in order to provide
the necessities outside to keep the farm operation going as it is very
tough to pay expenses in spite of the fact people think we are so rich.
(Conlin 1974)

Conlin points out that before this law was changed, it had deprived
3,600 women of their property each year. Even greater difficulties were
faced by divorced farm women.

Farm wife married fifteen years, three children, started with nothing and
bought a $100,000 farm. She worked during his final year of school, had
her babies and continued to work part-time in town as well as raise her
children, keep her house and of course, help generally with the necessary
farm work. After their fifteen years of marriage, he wanted a divorce. The
court awarded him the farm, and the machinery. He also, of course, kept
the college degree she had helped him earn. She on the other hand got
one third of the value of the land, and the children to raise on her own
while attempting to train herself for a paying job.

Farm women are beginning to communicate with each other about
many of these issues that affect them so vitally. For example, an issue
of *Do It Now*, the publication of NOW, has as its theme "Rural Women"
(Knaak 1977). Theme editor Nancy Knaak describes her life as a farmer,
the experiences of others in such groups as the Cowbelles and Porkettes,
and problems with tax laws. She reviews *Country Women* by Tetrault and
Thomas (1976), and reports on the Women's Educational Equity Act
study of "Rural Women's Educational Needs." She announces plans
for a 1977 summer conference in rural Missouri of NOW's task force,
Feminism in Rural Life.[16]
Rural feminism also poses a direct challenge to political/economic

structures. One of the most recent projects in NOW's Compliance (employment) task force is the project on Women in Agribusiness.[17] The NOW chapter in Des Moines has worked closely with agricultural and migrant issues, for example, the local Grape and Lettuce Boycott Committee.[18] At last report, other women in that city have enrolled in the community college Agribusiness Orientation course, and have formed a study/action group of agribusiness workers. Some members of this group recently attended a San Francisco conference titled "Multi-national Corporations and the Food System in California."[19]

Rural feminism has a unique constituency; most of these women do not have several generations of urban industrial, highly stratified workers behind them.[20] Their experiences provide them with potential different from that of their urban sisters.[21] As the growth of agribusiness subordinates women and the womanly, it helps create feminist awareness and protest. At this point, the protest promises to help clarify antifeminist implications in our economic and political systems in general, through a focus on agribusiness in particular.

NOTES

1. This project was funded in part by a Ford Foundation Faculty Fellowship to study women's role in society, Drake University, Des Moines, Iowa, 1973–74. I explored telecommunications and agribusiness, and, with Irene Talbott, printing and publishing, and insurance industries.

2. "Corporation farmers" refers to groups of four or five family farmers who incorporate for the protection it affords. It should not be confused with corporate "farmers" such as Dow Chemical, Tenneco, Standard Oil, Del Monte, or H. J. Heinz Co.

3. More recent data indicate a trend toward *increased* participation in farming on the part of women (Joyce 1976, 3).

4. See *Country Women Magazine*, published in Albion, California, and Tetrault and Thomas (1976); see also a fascinating book by Annette Kolodny (1975). Kolodny suggests we will have to change radically the metaphors we use to think about both gender and nature.

5. In a study of British industries, Joan Woodward (1965) found the application of "scientific" management irrelevant to business success. A firm's technology has an overwhelming impact on social relations. These relations become more hierarchical as one moves from unit to mass to process (for example, oil refining) production technologies. Her view, however, ignores the fact that men carefully choose the technology they want.

6. For an analysis of the interlocks between agribusiness and large farming cooperatives, see Linda Kravitz (1974). We visited several Land O'Lakes Cooperative locations, for example, the turkey plant and the dairy. Land O'Lakes, one of the eight largest U.S. cooperatives, is described in Kravitz's Appendix (pp. 120–22).

7. This is also discussed in an Agribusiness Accountability Project report (Nolan and Galliher 1973). Cargill, the corporation location we visited, is described on pp. 16ff.

8. The number depends on who's counting. A federal agency reported around 2,000 migrants, a state agency reported only 637. The difference was that the latter did not count those who stay in the state six or eight months for work in the plants as migrants, but as residents. A migrant committee in southern Iowa recorded more than 1,000 migrants in their three-county area alone.

9. Hightower and DeMarco (1973) document agribusiness's rip-off of land-grant college research and other resources intended to help poor farmers. Their title comes from the development of hard tomatoes for the mechanical fingers of the picking machine, which was developed, in part, to replace troublesome field laborers.

10. The United States has slipped to the rank of sixteenth among industrialized nations ("Infant Mortality Rates for Selected Countries," data from United Nations Office of Statistics, February 1975). These data appear in literature from *Mother*, founded by Carol Downer, Edith Berg, and Ginny Cassidy, San Diego, California, to reclaim birth and motherhood for women.

11. See an account of intermediate agricultural technology in China in *China: Science Walks on Two Legs* (Rothschild-Whitt 1974).

12. I might have learned more. For insight into college, university, and corporate resistance to this research—lying, distortion of data, secrecy, delaying—see Chapter 3.

13. Esther Boserup's *Women's Role in Economic Development* (1970) outlines the way in which Western technology deepens the subordination of farming women in Third World countries as well.

14. For alternatives, see Kornegger, "Anarchism—the Feminist Connection" (1975). See also Barton Hacker, "The Prevalence of War and the Oppression of Women" (1977a), a paper that analyzes military institutions as core institutions of "civilized" societies, and women's oppression as the cornerstone of such institutions.

15. Marglin (1974) points out that technology that increases control over workers is often chosen over technologies that would merely increase profits, but leave workers more autonomy.

16. Task force coordinators were Mary Rhodes, Anita Wasik, Jennifer Hipp, and Sally Hacker.

17. Task force coordinator was Judy Goans, Knoxville, Tennessee.

18. The contact there was Elyse Weiss, Des Moines, Iowa.

19. The contact for the group was Lynn Price, Des Moines, Iowa.

20. On the other hand, we share a social context similar to that of the "moral crusaders" of the nineteenth-century feminist movement, as analyzed by Alice Rossi in "Analysis vs. Action" (1973a) and "Social Roots of the Women's Movement in America" (1973b). While noting similarities, Rossi contrasts rural, small-town moral crusaders such as Stanton and Anthony with their more sophisticated urban sisters of the later eighteenth century. Crusaders organized, others analyzed and wrote. Crusaders, however, held back from a radical challenge to church and family.

21. Perhaps because of smaller-scale or intermediate-scale social organization, rural feminists explore utopian possibilities. Des Moines, for example, is a center of anarchafeminist action and analysis of political and economic structures rooted in sexism. The fragmentation afflicting movements in larger areas seems slow in coming, and may be circumvented altogether; lines of communication across ideological differences are remarkably open. People seemed to be developing a hardy, earthy mix of analysis and action as they went along.

Chapter 3

Technological Change and Women's Role in Agribusiness: Methods of Research in Social Action

The most powerful social research, regardless of ideology, is embedded in social action. One informs the other and interaction often yields new ways of knowing and doing. When research and action promise to reduce uncertainty in order to achieve organizational goals, integration of research and action is encouraged (Freeman 1973). It is a rich mix. The union of military action and professional research, for example, produced the methodology of systems analysis (McDaniel 1964; Hoos 1972; Lilienfeld 1975). Other military-corporate research furthered personnel assessment methods by which ever-larger groups of people may be differentiated into appropriate occupations. This research/action effort was then transmitted to industry and public education (Noble 1977).

However, when research may reduce uncertainty for those at the bottom of an organization's occupational structure or outside it altogether, potentially threatening management security, normative prescriptions are likely to sharpen the boundaries between research and action, forcing differentiation. This separation retards the development of a methodology more appropriate to a critical perspective; it works to weaken both its action and research (Marx 1972).

A sufficient information base is crucial within any methodological framework. As Noll (1976) points out: "Strategic use of information to generate greater uncertainty for others as a vehicle for reducing one's own uncertainty would not be particularly troublesome if everyone had access to the channels of information . . . [but] one source of difficulty is that information is expensive." The critical researcher is thus disadvantaged compared with a powerful organization's ability to generate and organize information sufficient for its needs.

In 1973 I began research on planned technological change in four Iowa industries—telecommunications, printing and publishing, insurance, and agribusiness—as that change affects the role of women.

89

Critical research in this area had yet to take women into account, conceptually or empirically. In this chapter, I focus on agribusiness alone and report experiences with traditional and nontraditional research methods. My credentials were those of a grandmotherly sociology professor teaching in a conservative private university, doing research on a Ford Foundation Faculty Fellowship. My question was, How does technological change in this industry affect divisions of sex and race in society, and particularly in the occupational structure? I was an outsider, asking questions about corporate planning, and about the impact on women and minorities in the occupational structure. Any of these properties introduces barriers to the free flow of information; the combination increased the need for an unconventional methodological approach.

I focus here not on the substantive findings of this research, but on organizational response to critical research and what might be done to overcome such obstacles. The substantive findings are reported in Chapter 2.

RESEARCHING AGRIBUSINESS

Powerful organizations have a peculiarly significant impact on daily life in this culture (Braverman 1974; Noble 1977) and in the Third World (Boserup 1970; DeMarco and Sechler 1975). This is perhaps · nowhere so evident as in the directed transition from agriculture to agribusiness, and particularly in concomitant changes in the role of women. Nolan and Galliher (1973) report techniques used by the Agribusiness Accountability Project (AAP), a small, privately funded group that researches the complex of industrial, financial, academic, and governmental organizations constituting major agribusiness interests. The title of their article is "Rural Sociological Research and Social Policy: Hard Data, Hard Times."[1]

AAP researchers describe organizational reactions—delays, refusals, and dissembling. Their techniques included wide sampling of data sources and interviews with officials so single-minded as to recognize no other point of view, so chauvinistic as to release information to the AAP women whom they didn't take seriously.

Nolan and Galliher were concerned with the lack of policy relevance in much of the well-funded research in rural sociology. In contrast, the men and women of AAP produce thorough and highly relevant materials on a shoestring operation. In hard times, the authors suggest, one might turn to the alternative research methods employed by the AAP. The significance of AAP's methodology, however, is not its efficiency, but its relationship to action. It stems from the desire to affect social policy. This led to a primary focus on findings, not on methodology; if findings could stand up under congressional cross-examination, the data were sound enough. They avoid the technical fix on rigorous analysis of easily accessible data, a fix that can paralyze imagination in social research.

The new methodology called for in researching the powerful is variously called "muckraking sociology" (Marx 1972), "people's research," "insurgency research" (Sagarin 1973), "adversary research" (Nolan and Galliher 1973), or "investigatory reporting" (Sjoberg and Miller 1973). A major concern, as illustrated by a special issue of *Social Problems* (Sjoberg and Littrell 1973), is the social control of social research—in particular, the difficulty of getting information about powerful organizations when those who run them don't want you to have it.

People's methodology combines familiar techniques and data analysis, as did that of earlier critical researchers in times of trouble. One used documents, interviewing, participant observation, content analysis—with an awareness of the ways in which special interests affect the existence, amount, and nature of information available. The purpose of this approach is to illuminate and thereby weaken a concentration of power (Nolan et al. 1975).

I did not begin this research with an eye to obstacles as a major source of data. As it happened, however, they are such an important source we need to give them some analytic attention. Others have begun to analyze obstacles to critical research. Gary Spencer (1973) offers an 11-category typology of tactics used by West Point to inhibit critical research of that organization. Harassment and discrediting (Spencer's categories 9–11) were more likely encountered in his experience as an insider—a major disadvantage to this otherwise advantageous position—than in mine as an outsider. I use a revised version of Spencer's typology:

1. barriers to physical access: gaining entry, being able to see what is going on; meeting informally with those at the lower levels of the organization; interviews with top-level executives and middle management for rule-of-thumb, general perception about the structure and operation of the organization (Spencer's category 1)
2. barriers to recorded data: legal barriers, concealment, distortion, delays (Spencer's categories 2–8)
3. barriers to ideological orientation: management beliefs and interests (Spencer deals with this considerable problem in a separate section, pp. 92–94.)

I also encountered a fourth obstacle, not necessarily a problem of a highly developed military organization or a conscious tactic to inhibit research:

4. lack of systematic data on the structure and coordination of the organization

Here, I deal primarily with four organizations with which I had the most extensive contact: a community college vocational agribusiness program, a land grant university, a cannery that was a subdivision of an agribusiness corporation, and a large, owner-operated poultry plant. In this case study, obstacles to critical research were not related to major organizational goals (educational versus profit), to public versus private ownership, or to independence versus subunit characteristics of the organizations. With the exception of the fourth obstacle, and related to that exception, obstacles of each kind were greater in organizations with more sophisticated management (the university and the canning plant) than in those with a simpler management component (the community college program and the poultry plant). A highly developed technology of information gathering, processing, and use appears to lead to mechanisms that protect technology from disturbances and uncertainty in the environment, such as critical research.

THE COLLEGE AGRIBUSINESS PROGRAM:
PARTICIPANT OBSERVATION

My background is rural/small town. I had a fairly good sense of the content and rhythms of that life and, later, of a highly urban context. I wanted to experience some formal processes of change from one to the other. I decided to prepare for research by auditing a three-month series of courses in agribusiness at a local two-year community college in the midwestern state where I worked.

As with any instance of participant observation, the work was time-consuming but incredibly valuable. Access to courses was readily granted. The summer session was part of a two-year program oriented toward the sons of lower-middle-class farming families (I was the only female). Generally, the more fortunate go to the land-grant university; the poor do not go to college at all. Students were rarely encouraged to think about the role of corporate executive or scientist, but were given exposure to the skills necessary for middle-level occupations such as sales and marketing.

Agribusiness interests and ideology were explicit in courses on sales and marketing, animal science, soils, crops, fertilizers, and petroleum and petroleum products. Political education was most obvious in the class on sales and marketing. The virtues of profit and expansion were espoused throughout all classes—in guest lectures by representatives from industry, the Farm Bureau, the State Development Commission, and in texts, class discussion, tapes, and films produced by the check-off system.

A masculine, aggressive, business management orientation rather than a farming orientation was clearly a major goal of this experience in adult socialization. Comments on the use of wives and women in the labor force for detail and routine work—setting the mind of the manager free for decision-making—were interwoven through classroom discussion, lectures, and other materials (see Chapter 2).

Agribusiness literature lined the walls of the classroom. The role of women indicated a dichotomy between the hardy farm wife and the frivolous city woman. The latter was related to the threat of organized labor and federal controls on industry through her capricious behavior at the supermarket. She was unknowledgeable about food and dangerous in her capacity to boycott high-priced products. The "good" farm wife, on the other hand, organized against the boycotts, lobbied for industry in the legislature, did public relations to increase consumption of industry products, took action against migrant workers, and otherwise volunteered free labor for agribusiness industry (see Iowa Cattleman's Association 1973a, 1973b, 1973c; *Nation's Agriculture* 1972).

Impressions gained in classes were valuable, but even more enlightening were field trips to agribusiness corporations and cooperatives (Kravic 1974), in this and a neighboring state. These trips provided the young men opportunities to view the system in action and to observe the number and variety of nonfarming occupations available. Persisting in the face of a faculty suggestion that "a woman might be in the way" on one such trip, I found that it did indeed provide an opportunity to view available jobs. Men worked as craftsmen, managers, researchers, salesmen, technicians, brokers, crane operators, truck drivers, and the like. A few female technicians and nutritionists worked in a research kitchen; all other women observed in place after place worked as clericals, or as operatives on mass-production lines in packing and canning plants. When I asked about the role of women in agribusiness, a faculty member replied, "The gals on the line? They are not considered a part of agribusiness. They do no decision-making at all."

THE UNIVERSITY:
SUPPORT SYSTEM FOR AGRIBUSINESS

As Jim Hightower (1973) explains, land-grant universities provide
agribusiness with its technical and professional personnel, research,
and other services. In the nearby land-grant university, a number of
us researched the role of women and their participation in academic
programs related to agribusiness. We wanted the distribution by sex of
faculty and students over these various programs and the per student
budget for each of the several colleges. The data did exist and were
public information by law. University officials, however, stated that
the cost of a computer run to organize the data in that fashion was
prohibitive. In this instance, the research group was more fortunate
than most. A friend emerged from his stall in the men's room to find
a stack of ten copies of these data on a washstand. New to campus
and inundated with information about the university, he assumed this
was more of the same, picked up a copy, and took it home. When he
discovered its importance to the women's group some weeks later, he
passed it on.[2]

The primary focus of the research was the great majority of
women in agribusiness who worked in the fields and plants across
the state. For careful study, I wanted to locate plants that had
recently introduced new technology or were planning to make such
a change. The university housed a center for engineers that provided
consulting services to the community; a perusal of their catalog
of clients for the last year revealed these to be largely private
corporate interests. I approached the director and asked for suggestions.
He referred the question to his staff. The following memo was,
perhaps inadvertently, returned to me by the center's secretary:
"Is [our organization] to be identified as to the source when Ms.
Hacker calls? If so, we'd best give only those examples where
the impact on women was a plus." This was followed by a list
of suggested corporations for research. The problem of controlled
access to information necessary to explore the effects of mechanization
or automation is not a new one. In 1959, Walter Reuther testified before the Subcommittee on Automation and Energy Resources,
documenting the disastrous effect of displacement of workers and
their children. In lieu of more direct figures, he used public school
data on the weight lost by displaced workers' children. He went
on to say:

It is true that the Department of Labor has done a few studies of the
impact of automation on specific instances, but the employers who have
been willing to cooperate in making such studies possible appear to be

those for whom automation has presented no serious problems of worker displacement.

Things haven't changed much.

AN OWNER-OPERATED POULTRY PLANT

Forgoing systematic selection, I made a more informed choice of firms I knew employed both Anglo and Chicano workers. These choices were an owner-operated poultry plant and a large canning plant that is a subdivision of an agribusiness giant.

I wrote and called the president of the poultry plant for an interview. He refused, saying he didn't really want to get involved in such studies. He had recently suffered negative publicity over the housing he provided the migrants who worked peak seasons at the plant. Besides, it was 200 miles away and he was sure I didn't want to travel in the cold, midwestern winter. I assured him I'd be delighted, saying I had a new motorcycle that made the prospect of any travel more exciting. As it happened, he was a cycle enthusiast and relented.

I arrived at midnight the day before the interview and asked the night foreman, the president's nephew, for a tour of the plant, to which he agreed. He spoke of recent problems—labor costs and labor unrest. "People won't take these jobs even if we paid them $5 an hour. Women and migrants will because they expect less." When asked about proposed solutions, he wasn't sure if future plans were for more mechanization or moving further west, where American Indian labor was reportedly less troublesome than Chicano labor.

Another source of information was the patrons of a nearby bar where workers stopped after the second shift. A middle-aged woman I spoke with knew of no plans to automate, but talked about the practice of hiring high school students as strikebreakers.

The following day the company president gave no hard data on changes in the occupational structure by race and sex, or plans for changes in technology or location. He said, and I believed him, that most management would refuse to meet and talk about planned changes at all. He did offer the information that the plant employed some 400 people, 90 percent female by day, 50 percent by night. (The latter figure grossly underrepresented the proportion of women I observed on the night shift.) He said he kept no information by race, but considered women right off the farms to be the best workers, since they were accustomed to hard work. Men (who tend to work in beef packing rather than poultry) were more accustomed to being their own bosses, moving around more freely, not having their work monitored as closely. He reported no plans to install new machinery, such as the automatic deboning machine used by a competitor, because of the expense. Business—largely contracted from the Office of Economic Opportunity and the military—was picking up, but he anticipated no great changes.

The president referred me to a local social worker who had worked with him on migrant problems. Among other things, she reported an increase in bone and joint difficulties in the hands and wrists of the older women workers. This indicated to her that the tempo of meat stripping had increased lately. (Speed-up sometimes precedes automation.) Some months later, the work force of this plant was reduced from 400 to 225. It then closed altogether for "renovation." A former union official informed me recently that the plant never reopened, but moved out of state. She did not know where it had relocated.

THE CANNERY

The second on-site visit was to a large canning plant, a sub-division of a giant agribusiness corporation. I made appointments, after some delay, with the production manager and the head of the cannery's agricultural division. I asked the production manager for the distribution of workers by sex and race over occupation, hopefully covering some past years during which the plant's technology had changed, and for future projections by occupation. The production and personnel managers said they were sorry, but the plant kept no such records, nor did it make short- or long-term projections for labor-force needs. In conversation about the content of the production manager's job, however, he described one function: to keep records and make projections of labor-force needs for the plant. Reminding him that these were the very data I needed for careful research, I asked again if I could see past records or future projections. I could not, he said; that was "proprietary information." "How was one to do responsible research without such data?" I asked. "It's tough, isn't it?" he replied. He went on to explain: "Companies are scared. Particularly the big companies. So many regulations. Everybody supports the underdog. If you give them some data, they want it all." A tour of the plant was out of the question because of "health regulations." He foresaw no further automation in the plant, due to the visual work necessary to sort vegetables by color and quality.

I interviewed the head of the cannery's agricultural division. This division formerly contracted migrant labor for work in the plant and on the area's middle-sized farms from which the company bought its produce. The division no longer took contracting responsibility, having sold the migrant camps to the local farmers.

The head of this division said he had no information on farmers' plans to further mechanize field work, nor would he provide a list of the growers under contract to the company: "They prefer their names to be a private matter." He thought mechanization and large corporate farming had no future here, however, because the farmers were too "old fashioned" and "individualism was too strong." He did give the name of one farming family in the area—but they were out of town on vacation.

The land-grant university maintained a research station in the area; the horticulturist there had observed experiments on mechanization and genetically altered produce appropriate for mechanical harvesting. In response to questions about local growers' plans for mechanization, however, he said, "I just prefer you get that information from [the cannery]."

So far, no good. However, I had worked on the Grape and Lettuce Boycott Committee in this state, and through that work knew of the local migrant health committee. It was through the committee that I was able to make the contacts I needed for research. The committee suggested interviewing a local county official with a chatty and overly familiar style. He revealed that growing frustrations of area farmers indeed led to mechanized harvesting, even though the equipment was not entirely satisfactory on the smaller farms and softer soils of this midwestern area, compared to California. I returned to the horticulturist, who confirmed these reports, assuming the information had originated with company management.

The migrant health committee also helped circumvent the cannery's refusal to give the names of its growers. The health committee had compiled such a list by asking migrants where they worked. I was able to locate and talk with farming women from this group. Contrary to cannery management statements, they had no hesitancy about being interviewed. They reported some dissatisfaction with the company, primarily for the recent shift of responsibility for migrant housing from the company to the farmers, with no additional compensation for this added financial responsibility (Hacker 1977a). In one case, the family had decided to move to mechanization of field work, although they were hard-pressed to afford such a move.

A final word on data gathering. One might think the straightforward approach lies in the documents produced by various levels of government. Here, too, caution and awareness of special interests are necessary. Such awareness was exhibited by one farmer in his letter to the state newspaper:

Those [Census of Agriculture] statistics are available to agribusiness and marketing organizations. I'm sure [they] are immensely valuable to such firms and greatly reduce the risk in their decision-making. Yet I've never heard of a census of agribusiness or marketing organizations so farmers could know what prices they might have to pay for fertilizer and fuel. . . . Is it really helping the farmer, or is it just another aid for the USDA [United States Department of Agriculture], marketing firms and large agribusiness? (*Des Moines Register and Tribune*, incomplete reference)

Government statistics present difficulty for the researcher as well. It was hard to determine the growth of large corporate farming in this state. As Senator James Abourezk (Democratic senator) reports for a nearby state:

In analyzing corporation tax returns in Wisconsin, [Richard] Rodefeld [of Michigan State University] found that USDA had missed 252 farm corporations altogether. Further, they had underestimated the number of acres owned by corporations by 37%, acres rented by 269%, the number of cattle fed by 80%, and acres of vegetables by 37%. . . . I think that a census conducted by people who are sympathetic to corporations is not going to reveal information unfavorable to corporations. (Hightower 1973)

This statement is followed by a list of agribusiness corporations on the federal Census Advisory Committee on Agricultural Statistics.

Obtaining an accurate count of the number of migrant workers passing through the state was also a problem. The state's Security Commission reported the total number of migrant workers in 1973 at 637; the Department of Labor reported more than 2,000. The local migrant health committee, with close day-to-day migrant contact, reported more than 1,000 migrants in their three-county area alone. Their records and knowledge of farmers and farming practices year by year also allowed analysis of the reduction of migrants due to mechanization. Jobs for migrant workers—men and women alike—in this area suffered a 15 percent reduction in one year, due to mechanization of field work. Unemployment for female operatives was the highest of any sex-occupational group, but, with one exception, it was difficult to assess the relationship between these unemployment rates and technological change, or runaway plants on a firm-by-firm basis.

DISCUSSION

In this case study, organizational response to critical research did not appear to follow criteria by which we usually categorize complex organizations, for example, purpose, beneficiary, or public or private. Response appeared to vary by the sophistication of the management component. The university and the cannery had a highly developed and differentiated management system, staffed by men with specialized training in management skills. The owner-operated poultry plant and the agribusiness college program did not.

Physical Access

Access to classes, professors, instructors, administrators, and students is more difficult for an outsider at the university; for example, auditing courses often requires formal registration. One couldn't drop in at the university as one could at the college to chat with professionals about research; appointments had to be made. Students in the vocationally oriented courses at the college often wore uniforms coded by color—one color for printing, another for automechanics, and so on. Agribusiness and electronics were among those without this requirement, but students were still "batched" (Goffman 1963). They marched through the day to a series of classes, took coffee breaks and lunch hours together. These breaks were staggered against students in other courses, which provided a greater sense of community than in the more individualized programs at the university. It also provided a structured opportunity to talk with agribusiness students. Less homework at the college also meant more leisure, often spent with other classmates.

Access to the poultry plant was not easy, but it was not impossible as was the case with the canning plant's fences, guards, checkpoints, and other restrictions against roaming around. A tour was out of the question. Management at the canning plant gave no referrals to anyone who might have a point of view somewhat at variance with their own. The list of growers, for example, was "private." The president of the poultry plant volunteered such a contact with the social worker.

Access to Recorded Data

I found little resistance to dissemination of such data that existed in the college course. The director freely passed out what he had, usually from the State Development Commission, gave out names and addresses of people he thought I might like to talk with, tried to recall as much of past classes as he could. With the exception of one field trip, there was little resistance to participation and little withholding of information. The president of the poultry plant was not entirely free with what he knew, but he was not nearly so resistant as management of the larger plant in providing, for example, numbers of employees, what proportion female, and kinds of contracts. At both the university and the canning plant, people refused, dissembled, and lied outright.

Ideological Access

In the less sophisticated organizations—the college program and the poultry plant—people spoke their minds. Open access to an articulated ideology and the interests on which it rested was, to say the least, boggling. In the more sophisticated organizations, the ideology was less apparent. Reasons for noncooperation were ostensibly objective, factual, instrumental, and often false.

Existence of Systematic Data on Operations, Structure

Systematic data were present to a greater degree in the more advanced organizations. The university had data, the engineering center knew about technological change in local industry, the canning plant production manager had records and projections. In contrast, the head of the agribusiness program did not have, nor did he know of anyone else who had, records of graduate employment. Along the same lines, I doubt that the president of the poultry plant, his nephew, or the several others in management positions were involved to the same degree with record keeping and professional projections as was the production manager in the canning plant.

Finally, organized protest groups were in evidence, perhaps in dialectical response, in and around the organizations with a more highly developed management component—the university had its feminists, the cannery its local migrant committee. I had worked with both, and was now doing research with their cooperation. This collective work was most helpful in overcoming obstacles introduced by a sophisticated management. These protest groups in or around the more highly developed organizations had gathered information, helped me do so, or both. In the university, feminists had gathered some information on women's participation in agribusiness education, and had won visibility so that others knew where to channel new information as it emerged, despite administration refusals. The migrant health committee had also gathered information that was not forthcoming from management, for example, the list of growers. They also had more careful and accurate data on the number of migrants in the area than did government agencies.

CONCLUSIONS AND SUGGESTIONS

The pattern of resistance and control in this case study suggests that management sophistication may be a useful independent variable in the study of organizational reaction to critical research. Along with measures such as administrative intensity and hierarchical differentiation of a management component, I would also suggest exploring the proportion of management with formal management training. In such training, for example, the field of organizational behavior, we find a powerful integration of research and action uncritically joined. Some management skills transmitted to students may be more benign than others. Some, however, informally transmitted, may deal purely with techniques of manipulation, control, and other more obviously antisocial behaviors (Hacker 1978). Complexity or differentiation, technological sophistication, and resistance to critical research have all been conceptualized as mechanisms of social control (Braverman 1974; Woodward 1965). Secrecy, limited access, lying, and distortion may simply represent one subset of such management skills. Weber spoke for attention to control over the means of administration. Along with Acker (1973) and Kanter (1975), I suggest this is a particularly significant concept for those concerned with women's labor force experience and with critical research.

Certainly we should continue legal efforts to render organizational operations more visible to the public from which they draw their strength. Such efforts provided data for a careful assessment of the impact of technological change on women workers in the telephone company (Hacker 1979b). In my experience with four industries, AT&T showed the most sophisticated resistance to critical research—a smooth appearance of great cooperation and most convincing utilization of all methods of resistance noted above. In that case, however, a nationwide civil rights action eased access to significant data. Scholars continue fine research and action suggestions along these lines (Sjoberg and Littrell 1973; Noll 1976), but this alone leaves critical research several steps behind management which organizes that information (Barnet and Mueller 1979).

A second path is to fight fire with fire. At times, I obtained more information than I might have otherwise when my own methods approached the gray area between professional ethics and the standard operating procedure of management ethics. In gaining access to the community college courses and interviews, I was not as open as I might have been about the values from which my research emerged. (I had discovered how quickly doors closed when I was more explicit.) At the poultry plant, I arrived early and secured a tour. I didn't correct misperceptions of informants if that meant losing information. This experience is both unpleasant and less than hopeful. One does not wish to share the alienation of the powerful by fighting fire with fire—particularly in such an uneven battle.[3] Still, more useful information was obtained when I acted with some variance from openness and honesty—professional norms as I had formerly accepted them. This may suggest that some of the norms themselves function to protect powerful organizations—which don't play by the same rules—from critical research.

Another path is the reunion of social action and critical research. In my experience as an action researcher, this integrative process is most satisfying. As a side benefit, it was also the most effective approach toward sociological understanding through insight and better data. This process provided very good day-to-day education in special interests that can hide or distort certain kinds of information, ways in which that happens, and alternate routes around these obstacles. Short of being action-researchers, we could strengthen communication between researchers and people of action who share a critical perspective.

Coming full circle, critical action reunited with research should improve the discipline as a whole. Differentiating critical research from action weakens both, and lessens the discipline's significant function as a critical force in society. One-sided support of the integration of conventional action and research produces an uneven and distorted development in our collective sociological wisdom, particularly its methodology. This will reduce any sociologist's ability to make good sense out of social phenomena. We can look forward, then, to a better sociology when critical research is reunited with social action, and when "people's methodology" is more fully incorporated into courses on research methods—eventually into the texts themselves.

As Gouldner (1976) would correctly perceive, however, my argument for the general good—a better sociology—is secondary to special interests, the role of women in society, and the role of the activist/researcher in sociology.

NOTES

1. This is a turn on Jim Hightower's AAP book title, *Hard Tomatoes, Hard Times* (1973), which analyzes agribusiness influence on and through land-grant colleges. One agribusiness response to labor costs and difficulties was the development of a mechanical tomato picker and the subsequent need to develop a tomato with harder skin for mechanical fingers—hence the title.

2. Agriculture, veterinary medicine, and engineering showed almost no participation of women as faculty or students. Per student funding of these colleges ranged from $1,078 to $4,862. Education and home economics had the highest proportion of women, with per capita budgets of $750 and $950, respectively.

3. Secrecy, it has been noted, is also a hallmark of violent as opposed to nonviolent strategies, which should give us further pause (Lakey 1973).

Part II

Gender and
the Culture of Technology

DOROTHY: In these studies of the culture of engineering, you made a transition in your work. From looking at what corporations were doing to people, you're now looking at the people who design the technological changes displacing people. What led you to want to do this other kind of work?

SALLY: In the experience of studying agribusiness and AT&T . . . Oh, the managers I came in contact with, most of whom had had technical or engineering background. There was this kind of blindness to people. And the racist jokes, the sexist jokes—you know, the weird stuff about nature and sexuality—all of that was there and it made my skin crawl. There was something so sleazy about sexuality in their jokes, exhibits, pictures on the machines. I mean, it was just pervasive. It was blatant. It began to make you wonder, and the Marxist theories didn't help. It was a gaping hole in women's issues. There was no way to deal with sexuality—or we didn't find one. All that was there. I needed an approach that didn't require bad guys with bad attitudes and blatant sexism and racism and stuff like that, an approach that would let you look at the nature of the way the whole thing was put together—the way in which the schools were related to industry and the importance of the military—we were a little slow on the military, which I now think is crucial. [See the work of Barton Hacker.]

I was just thinking about the personal difficulties in the collectives—something I wanted to deal with in the book and didn't—how they turned so much around alliances, coupling, romances, and so on. Just about that time, my relationships in the collectives changed. So I wanted to move on. So again there was this opportunity of funding. About that time there was this application for a fellowship at MIT. Again I said, "I'm not going to take money from . . . " but Bart encouraged me to apply. I went ahead and applied, figuring that if they would let me do it the way I wanted, it would be just a delight to get inside MIT, which so represented . . . you know, after these years of talking to telephone engineers and agricultural systems analysts and managers and so on, to find someplace where business and industry were so tightly fused at the time. And again, like the Ford grant, I cast it in terms of "Do what you want to do and they can take it or leave it." I said I wanted to study MIT because that was the closest combination of management and an industry. I wanted to learn how technological decisions were made that shaped industrial technology. That was true. It was not the whole truth perhaps, but . . . [laughter].

DOROTHY: True enough.

SALLY: I wanted to know how they slept at night. Which is an interesting question. Ideology is powerful and we are so *creative*. We can think of many, many reasons to justify what we are doing. Industry and business are fused up and down, but MIT was the closest and I wanted to see how ideology was created, to see how it was passed on and how people were made into these "managers" that I had talked with. That was fascinating. But it was also true that my lover at the time in the collectives was messing around with somebody else and so

105

it made the decision whether to stay politically active in Des Moines or move out of town, a little easier to move out of town. And the reason I bring that up . . . I don't know if it will fit into this context or not . . . is that in honesty, it's those kinds of experiences, I think for women more than men, those personal things affect our decisions in important ways. But I guess in one way those opportunities had to be there.

The Ford Foundation grant didn't make getting access any easier. Maybe the credentials made it a little easier with AT&T and they probably helped a little in the agribusiness study. But having an MIT post-doc, 12,000 bucks, we're talking big money here! It made it a lot easier to begin. I wasn't quite sure what I wanted to do or how I was going to do it. I just wanted to be there and kind of soak it up. Just get the sense of the place—it was *big* and *cold* and people were weird and strange; the buildings are all numbers and there was very little attention to creature comfort—you couldn't find food! These are all clichés about MIT, but they are all true. Though it's a lot better now—they've got a lot of really nice cushy places for eating.

Having David Noble as my officemate made a lot of difference because I was still working on the AT&T stuff. And reading his work . . . all these AT&T executives who were working with the military to change the nature of engineering education, around World War I! That was an eye-opener, but still didn't become crucial at that period of my thinking. But I didn't know that I wanted to do *a study* yet, so it was mostly just sitting around—sitting around, listening, talking, beginning to get some stuff that was persistent enough to be a pattern. Just letting the institution and the culture soak in. But the jokes began to bother me. I was sitting in on classes, some very, very good classes, to learn more about the technology of telecommunications. One guy was very, very good in politics. He started out by saying, "I used to spend the whole first day or two talking about the political implications, but now we just have so much technical work to do . . ." This is really a neat guy, he's a neat person, but [sigh]. Then I sat in on this other class and the guy was so irritating and arrogant—he was an asshole—and his jokes were so stupid and they would put down people with less power than him. So, I got together with this friend of mine—a really nice guy who was getting his Ph.D. in electrical engineering but he was open to feminism—he was just polar opposites. I thought, if I am going to do a study of these jokes—I thought that the jokes putting down the body, making fun of bodily functions, would be the most frequent—hell, I know how to do content analysis, but it's so subjective. Here's the scientific approach coming in. So I asked this guy if he would help me. We decided that if more than three people out of a hundred in this class laughed, that that would be a joke—that was the empirical, the operational definition. It was a kick. So we would sit there, I would be counting jokes and putting down what they were about and I would be listening and he would say, "You missed that one." [laughter] [Dorothy: laughter] And then he would miss one and we would sit there elbowing each other. I feel pretty good about that. If I had not done it in that way, it would be real loose. I think that it was well done and it was a kick. Then comes the part of trying to put them together in categories. And then trying to make sense of why so many of the jokes had to do with things that were abstract, clean, technically elegant. Body jokes were actually the least. Women, and blacks and workers, were in the middle.

So I was doing that and that was helping to some extent, because by that time I was beginning to see that there was some very, very important role for sexuality in the construction of technology. Not just "gender," but "sexuality" . . . well, gender because the sexuality—the eroticism had to be gendered. This one professor, for example, referred to active elements as male. There would be this big formula, and then one term in the formula would be the one that made all the difference and it's "this little guy." It's like Ollie North—"this little guy"—you know, with sort of a grin. The women would do this too. This is what the women would tell me . . . "I'm not a feminist. They accept me as one of the guys." Cynthia Cockburn points out that when you become one of the guys you have to suppress your own sexuality. And spontaneity. And in a field like technology, I mean that's a lot of what you have to work with.

Anyway, I knew there was something going on there. I knew there was something going on with "women" and "gender" and "the natural world." I knew this from the radical feminist stuff and the agribusiness . . . listening to these agribusiness people in class—ugh! So I was trying to figure out how I would go about asking those questions in a random sample survey technique—again that's where I got my degree was NORC. I figured I could do it—not in questionnaire form, not in the yes/no forced choice—but in an interview schedule. Why I taped them, I don't know. But we got the tapes and we got them transcribed. If anybody is interested in looking at that. I talked with people . . . the year was running out and we, as the three of the four students who were selected for the program, and some faculty, were arguing for another year. But in the end they kept on David and Ray and got rid of me real quick—didn't like what I was doing, didn't like this notion of interviewing faculty about their sexuality. In the meantime I had three-quarters of it done, so I turned around and got odd jobs at different universities to finish it. What I was trying to get was some empirical verification of dominance over nature as linked to gender. Because there wasn't too much out, but [Mary] Daly's work was out; [Annette] Kolodny's was out; [Shulamith] Firestone's was out; I think [Sherry] Ortner's work was out—this "woman is to nature as man is to culture" theme. I liked it and I believed it; it explained a lot, but—and maybe it's this background or training—there wasn't any proof. I wanted some empirical data behind it, acceptable to the normal community of scholars. In a way it's like again fighting on their turf. There's danger to letting people define that. If that's all you do, I think you're down the tubes. But if you can do that *also*. . . .

So I talked with someone who had some travel money they wanted to use up before it had to be turned back. There was a guy there and we were talking about some of my earlier work on leisure. He said, "You know, you could do this in a leisure framework." And it just all made sense. Because I wanted to know, because of my own background, what they had enjoyed as children, what turned them on, what pleasures—the pleasures of childhood that lead to career choices later. That sounds very straightforward, but I wanted to know if they played with girls, what they thought of them; wanted to know the sexual, sensual experiences. It was the "sensual experiences" question that got me in trouble, you know, sunlight on landscapes and rhythmic music and texture and sounds and . . . They enjoyed talking about it; I enjoyed talking about it, but this is what I had to go to the Human Services Committee about.

So that's how that research got put together and done. There were a couple of people who were out of work who did some of the interviewing. I wanted male interviewers also, and one of the people that I hung out with had a degree but he was a musician and he played pinball machines to clear his head . . . but he was very computer oriented—wacky; and Bart did, I think, one or two. Did David [Noble] do any? So it was kind of a mix. I did most of the electrical engineers—I was particularly interested in them. It isn't "tight." It isn't a really good design. There wasn't that much money or time.

But that's what I did. I wanted to find out the ideology of power. How they put it together. What gender had to do with it. How that was linked, then, in the way in which the kids that grew up on it would then go out and organize industry. The way in which AT&T is put together. And "What did you learn in school today?" That is what the paper on the mathematization of engineering [Chapter 6] was trying to show.

The ethnography on learning mathematics that I did for that paper was after I came here [to Oregon State University, Corvallis]. I had time to do this ethnographic work that I wouldn't have had earlier when I was involved in more active political life. I wanted to learn about the mathematics learning from the inside, from experience. I wanted to know *what it feels like*. I called it "doing it the hard way." I wanted to learn about the mathematization of engineering, where it comes from, what it does, how it's organized, how it is passed on, transmitted. It was after moving out here and knowing what it felt like to be an engineering student after I did the ethnographic experience that I then came to do the historical work [on engineering]. Because I was just fascinated to know where all this came from.

But I must not have done the ethnography well enough, since so many people are getting it wrong. I've seen two reviews now which kind of dismiss it as saying—one was by a young woman, a computer scientist up in Portland, and then the other was just a half sentence in another paper—both of which say that my point

is that women can't do math. And everybody knows that's not true
. . . so . . .

DOROTHY: Okay, tell me how people are getting it wrong.

SALLY: They think the main point that I am making is that women
can't do mathematics and therefore we shouldn't have mathematics
as a criterion for getting into engineering. Rather than that, what I'm
talking about is that testing and training in mathematics is embedded
in a very masculine-shaped professional organization of knowledge
and evaluation. It's not math, itself . . . you know women can do
math perfectly well. Toward the end of the article, I said we should
take math testing away from engineering as a criterion to let people
in or out, because it's this whole dominance/submission game. It's
grizzly to see it and it's grizzly to feel it—even when you like math
and physics.

Of course, there may be, as we were discussing last night,
a discipline that is interesting—you know the focusing and the
clear-mindedness and the ability to cut everything else out of your
awareness . . .

DOROTHY: That's interesting. You haven't yet related that to the
culture of engineering as you've analyzed it. I mean the linkage
between that and the kind of discipline mathematics creates. Do you
think there is a linkage there?

SALLY: Yeah. I think that discipline is where patriarchy got the moon.
I think it's a way in which the energies, particularly erotic energies, are
so constricted in relations of dominance and submission. The models
of that discipline are found in the ancient schools of engineering, and I
think Bart's right that those, themselves, have their roots in the military,
which for thousands and thousands of years have been the primary
patriarchical institutions. So there is not just gender differentiation
but gender subordination from the git go. What I am looking at is
one small piece—how does that come down to affect the working
woman, and how that comes through the institutions of engineering
and engineering education to create the manager who thinks it is not
only okay but the best, most efficient, productive, smartest way to
organize the workplace. Now relate that to the things we were saying
about AT&T, that it was put together by geniuses to be run by idiots.
And you know, women are going to be the "idiots." Until they are all
mated out and then there will be new idiots.

I was trying to figure out how gender was implicated in that,
because my reading of any of the theories that were floating around,
the radical theories, Maoism, Marxism, you know, whatever, didn't for
me fully enough explain. The radical feminist theories in the beginning
seemed to be taking account of both exploitation and oppression. They
seemed to allow the entrance of sexuality and eroticism. But if you went
with that you lost sight of both the working women and the organization
of technology and capitalism. It was just so hard to get it all . . . and still
is. If we had it together we wouldn't have so many problems. The idea
of capitalist as "bearer" of capitalist relations ties in here. With his or her

peculiar twist of being both driven by and drawn to doing the work of capital. I do see the upper-middle class and the upper class as more caught in a mesh, a finer mesh, in terms of movement. I see them as a little more controlled on those levels—more controlled through their sexuality. And more likely to use it as a weapon against blacks, the poor, women. I think, sometimes, that children whose pleasures are overly programmed—dancing lessons, language lessons—one of my friends told me about her finishing school and how she learned to "sit"—the programming of the body in that sense seems to be part of the discipline that for both men and women serves the patriarchal institutions. It's nice to have escaped that.

Chapter 4

The Culture of Engineering:
Woman, Workplace, and Machine

MANAGERS AND THE CULTURE OF ENGINEERING

*F*or the past several years I have studied the impact of technological change on women workers in four industries in the United States—insurance, printing and publishing, agribusiness, and telecommunications. Over a three-year period of technological change in the telephone company, women lost 22,000 jobs, while 13,000 more jobs were obtained by men. Automation eliminated operator and entry-level clerical work, while it simplified male craft jobs to the clerical level, drawing women in, only to push them out again in the next round of automation (see Chapter 1). In agribusiness, automation and runaway shops have reduced employment for women factory operatives, Chicana[1] and white; mechanization of farm work has reduced employment among migrant workers, male and female. Women farmers faced a double threat—the economics of large-scale agrotechnology and politics that favored male over female farmers (see Chapter 2). Office automation in an insurance company slowed the growth rate in some clerical occupations, following patterns noted by Feldberg and Glenn (1980).

In a newspaper firm, "cold" typesetting (computerized, phototype-setting versus hot-metal processes) also threatened male craft work, as that work became clerical in nature and designed for women workers at much less pay. In this case, however, a strong, predominantly white male union retained the deskilled work for their members (who referred to it as "junk" work).

The more sophisticated technical work created by automation provided employment more often for men than for women—in engineering, management, sales, systems analysis, and the like. With some variations, the flow of workers through occupations during technological change appeared to proceed from white male to minority male to female, then to machines. In the newspaper firm, this process was short-circuited as white male labor gave way only to machines,

111

designed, managed, and often maintained by white males with more sophisticated technical skills.

In all instances, women's home responsibilities, lack of employment options, unresponsiveness of unions, and opposition of husbands and male co-workers inhibited women workers' ability to protect their interests collectively. Such factors, and the way in which work is organized, heightened female attrition rates, further easing the processes of automation. Most of these findings fit nicely into a Marxist framework. Sex and race effectively divided the working class, inhibiting solidarity and weakening class consciousness and struggle. Women and minorities functioned as a reserve labor army, particularly useful when a company moves rapidly to capture a new market or to change its technological base (Christoffel and Kaufer 1970; Braverman 1974). The benefits of technology go to the owners, not to society in general.

Some parts of the story did not fit quite so nicely, however, such as domination and exploitation of women by husbands, male co-workers, and unions, as well as by corporations (Hartmann 1977; Brown 1979; Sokoloff 1980). These factors suggested patriarchal elements at work. Observing the ways managers viewed women within the industries studied, I found views that justified exploitation of women, including easier manipulation of their labor during times of technological change. Such attitudes were prevalent especially among those managers with technical or engineering backgrounds. Most of the managers I interviewed in the telephone company, for example, had backgrounds in electrical engineering. The engineering/managers in industry seemed especially male centered, and prone to gender the social and physical world. Activities, styles of interaction, jobs, machines, devices, even bodies of knowledge, were often characterized as having masculine or feminine properties, appropriate to men or women. These gender-based perceptions were also stratified, or hierarchically ordered. What was womanly had low status; what was manly had high status. Considered dumb and/or sexy, women were viewed with suspicion and distrust, and were more closely controlled than men.

I was particularly struck by the way managers insisted that "ladies" didn't move. Touring a printing plant, where the head of Research and Development showed us the hand bindery, I observed middle-aged women sitting at a table, stuffing material into covers for binding. "This is the only place we hire girls in this department," our guide told us. When asked why, he said, "This is boring, routine, detail work. Men won't sit still for that kind of work." He referred to Ms. magazine, which the plant printed, as "the porno department."

In a poultry plant, I learned that "people won't take these jobs anymore, but women and migrants will because they expect less."

Management reported that farm women worked out best in deboning, because farm men were accustomed to greater freedom of movement and chose beef rather than poultry work. Telephone company job descriptions for traditionally female work read: "works close to the desk," "works under close supervision," "writes in small spaces." Men's work at corresponding tasks differed largely by the freedom to move about inside and outside the plant (Northwestern Bell Telephone Company 1973).

The tendency to polarize male and female, masculine and feminine extended to bodies of knowledge. In agribusiness, "manly" fields were beef production compared to poultry, crop production compared to horticulture, salesmanship (which stimulated needs) compared to womanly clerking (which simply supplied what a customer wanted).

Agribusiness training classes portrayed women consumers as ignorant, incapable of shopping without male guidance, and dangerous when exercising choice (for example, choosing vegetable additives, boycotting beef, protesting extensive use of agribusiness chemicals). Women were considered suitable for routine, detail work and child care, which freed the mind of man for decision-making (see Chapter 3).

These observations suggested a relationship between sex and dominance in the organization of industry; that the managers expressing these views most often shared a technical or engineering background seemed particularly worthy of note. Engineering contains the smallest proportion of females of all major professions and projects a heavily masculine image that is hostile to women (Rossi 1965; Ott and Reese 1975). Women are not easily accepted as colleagues by men in the field. Many engineering magazines are liberally sprinkled with advertisements portraying women draped suggestively over one piece of equipment or another. The *Iowa Engineer*, published at Iowa State University, came complete with a centerfold "E-Girl of the Month" and a dirty-joke page. At scientific/engineering conventions, attractive women in bunny suits staff merchandise booths; a tape measure on a scantily clad model illustrates the benefits of the metric system. A university fair booth promotes agricultural engineering with a leather miniskirted mannequin, a sign on its rear reading, "Ag Engineering, for a BROAD education."

These examples reflect a culture of engineering, highly male centered. Publications, fairs, and conventions not only reinforce this culture, but socialize young engineers/managers as well. An earlier, more powerful, socializing agent is the educational institution that trains these future managers. In order to explore further the development of this culture, I spent a year in participant observation and interviewing at a prestigious institute of technology in the eastern United States where the interests of management and technology are closely linked.

I sought to find out how and why in this culture the social and physical world may come to be gendered and how and why gender-linked characteristics come to be elevated or subordinated.

What I found were significant mind/body dualisms, a male-linked mind superior to a female-linked body. In the following section I describe findings of my research at the institute that support this view. In the third section I speculate on the meaning and implications of such dualisms for women, workplace, and machine.

AT THE ENGINEERING INSTITUTE

The institute was a major point of origin and transmission of engineering culture, as exhibited in the behavior and attitudes of both engineering students and faculty, and in classroom procedures and general atmosphere. I participated in and observed classrooms, seminars, lectures, and social gatherings, and conducted a systematic series of in-depth interviews with engineering faculty and a comparable sample of humanities faculty members.

My first impressions reflected perhaps little more than a stereotype of what was a technological milieu. The buildings were large and austere. The place was quiet. Dominant elements appeared to be mechanical and physical rather than social—sophisticated laboratories seemed to both shape and reflect the nature of social interaction. Compared with other campuses where I had studied or worked, presentation of one's physical and social self seemed less meaningful to students, and I met less affect than elsewhere. Male students encountered difficulty with community or cross-campus parties, where the very mention of the institute "turned off" women, and they were occasionally referred to as "turkeys." Many students identified their bodies with machines.

Snyder (1971) has contrasted metaphors among such students ("I need a tune up," "retool," "add gas," "get the carburetor adjusted," and the like) with organic metaphors (for example, "cultivating," "nurturing young plants") common on a nearby women's campus. Students were encouraged not to develop serious relationships with "girls." Relationships with females, other than for immediate, specific sexuality, would distract them from their work and drain their energy (Snyder 1971); hence the qualified acceptance of women students only as "one of the guys."

My in-depth interviews with a random sample of members of the engineering faculty—a procedure that produced an all-male sample—and a comparable sample, then, of men in the humanities faculty (N = 40) were designed to follow some of these issues in the culture of engineering. I wondered about gender-assigned tasks and behaviors in childhood, such as intimacy in social relations, early experiences with girls, attitudes toward characteristics considered womanly, and toward nature, and the sexualization of technology itself. I hoped to find links between childhood experiences of elite engineering professors and their current values.

When questioned about intimacy in childhood family and friendship relationships, engineering faculty reported little: "Close, within reason"; "Never very warm in exchange of feelings"; "Never dependent on others in an emotional sense . . . could be quite happy on a desert island"; "I didn't have personal feelings as a child"; "Most men even now seem to be able to form warm relations . . . but not especially intimate." Others described themselves as shy, and suggested that "an interest in learning how things worked" might insulate one from social relations or substitute for them. Humanities faculty recalled a little more intimacy, but stressed the negative as well: "Close and contemptuous." More typically, they also recalled "strong barriers to communicating emotional things."

Relationships with girls were not a source of childhood pleasure for either group. One engineer said, "They weren't my ball of wax." Others were "intimidated by girls"; "ignored them"; "felt insecure about them." Most spoke of all-male play groups, schools, and colleges. At one boarding school, boys were punished for talking to girls in town. Some humanities faculty reported friendships with girls in childhood, but most were like engineering faculty in being segregated from girls and "puzzled" or "mystified" or "frightened" or "shy and insecure."

Questions about sexual experiences tended to yield mere yes or no answers. But another question touching on physical pleasure of a particular kind—"Were you good at, or interested in, sports or athletics as a child?"—produced some unexpected responses. The engineering faculty I interviewed were generally attractive and robust in appearance, but two-thirds of them painfully recalled children's bodies that would not do what they should: "I was fairly uncoordinated"; "painful experience"; "never very good at sports"; "started out roly-poly and pudgy"; "I was really awful"; "a sissy"; "sickly"; "I wasn't courageous." One recalled being picked last for the playground team; another, his fear of having the ball hit toward him as he stood alone in left field. Another worried about embarrassing a gung ho father. Others recalled attempts to compensate for physical shortcomings by "being head of the class" in everything else. (These results were shared with those interviewed. One pointed out they had likely advanced in school grades more rapidly than their peers, and were therefore two or three years younger than classmates.) In contrast, among humanities faculty, many also had felt incompetent in sports as children, but did not seem to care that much.

Only one, with a long history of interest in things technical, recalled the strong and painful feelings typical of the engineering faculty.

To explore sensual pleasures, I asked for recollections of pleasures such as the play of sunlight, colored lights, quality and texture of materials, pleasurable tastes and smells, and music and good rhythm. About half of the engineers, chiefly those in the more abstract, scientific fields of engineering, recalled no such pleasures. Some thought them abnormal for men, unmanly, or "my wife's concerns." (A few recalled visual pleasures of a kite against clouds, reflections from a lake on clear summer evenings, the ripple of sunlight on moving waters; aural play, for example with echoes; tactile pleasures such as sanding wood and walking on snow.) In sharp contrast, almost all the humanities faculty recalled sensual pleasures as a source of much gratification in childhood.

About half of both groups remembered pleasure in being outdoors, in the natural world. Some recalled the pleasures of solitude, "loved the stillness" of hiking. Most, however, stressed the skills of manipulation of cognitive control, classifying or analyzing, scouting, changing or improving what one had found.

I asked these faculty why "woman" or "womanly" was associated with nature, why we tend to see nature as female. Avoiding the obvious "Mother Nature," I quoted Bacon on pursuing nature in her secret paths and similar passages to suggest what I wanted to learn about. No respondent made the association between women and nature himself, but when asked why others might, engineering faculty replied: "because of the whole cycle of having periods and all that"; "[to protect women], men are more aggressive"; "Women end up at home without a direct role in survival. . . . childbearing . . . is a little more obviously relevant to nature than to man, nature being growth and reproductive"; "The earth gives plants as woman gives children"; "It's a very basic and primitive image"; "People's interpretation of nature, emotionally, is out of my field . . . the hard side of nature is my business"; "Women and nature look nice"; "Nature is where everything comes from, including babies."

For engineering and humanities faculty alike, reproduction is the key linking women with nature in the minds of men. But humanities faculty, unlike engineers, were also apt to comment on aspects of both women and nature seen as unpredictable, uncontrollable, and dangerous.

Engineering faculty ranked technical expertise as more valuable than knowledge of social relations. They described social sciences in womanly terms: soft, inaccurate, lacking in rigor, unpredictable, amorphous. Very few felt inadequate because they lacked knowledge of social relations or social systems. Almost all, however, felt engineers more qualified than most to move into management. They perceived little difference between managing people and managing technical systems.

At the institute, I found that fields within engineering were also ranked, informally, along an "earthy-abstract" continuum. Electrical engineering (EE) carried more clout and status than, say, civil engineering. The former was considered "cleanest, hardest, most scientific," the latter far too involved in physical, social, and political affairs. Most engineers agreed with the stereotype of EE, although those outside that field resented its power and status, merely because the field was closer to abstract science.

In *The Existential Pleasures of Engineering*, Samuel Florman (1976) stresses the sensual and physical, as well as intellectual, pleasures derived from the practice of engineering. However true this might be of others, it was not the picture most electrical engineers painted of themselves.

When asked what it was about their work that gave them most pleasure, their answers suggested something quite different: "The best hard science is flawless, with simple systems [so large] you can deal with them by statistical methods"; "The mathematical symbology seems to me very pretty . . . can represent so many different things and rather subtle connections"; "It's very hard to remember enough to put order into nature. You have to have some structure for it always, and that structure is beautiful"; "reducing to rationality, although it is right on the border, just barely rationalizable"; "My mother was a hysterical woman. . . . I think somewhere along the line I felt the need for things you could trust. . . . That was the attraction of mathematics"; "some degree of elegance, aesthetically and technically"; "the beauty of finding that single equation that sums up everything, that explains everything."

These are pleasures not unlike those derived from empirical social research. The question is not only why this work is enjoyable, but also why it is so prestigious and highly rewarded. Further, little is to be seen here of the "crafting" about which Florman waxes so eloquent. That crafting is more likely now left to people without managerial or decision-making functions, or is incorporated into the machine.

A final question invited comparison of traditional ways of organizing work in industry, along hierarchical lines, with newer nonhierarchical forms: those that rotate tasks and allow workers and professionals to teach each other their skills. One engineer at the institute had in fact reorganized his laboratory so that engineers, technicians, and bottle washers did rotate tasks and share skills.[2] Most of the engineering faculty that I interviewed thought such an approach would be wasteful and inefficient. "Science can only be done by a highly trained elite." "The Chinese are lying about what they've discovered [working nonhierarchically] or about how they've done it." "It would only give them [lab workers, secretaries] something to talk about at cocktail parties." Although a few thought some sharing of tasks, especially crafts, would benefit engineers, no one considered that sharing clerical work would be helpful to them. The humanities faculty contrasted with engineering in that most favored a more egalitarian organization of work. Some of the responses seemed to reflect a common masculine experience among members of both groups. Many men on both engineering and humanities faculties had learned to find pleasure in ordering the natural world. They experienced sex-segregated childhoods and subsequent anxiety about "girls." Almost all explained the woman-nature identity in terms of reproductive ability, but humanities faculty added that both women and nature could be dangerous. The engineering faculty tended to differ from those in the humanities in recalling less pleasure of involvement with social or sensual experience, more discomfort with sports or distress about the way a young boy's body should behave. Engineering faculty had also learned to place greater value on hierarchical relations as rational, and on abstract and scientific skills as worthy of greater social rewards than other skills.

In the privacy of an elite institution, where a consensus on some basic values might be assumed, this emphasis on hierarchy was taught to the next generation of engineers/managers in various ways. Classroom humor was an unexpected but clearly effective way to transmit key social values along with technical expertise. In various classes and seminars I audited (electrical engineering survey, decision analysis, telecommunications, artificial intelligence), professorial humor seemed markedly different from that in the social sciences. In these elite engineering classrooms, it seemed that wives, students and others with relatively little power were frequently the butt of jokes; there was a fair amount of mildly scatological humor as well.

With the help of a graduate student in electrical engineering, I conducted a systematic content analysis of jokes in a course on telephone technology taught by two professors and an engineer from the telephone company. This analysis showed students encouraged to laugh at, in order of frequency, (1) technical incompetence; (2) women, and to a lesser extent blacks and workers; (3) honesty or everyday morality; and (4) the body and its functions, through mildly scatological references.

By far the largest proportion (44 percent) of the 129 jokes recorded in this way focused on technical competence. Things overly compli- cated, messy, slow, redundant, cumbersome are the mark of a poor engineer or outmoded engineering; the work and the people responsible for it are the butt of the joke:

1. After drawing an earlier relay circuit, says, "OK, let's stop fooling around," and draws a very simple diagram of today's device.
2. "The picture of the Line Finder has an interesting error—it's printed sideways and since the function of gravity to restore the switch is a vital part of it, the Line Finder as pictured wouldn't work very well."
3. "You could tell when a line was busy in those days . . . there was wire in the jack."

This apparently harmless humor, which appreciates sophistication, difficulty, and complexity of purpose coupled with speed, elegance, and simplicity of design and construction, can be a source of pleasure in engineering or any other science. Such humor also heightens awareness of the technically competent class with which one wants to identify as against the class of incompetents one wants to avoid. Given a somewhat different emphasis, however, jokes of this type also reflect the way in which some professors made difficulty and competition ends in themselves in order to "separate the men from the boys." With such stress on the rational and technical and on competition for grades rather than on comprehensive understanding, the most creative and sensitive students opt out; those who recognize and accept the game continue (Snyder 1971).

Humor also reflected the great disdain of some professors for the social sciences:

4. "Scientists and engineers stand on the shoulders of giants. Social scientists stand on their faces."

Although engineering education apparently seeks to separate technology from its social context, social relations are very relevant to today's engineers/managers. I found that appropriate social values and behavior were often conveyed informally through classroom humor. In this second most frequent category of jokes (26 percent), the status of engineers was elevated over that of students, workers, ghetto dwellers, and, most often, women:

5. "A girl in (M) dorm wanted help with her homework. She called guys, either in her class—or one year ahead. [laughter]

She'd say, 'Where were we when we were cut off, wasn't it on problem three?' The guy would go along with this usually. Once she got a phone hacker. By hitting the button a number of times, you could tell which lines in the dorm were busy. . . . He did this while talking to her about 20 minutes, and only one other line was consistently busy. [By a simple calculation] you can get the room number from the phone number. So he says, 'By the way, how are things in 543?' "

6. "Multiple switchboards determine how long an operator's arms have to be. [The institute] used to have operators; when they walked down the hall their knuckles would drag the floor. They could serve 700 jacks depending on their position."

7. Workers, often black, were referred to as "coolies."

8. Comment after a tour of a switching system located in a black neighborhood, which was to be automated with the electronic switching system: "You may have noticed coolies running . . . here and there 'tweaking' [the system], and that's an expensive operation."

(The workers, many of them minority men, faced a 60–80 percent reduction rate after the change, according to a guide.)

9. Same tour: "Shall we take a bus or an armored car to get there?"

Third in frequency (17 percent) were jokes about morality or ethics—bluntly, about how to "rip them off."

10. About computers: "In the telephone, speed doesn't matter that much. Depends on who you're competing with. And accuracy—it's fixed so that the subscriber will believe it's him."

11. Joking references to stolen equipment.

Professors' jokes elevate the status of those who can break the rules and get away with it.

Last in frequency (13 percent) were jokes drawing some analogy between machine and body function, or simply a reference to such functions, most often scatological.

12. "The early version of an ESS [electronic switching system] looked like a well-built outhouse."

13. Answer to a question: "Weelll, this is all men's room hear-say . . . "
14. "You don't know when transistors are unhappy. Relays smell when they're unhappy."
15. Reference to timing the load of calls and flush toilets: "We all know that water pressure is correlated with the time of TV commercials."

Professors' jokes transmit values, warning the students what to avoid and what to emulate, approving the higher status and benefits of mental work, particularly of an abstract or scientific nature. Poking fun at the body and its functions may be the other side of this coin; putting down the body elevates the mind.

Among the several approaches to the analysis of humor, LaFave's (1974) seems most relevant to these data. His model explains the butt of a joke as opponent or competitor. The Marxist critique of capitalism more readily explains why workers or honesty might be viewed as opponents. The concept of a reserve labor army, which demands a divided work force such as that observed in the research on technological displacement, might explain the tendency to subordinate women and minorities further. But for understanding the elevation of abstraction and technical competence or putting down the body, we must look elsewhere—to the cult and culture of technology itself.

MIND/BODY DUALISMS:
WOMEN, WORKPLACE, AND MACHINE

In the industrialized world, technology fused with science pro-duces a new notion of the Good, a technical ideology held most strongly by engineers (Gouldner 1976). Technical skills compete with skills of nurturance and responsiveness to the ends of others (Rossi 1965), and the competition is pretty one-sided. Technical expertise is also closely related to what some consider modern day's most exciting and engrossing work, such as the design and development of advanced weapons systems. This work of protection and defense is most highly rewarded. But there are costs as well. Marcuse (1964) suggests that for technical rationality to "work" (as an ideology to shore up hierarchy in social relations) it must be divorced from sexuality:

> True knowledge and reason demand domination over—if not liberation from—the senses. . . . The link between reason and sexuality or eroticism

is broken; scientific rationality dominates. As nature is scientifically comprehended and mastered . . . the rational hierarchy merges with the social one. (p. 166)

The question, of course, is why this seems necessarily so, and why someone is willing to pay such a price. My exploratory work can only suggest areas for more thorough or systematic inquiry into such dualisms, their origins and meaning.

The research and observations presented here highlight strong elements of mind/body dualism in the culture of engineering. Such dualism also seems firmly linked to a preference for clearly defined and hierarchical relationships such as those found in the organization of industrial work. In Western society, the highest places in a social hierarchy are not held by those with qualities of the divine, but by those with qualities defined as scientific or technological rationality. The lowest places, the fewest rewards, are held by those with qualities of the womanly—nurturance, routine maintenance, intimacy, sensuality, social and emotional complexity. Possible origins of such dualisms are suggested by some to correspond to changes in social organization, such as increased fertility, women's subordination, and the separation of man from woman and child (Nielson 1978; Stanley 1980; for speculations relating to military institutions, see B. Hacker 1977a). Ideological justifications for such significant social transformations can be found in both myth and religion. Lewis Mumford (1970), for example, traces the "deity that presided over the new religion and the new mechanical world picture" of the sixteenth and seventeenth centuries to the ancient "Atum-Re, the self-created Sun, who out of his own semen had created the universe and all its subordinate deities . . . without the aid of the female principle" (p. 28).

Scatological humor, an almost exclusively male prerogative in modern society, may further reflect the evolution of men's concern for increasing female fertility during these transformations, and their separation from women and children. Philosophical and anthropological literature on scatological jokes and myths suggests that these also reflect man's concern with his creativity and sexuality, and the anxiety about his minimal role in reproduction. Dundes (1962) also discusses male envy of pregnancy and childbirth as a source of male creativity. His data on excretory myths offer examples of male fantasies of anal birth. These myths, he finds, serve a similar function:

The creator is able to create without reference to women. Whether a male creator spins material, molds clay, lays an egg, fabricates from mucous or epidermal tissue or dives for fecal mud, the psychological motive is the same . . . , a flaunting of anal creativity without the participation of women. (p. 1046)

In the fields of philosophy and science, both al-Hibri (1981) and Keller (1980) illuminate this male desire for generative power, the power to reproduce without women's participation. The mind is the instrument of creation; woman has been identified with the body. Today, as well, the mind is clearly superior to the body, which is dumb and sexy, unpredictable, and much in need of discipline and control.

Persistent mind/body dualism may well be the root of a central concern of present-day socialist analysis of technology (Braverman 1974), the separation of mind and hand in the labor process as management transfers craft knowledge to machines run by cheaper and less skilled hands. But the separation of mind from body followed the earlier social separation of man from woman and child. Socialist analysis may need a more extensive historical approach to integrate questions of women's place, and of sexuality, with the inquiry into the degradation of labor.

I believe such dualisms help explain both technological displacement as it varies by race and sex as well as class, and female exclusion in the culture of engineering. In Western society, it is a technological rather than a religious ideology that justifies the existing order. In the everyday lives of engineering/management, and in the early lives of leaders in elite engineering education, we see reflections of man/woman and mind/body dualisms, related to strong notions about hierarchy in the world of work.

Material conditions leading to a patriarchal ideology in history may parallel socialization experiences of both the engineering and the humanities faculty interviewed. Boys are separated from girls; both learn that females have babies and therefore have a closer link with nature. Women are viewed as better suited to child rearing as well as to childbearing than are men. Men benefit by relief from child care, by free home and self-maintenance, and by lack of competition for better jobs in the paid market (Sokoloff 1980; Brown 1979).

As Chodorow (1974) suggests, when only women do the parenting, boys learn to develop skills of cognitive control rather than of nurturance, intimacy, and the maintenance of daily life. They also learn to believe the former set of skills are more valuable than the latter; those who protect and provide for the others deserve a greater share of goods and services than do the protected.

Men on the engineering faculty shared with those in the humanities this general alienation from women, centering on reproduction, denial, or suppression of intimacy in social relations, and a desire to order the natural world. In childhood, however, men in the humanities faculty may have learned to accept conflict as naturally inherent in intimate social relations. But now they showed more concern than engineering faculty over the power and unpredictability of women. This is a pattern described by Fatima Mernissi (1975) in Muslim societies—a fear and respect for the power of women's sexuality—which, in those societies, is dealt with firmly and directly. This view of women does not seem to predominate in Western culture, where the individual is expected to control her/his own sexuality. Perhaps the engineering faculty epitomizes this more peculiarly Western view, one that places ever-greater emphasis on man alone and on his ability for rational self-control. Whereas men in the humanities in this research may have expressed concern for the unpredictability of female sexuality, the engineering faculty by comparison seemed more concerned with their own.

The men who chose engineering had early life experiences that emphasized aloneness, that allowed them greater distance from intimacy or the pleasures and dangers of "mixing it up" with other people. Many became fascinated instead with things, and how they worked. These experiences heightened the value placed on abstractions and control over the natural—women, reproduction, emotions, intimacy, sensuality, their own physical selves. It is only the body, however, that cannot be literally distanced to obtain such control.

Later in life—here, from observation in the classroom as well as interviews—engineers tended to learn that other men also, or the work qualities they represent, such as blacks, workers (Adamson 1980), social scientists, and finally even those in some fields of engineering, have womanly characteristics. Rather than being clean, hard, abstract, such nontechnical men or their activities show characteristics of emotionality, sensuality, or interest and skill in social complexity. A technological ideology justifies control over these other men as well, which in its turn brings greater reward for those with the skills of greatest abstraction and greatest technical competence. Social hierarchy along these dimensions appears the most rational way to organize people to accomplish work. This is a fairly well-articulated ideology of technology, as expressed by the engineering faculty in this study.

Gouldner (1976), however, in his work on ideology and technology, pictures a paleosymbolic system "older and earlier" than ideology. Preceding a publicly articulated ideology, the paleosymbolic, the "old snake brain" of beliefs and symbols, rests on a more private kind of communication. Its language is learned in childhood, linked "to [the] provision of gratification and security for the self of the learner, and hence with the most elemental system of affects." This language may generally be spoken only "to intimates in private settings," or among those presumed to share similar interests (pp. 224–25).

Gouldner's analysis is applied to the way management's needs shape the ideology of technology. But what I perceived among both engineers/managers and the way they viewed women workers and what I saw in the institute was an "old snake brain" of patriarchal beliefs, justifying male dominance. These beliefs underlie the new articulated ideology of technology, and may become more visible as the technological base and work force of industry are being substantially transformed.

A challenge to the technological worldview may very well be perceived as an attack on reason itself. But such challenges—women's entry into engineering or the crafts, for example—may bring to light more of the "paleosymbolic" elements beneath a technological ideology.[3]

These elements bode well neither for women nor, it appears, for the fruits of engineering, which may be shaped in ways many engineers themselves would not want to see (Garson 1977; Melman 1970; Hoos 1972). Such patriarchal elements in technology as they affect women, work, and workplace need also to be explored in relation to capitalism, research that I am pursuing for internal contradictions, as well as for the convergences and contradictions of the two systems. For example, increasing specialization and hierarchy have been linked to declining productivity and technical malfunction, as the number of organizational levels increases and with them the distances between engineers/managers and the workers and machines they must coordinate. Within engineering, automation produces demands that may lead to deskilling, now and in the near future (see Chapter 7). These changes may provide new conditions, perhaps new opportunities, for women. As Joan Acker (1980) tells us in her review of the literature on sex stratification: "The interesting and potentially useful questions are not how individuals get into certain slots, but how the structure itself is formed and what its changing contours are" (p. 29).

My central concern is to develop a framework that will help us understand those changing contours and how they will affect women, technology, and the workplace. The work of both Marxists and radical feminists can give us valuable insights. If this research approach aids us in reducing the imbalance of power between men and women, and in reversing the process of social hierarchy, it may also help transform the shape and direction of our current technological endeavors, our troubled relationships with others, with the natural world, and with or own physical, erotic selves.

NOTES

1. The term *Chicana* is used here to indicate women of Mexican-American descent, largely from the Texas migrant stream.

2. There were other notable exceptions to norms expressed by the randomly selected faculty. One professor in telecommunications devoted his first lecture to a brilliant analysis of social and political ramifications in this field. He noted that the increased amount of material to be covered no longer allowed him to integrate his analysis with technical instruction. Others worked uphill against the increasing tendency toward technical rationality. A professor in electrical engineering conveyed the rich language and context of Newton's work on color optics; a chemist analyzed the implications of military research and development in the field; many explored ecologically centered technologies; the director of a technology and values program struggled to salvage it from strong management-oriented influences. These were important but definitely variant efforts at the institute (Hacker 1983).

3. Like scatological myths and humor, popular culture and even everyday conversation about technology often reflect a masculine concern for creativity and reproduction. Florman's (1976) work reveals that sexuality and reproductive creativity are often channeled toward the machine, with metaphors of potency, creation of "new forms" of life, feelings of love, and so on. The very phallic imagery of defense technology is a cliché, as in a film by the aerospace giant, McDonnell-Douglas, "We Bring Technology to Life!" which portrays repeated views of rockets being erected and slow-motion shots of ejection. This portrayal parallels an engineer's comment about the "drive" introduced into electrical engineering by its increasingly tight links with industry, as the "electric penis approach." If we have here some elements of the patriarchal desire to create "without the participation of the female principle" that Mumford (1970) noted, we can hardly wonder that women are hard-pressed to enter and remain in blue-collar crafts or technical professions such as engineering.

Engineering the Shape of Work

E ngineers are the agents of the most radical social change. The profession designs and builds the physical world in which we live. Incorporated into that design are also new forms of social relations, brought about by transformation in transportation, communications, food production, and the like. Yet engineers often hold the most conservative beliefs about social and cultural change (Ferguson 1981). It is the purpose of this chapter to suggest that the radical changes brought about by engineers and their patrons must at least be matched by radical changes toward a more democratic society. I think that the problems of responsibility in engineering may not be fully addressed unless such change occurs in the structure of organizations within which the engineer him- or herself works.

Here, I will explore the engineer's responsibility in one environment—the workplace. As the engineer shapes industrial technology, he or she also gives form to social relations at work. The structure of these social relations can enhance or inhibit responsible behavior of individuals.

Bureaucratic organizations make responsible behavior difficult. They tend to foster a "who cares?" attitude at the lower levels of the organization, and the appearance of a "not me" attitude at the top (Gouldner 1976; Garson 1977). Those who choose engineering as a profession are likely to work in large bureaucratic organizations, but are less likely than most to have an interest in social structure or the complexities of social relations (Rossi 1965). Further, engineering education does little to increase students' awareness of these phenomena. And so the engineer is often oblivious to ways in which he or she both affects and is affected by patterns of relations on the job.

If engineers do have a "blind spot" about social structure, altering current patterns and finding alternatives to bureaucratic organization will be most difficult.

127

ENGINEERING/MANAGEMENT:
IMPACT ON OCCUPATIONS

I will begin by summarizing several years' research on engineering's impact—through mechanization and automation—on female and minority employment. This impact has often been devastating. I became curious about the apparent lack of interest or concern on the part of engineers/managers about how their decisions affected others, or even the structure of their own profession. In the second part of this chapter I present information gathered from interviews with engineering faculty in a prestigious eastern institute of technology. This report concerns faculty attitudes toward their own work, toward social science, and toward radical changes in industrial organization suggested here.

In previous research (reported in Chapters 1, 2, and 4), I studied the impact of technological change on employment of women and minorities in four industries. Expensive agribusiness technology makes farming all but impossible for the average person, especially the family woman. In the telephone company, and in printing and publishing, craft work was routinized into clerical work; in these and insurance, clerical work was automated. In agribusiness, mechanization eliminated migrant work in the fields; automation reduced employment in canning and meat-packing firms.

The flow of workers through occupations during the process of mechanization and automation showed that white male craft workers were replaced by minority male semiskilled workers, who were then replaced by women clerical or factory operators, themselves replaced by machines. New jobs created were computer related, and often filled once more by white males with technical/scientific training. The technical division of labor in industry thus interacts with the social division of labor based on sex and race (Braverman 1974). In this way, inequalities of opportunity are maintained in society.

During the several years' work on technological change and its impact on workers and work, I noticed that almost all of the managers with whom I spoke had technical backgrounds, particularly in engineering. We spoke different languages. I would ask about numbers of people and jobs lost to automation; most were truly puzzled, and replied in terms of time and dollars. Most vaguely believed automation created jobs, but had not explored the fact that new work generated was largely computer related and performed by technically trained white males, while that which was eliminated was work performed by working-class white men, minority men, and women. Few argued with the data when they were presented, but this was a problem none had thought about. Nor had they thought of the impact on a community, especially its young and relatively disadvantaged, when entry-level jobs are eliminated.

In the telephone company, for example, company-level engineers/managers had not deeply considered the social impact of the electronic switching system on employees. This system centralized many operations, and, in Iowa for example, led to the closing of rural offices. Older women workers in these offices were faced with the prospect of taking severance pay, early retirement, or tearing up roots and moving to the city.

At Bell Labs, high-level systems groups (BISP) were charged in part with eliminating "the need of tedious handling of large volumes of paper work," but not, also, with the problem of female unemployment. Another system (BSCUS) reduced employment in customer records and billing, up to 50 percent. (TDAS, TIRKS, SCOTS are also aimed toward the elimination of much clerical work.) Earlier innovations in placing and recording calls continue to eliminate the need for telephone operators. In a recent three-year period, technological change eliminated 36,000 jobs at the level of operator and lower-level clerical (see Chapter 1). Fiber optics should reduce the labor force, especially in repair, by 10 percent. Framework can be fully automated and switchwork markedly reduced (some 80 percent in one Boston office, by their report). "Clip and take" and phone store service reduce the need for installers.

Most telephone company engineers/managers, as I say, had not considered the disadvantages of such progress. At the very top of the corporation, however—at Headquarters and Bell Labs—awareness was greater. In fact, there had been considerable long-range planning to substitute the cheaper labor of women clericals for male craft workers after automation. Corporate leaders also explicitly suggested moving women into craft work scheduled for automation, because women "resist displacement less than men."

Engineering managers and owners emphasize values of efficiency, productivity, profit, and control. Lower-level engineers are expected to identify with the interests of the organization as articulated by those at the top. This expectation is explicit in engineering education, in lectures and texts.[1] As Gouldner points out, however, management interests are at times contradictory to good engineering—a condition that may foretell more difficult relations between engineering and business than exist at present. Here, I am interested also in the ways a management ideology encourages the engineer to ignore the impact of technological change on the community, in particular on workers. This effort is most successful within organizations structured to separate those who make decisions from those who carry out the work.

The telephone company is said to be a system designed by geniuses to be run by idiots. According to Eleanor Langer (1970), a writer who worked as a service representative for some months, the logic of training is to "transform the trainees from humans into machines. The basic method is to handle any customer request by extracting bits of information, by translating a human problem he might have into bureaucratic language so that he might be processed by the right department." Another author describes the organization of work in the phone company as follows:

> The ideal is an army of lower echelon workers behaving like parts of a precision machine, like flawless relays in an exchange circuit. A service rep's duties are as programmed as a computer. Instruction booklets describe any possible contingency she may expect and prescribe the precise way to handle it right down to the proper tone of voice. This programming is universal throughout the Bell system. A rep trained in New York will be able to sit down in Boston or San Francisco and perform her task flawlessly. Like a part in a machine she is interchangeable with identical parts anywhere in the system. (CULA 1972)

Bell does, however, know how to organize things so that people perform interesting work and perform it well. The role of the engineer at Bell Labs is defined in contrast with the oppressive conditions of women working at the bottom of the occupational structure. From *Mission Communication: The Bell Lab Story:* "Engineers need intimate contact among scientists and other engineers." There is a "need to relate to the outside world; a need for meetings, symposia, exchange with universities, postgraduate education for lower staff levels." "Money is important but one must also provide the opportunity for pride in workmanship. You need the respect of other men who understand what you've done." You have a "pride in skills and knowledge." You have "a free play of creative minds," "stimulating, challenging atmosphere." Achievement is important. Let them "exercise their creative power," for example, in the words of one, in finding great satisfaction in "the elegant solution." An organization structured like this, which treats its employees so well at the top and so poorly at the bottom, will not foster a sense of participation and responsibility among them all. They are likely to work at cross-purposes.

ENGINEERING EDUCATORS: ATTITUDES TOWARD THE STRUCTURE OF WORK

When work is organized by "idiots"—not uncommon in Western industrial organization—the work and the workers will suffer. Even the responsible, concerned engineer may find institutional pressures overwhelming, and the institution unresponsive.

Some researchers say that these processes also adversely affect the quality and practice of engineering. Woodward's (1965) study of British industries, for example, shows that more sophisticated (process versus batch) technologies add levels of occupations to an organization, particularly within the management component. Too many levels of occupations between the engineer and craft or production work in industry impairs communication and awareness. The separation of cognitive (design, decision-making) work—performed by the engineer—and the eye/hand work of the technician, operator, or craftsperson may lead to system failure, particularly in large-scale systems (Ferguson 1977; Noble 1980; Sandkull 1980; Rosenbrock 1977). Part of the problem facing the profession, then—quality engineering—may be embedded in the very social relations created by new technologies.

To explore engineering ideology "at the top"—where the interests of engineering and management are highly fused—I interviewed a random sample of the engineering faculty at MIT (N = 30). I was interested in the beliefs that perpetuate blindness to structural factors, such as technological displacement, callousness to the needs of relatively powerless groups, and a sense of entitlement for their own profession. I wanted to know their views on the study of social sciences and the organization of work, especially nonhierarchical forms of organization.

In the interviews, I described some alternatives to the bureaucratic organization (Johnson and Whyte 1977; Rothschild-Whitt 1974, 1979). These are radically alternative social structures that "flatten" the hierarchical or vertical dimension, encouraging skill sharing and rotating routine work with work that has management or decision-making content. One question described an experiment in China, wherein uneducated housewives, workers in a new computer factory, taught engineers and scientists how the computer was built on the shop floor. Engineers and scientists in turn taught the workers some of the fundamentals of electricity. Other illustrations—from agriculture, from heavy industry—indicated ways "elites" and workers shared skill and knowledge with each other, and ways in which new developments in science (for example, new forms of hybridization) emerged. I asked how appealing these nonhierarchical structures were. Would the faculty like to share skills with workers such as machinists and technicians?

There were various reactions. Most found the suggestions appalling:

> *Computer scientist*: I think that will destroy Chinese science.

Electrical engineer: I don't mean to be snobbish about this, but the help [laugh] you know what I mean, the other people around here—I think a lot of the innovative type work that we're doing doesn't involve hairy, hairy science and in that sense I think people around here working with us can't understand, in many cases, just what it is exactly that we're doing. But the connection between that, what we're physically doing and the way it works is often very, very difficult. The reason that people are simply here as helpers rather than as active participants is the reason that they cannot be terribly well keyed to what we're doing. A lot of people who are technicians don't really have skills, the basic skills that would be necessary.

Electrical engineer: Oh, no, that's only for China. China is such a society that you tell people to do something and they go out and do it. There was a joke that Mao could have 600 million Chinese jump all at once and it would shake the world. It would make the world jump out of its trajectory. Places like China you can do all kinds of things. I don't know what they get out of it, but I don't think it is possible or useful or, it will just waste a lot of time, of other people's time. And I don't think anything will get out of it.

Civil engineer: I think in order for me to do my job of design of structure I get to know how the structures are built. Years ago I worked as a laborer on construction and I still go out on the project. I can run a bulldozer, I have a bulldozer. I build things with my own bulldozer. Built a road on Sunday. Built a reasonably nice road. So when I go out on a project I know what the bulldozer can do and I know how to build it, so I think that's important, yes. But whether I think I ought to be out working up here with Vappi, working out and talking with his laborers, I don't think it would help them and I don't think that's a good use of my time.

Mathematician: When the Chinese talk about some of their accomplishments, I'm just completely skeptical. My experience is such that either I think they're lying and didn't discover it, or they did discover it and they're lying about the way they did, and the fact that they've got a whole bunch of highly trained elite people who concentrate full-time on what they're doing hidden away and exempted from the rigors of the system. OK, because I just don't believe it. From my own experience, from the experience of everybody else, I know who's good at it. To do good science, to really do the kind of—or good engineering—to do the really creative original demanding stuff, you just have to be obsessed with it and you have to have the time to devote your whole self to it. And if you're being distracted with teaching elementary courses and working in the fields and participating in political discussions and so on, you just can't—child care too—I'm sorry for my sexist orientation.

Civil engineer: It really sounds to me like a waste of time and a waste of talent. I don't really believe that that is a most effective way to do. I do not believe that all people are equal. I believe in all liberal programs as long as things don't affect me.

Chemical engineer: No, I wouldn't care about interacting with technicians particularly.

Some felt one-way sharing would be fine, as the engineer learned more craft or hands-on practice. But it would be a waste of time to teach elite engineering skills in return. Besides, the justification went, few would want to learn.

Physicist: If you are working in a laboratory you generally have some other people working there who have some different skills from what you do, and generally if they're good at their job and you're good at your job you develop a mutual respect. I don't know that you have a great deal of intellectual exchange, that is, you don't go around trying to teach a machinist how to do difficult mathematics; first of all, he doesn't want to see.

But surprisingly, many rather liked the idea, even though it might be "inefficient":

Electrical engineer: We have one of the most successful plasma groups here in the country. There are theoreticians and there are experimentalists and the two will not cross over. It's terrible what it does to me. I refuse to accept that—I just will not.

What I've been describing with my equations, I would like to see and I would like to probe it. I needle it, criticize it from firsthand, look at it. They [Chinese] go out and do it for themselves—every engineering student has to spend every third year in the countryside. It's certainly inefficient. That's certainly a price paid for. [But] I find it immensely appealing that people would be able to do both [work with body and mind]. . . . I have a student with a 5.0 who cannot build a Heathkit.

Mechanical engineer: It [skill sharing with machinists] sounds like a good idea . . . one of the powerful and satisfying things about MIT.

Electrical engineer: I think that's a wonderful idea. I see no reason why you shouldn't do that.

Civil engineer: Definitely. I think there are new ideas that come out of us. Both sides. You get much better cooperation.

One chemist at this institute, but not in this sample, had in fact organized his laboratory so that scientific personnel, technicians, and bottle washers shared skills and rotated tasks.

Next, I inquired about an even more radical change having to do with sex division in the labor force. I asked the faculty their opinions on sharing skills, rotating tasks with clerical workers.

Some mistook friendly relations for real sharing. Others said they had their secretaries "do many things" such as film processing, to add variety to their work. But most objected to this notion outright, as wasteful and inefficient:

> *Electrical engineer*: People earn the right to do what they do. So if someone works with me, I'm not going to arbitrarily say we're equal, therefore I'll do half the typing. This is nonsense, just crazy. It isn't true.

> *Physicist*: There is a level of preparation that you know that you are not going to be able to change overnight and nor do people, in general, want to change. I don't know a lot of people who wished that they were interested in a lot more subjects. So that it doesn't mean you can't have some, you know, that you can't both respect what each other does and have reasonable exchanges on other topics. But it rather means, you know, that it rarely happens that I discuss the Second Law of Dynamics with other people in the office. If someone is typing notes that I have written on that, I doubt very much if they seriously think, "Gee, I would like to learn more about that."

> *Electrical engineer*: I don't think it could be helpful in most cases. . . . There are a lot of things a secretary can do which is very creative . . . but someone who isn't conversant with the concepts of the field couldn't make much of a contribution.

> *Mathematician*: I guess the answer to that is "it might be." But I'm inclined—with the particular kinds of concerns that I have—mathematical concerns, I'd be inclined to doubt it. I mean we're talking about intellectual disciplines that have been stable for a couple hundred years, through many cultures. It's hard to see how suddenly encouraging a bunch of minority students and women to get into it full-time is going to significantly alter its central intellectual core. There have been a couple of truly outstanding women mathematicians and they're considered outstanding women mathematicians because they met those transcendent criteria of mathematics, which were not set by men or women or by anybody else but are just sort of there.

Others felt that secretaries might benefit socially by math and science skills, for example, to "sound good at cocktail parties." Some, surprisingly, did most of their own clerical work so that they had better access to their own files. In general, however, this notion of open movement between clerical and professional work was not appealing to the engineering educators. One did note that people with different skills were differently rewarded by society, but attributed this to different investments in education and responsibility—the "human capital" theory of the labor market. (It is quite possible, however, that the average secretary at this institute has as many or more years of education as the average engineering graduate.) Only recently have activists and scholars addressed the way in which institutions such as the family and education track women into sex-segregated occupations, or that even work of comparable worth is devalued if that work is performed by women (see Sokoloff 1980). Among these engineering educators, there was a strong belief in meritocracy—the truly talented will rise to the top, and should be entitled to the privileges currently associated with such positions.

These radical questions about the structure of work are unlikely to emerge in the engineering curriculum. They are somewhat more likely to be found in the social sciences. I asked the faculty their opinions about the social sciences. Few were attracted to them:

- "I'm too accurate."
- "They're softer, noisier."
- "Woolly minded. Too soft."
- "Soft. For engineering dropouts. Engineers are an elite group."
- "Economics is OK . . . deals with mathematical systems."
- "I have few abilities in interpreting relationships. I have no gift for it."
- "Least rigorous . . . most variables."
- "Engineering questions and systems are much more controllable."
- "Softer . . . amorphous."
- "Engineering is more rigorous. You get a definite yes or no."
- "I don't think much of them."
- "I don't understand them. What use is it if you can't control the object of study?"

Rather, they were attracted by elegance and abstraction of physical phenomena. This was particularly marked among electrical engineering faculty. When asked what gave them the greatest pleasure in their work, they responded:

- "It's an orderly subject . . . the procession of signals, the way signals are manipulated."
- "To be able to put things into a certain logical pattern which is what I am doing now . . . putting things in a framework is just a lot of fun, I guess."
- "The challenge of struggling with an intellectual problem with things; solving the problem is very much like a giant three-dimensional

crossword puzzle, you try to put all the pieces in place and the result when you get it is intellectually pleasing."
- "Some degree of elegance, technically or aesthetically."
- "The beauty of writing that single equation that sums up everything, that explains everything . . . the beauty of the elegant solution."
- "The beauty of a neat solution to a problem and the thrill of having solved something, or built something."
- "My mother was a hysterical, very unreliable woman. I think somewhere along the line I felt the need for things you could trust, be absolutely sure of. That was the attraction of mathematics."

These are truly different skills from those required for traditional women's work, or for the social sciences or humanities. One of the important questions we might address here is how one set of skills is rewarded so much more than others. A traditional education will leave such questions unasked, or will suggest that engineering/scientific skills are more valuable to society than, say, child care, art, history, or sociology. If, how, and why that is true are questions left unexplored.

These are the kinds of questions, however, one must ask if the structures of social relations—for example, hierarchy in occupations and great differences in rewards—are to be altered. The structure of social relations in industry can be transformed so that participation and responsibility are encouraged among all members (Johnson and Whyte 1977).

CONCLUSION

As engineers move into management, and as they create the technological background of industrial work, they also shape the social relations of that work. It is these social relations that present the responsible engineer with so many of the constraints within which they do their work. If engineers change technological structures radically, they must be aware of concomitant changes they bring about in social structures. Who benefits, and how, by such changes? Who pays the price? How will such changes affect the quality of engineering and related work? How can we move toward a more democratic, rather than authoritarian, bureaucratic society?

These seem unlikely questions for engineers to address, given the stereotype of those in the field. Yet, in one of the most prestigious technical institutions in the United States, a sizable minority of engineering educators indicated pleasure, willingness, or curiosity to explore radically different forms of industrial organization. Some expressed the belief that such a different order to things might lead to better engineering. That this openness to new social relations did not yet extend to clerical work or to the sex-based division of labor in society is not surprising. No field at this point—even my own—has seriously tackled these issues.

It seems to me that responsible engineering education must teach the student how social relations at work are built into technological systems. Current forms of organization encourage lack of responsibility on the part of most workers, and lack of responsiveness to the concerned engineer.

NOTES

1. Based on participant observation at MIT and as an engineering student at Oregon State University. The latter is described in Chapter 6.

Chapter 6 ———————————————————————————

Mathematization of Engineering: Limits on Women and the Field

The main function of mathematics in advanced capitalist society is the maintenance of social stratification. Our courses . . . are the feature of formal education which performs the most decisive winnowing of students. Society tells the student, even the working class student, you may be a dentist if you pass the test, you may be a military officer if you pass the test . . . and the decisive test is in math. . . . The aridity of our courses, their remoteness from students' human concerns—together, of course, with their difficulty—make them especially forbidding, hence especially good as selectors of students with superior capacity for self discipline (sometimes called repression). (Professor Chandler Davis, Department of Mathematics, University of Toronto, 1980)

MATHEMATICS AND ENGINEERING: BACKGROUND AND AN ARGUMENT

*A*mong the most striking results of my research at a prestigious American institute of technology, reported in the previous two chapters, was my observation of the faculty's pervasive attraction to abstraction, elegance, and simplicity—the qualities embodied in mathematics. Faculty members approached mathematics with playful insight and appreciation. The pleasure and ease with which men at the top exercise these skills is one reason mathematics weighs so heavily in engineering educational success.

When I later attended engineering and technical courses, at this and other institutions, I learned something else important about engineering and mathematics. A world of difference separated the pleasures of mathematics at the top from the grind at the bottom, where engineering students struggled to achieve the required C or better in calculus or statistics examinations. Clearly, mathematics and the methods of teaching it served to stratify access to the profession—to "weed out" those not proficient in taking mathematics tests, or not delighted in the abstract, from those who were. Only the good test takers pursued the program successfully, won their degrees, and gained access to the profession. Mathematics tests serve as a major criterion for success in today's educational system—particularly engineering education—and more generally in the world of work. Selecting successors by the criterion of math testing may, perhaps inadvertently, assure cultural homogeneity in the field. Such a one-dimensional perspective in this significant profession affects us all.

I do not here address the issue of gender-differentiated ability in mathematics, a subject fully treated by others (Russo 1981; Sells 1978; Tobias 1978). Contrary to popular misconceptions, the data suggest that women are just as competent as men in mathematics. Yet, women continue to be grossly underrepresented in the math-based professions, such as engineering. Women's mathematical ability went unquestioned in the early twentieth-century reports by the U.S. Bureau of Education (1911a, 1911b, 1911c), one of which noted that women were outperforming men in college mathematics (1911a). The search for sex-related differences proved largely fruitless, although men displayed a more "rugged" attitude toward the subject. Interestingly enough, the report suggested stressing courses that would "develop that proper sex difference which is so generally recognized" (p. 30). Things have not changed that much since. In showing how mathematics testing has operated to stratify and structure the engineering profession, this study may add an important piece toward solving the puzzle of women's technological exclusion.

Women can surmount the barriers to male-dominated professions, in this case, perhaps, by "overcoming math anxiety," as Sheila Tobias (1978) titled her excellent work on the subject. But if a primary function of mathematics courses is limiting the number and kind of applicants to a field, then large numbers of women (and men disadvantaged by race or class) mastering mathematical test taking would simply cause the criteria to shift. (I discuss below the possibility that this may, in fact, be a shift now occurring.) So, at the same time as we learn "how-to"—today's fashion in literature, courses, and programs—we also need to understand how and why the professions select the standards of excellence they do. Otherwise, most women will remain at least a step behind. A second commanding reason for this broader perspective challenges the criteria themselves; we must understand not only their creation but also their subsequent impact on the field, its services, and its products.

Thus, two issues seemed vital to pursue further: First, how and why—beyond technical considerations—did mathematics become so important to engineering education? Second, how does this link between mathematics and engineering education affect the practice of engineering in our society generally, and the structure and organization of the work force in particular?

THE DISCIPLINE OF MATHEMATICS AND ITS ROLE IN ENGINEERING EDUCATION

In this section, I shall examine the discipline of mathematics and explore some of the nontechnical reasons why it became integral to engineering education. Mathematics tests serve as major determinants of success or failure in today's educational system, particularly in engineering education. This bias extends to programs outside formal education, where a growing number of people actually receive training, as in apprenticeship programs. Scores on mathematics tests (as well as high school shop courses and "attitude") play a major part in assigning the points that determine whether or not an applicant will enter a program.[1] One reason for these practices lies in the real and growing technical demands of science-based industry, which makes mathematics seem particularly important. But mathematics is not quite the arid, neutral subject of some critics—"the most objective, most coercive type of knowledge, and therefore . . . least affected by social influences" (Mehrtens et al. 1981, ix). Critical scholarship has begun to show how strongly social factors affect the content and direction of mathematics (Ernest 1976; Grabiner 1981; Mehrtens et al. 1981). The impact of social factors on engineering is even more pronounced, mathematization itself being one such social factor affecting the nature of engineering.

Mathematics has long been emphasized for nontechnical, or "cultural," reasons. In nineteenth-century France, for example, mathematics "represented rationality." Its study was not for the masses but for the "relatively large and unformed elite" (Hodgkin 1981, 63). In England, "mathematics was used to educate gentlemen, not to train mathematicians" (Enroe 1981). Historically, other courses have served the stratifying function Davis assigned mathematics (in the epigraph, above)—"weeder" courses, the students call them. When the church controlled higher education, Latin was the obstacle. Theology gave way to aristocratic classical studies, then science, as control shifted from one ruling segment to another. Classicists, then the bourgeoisie, challenged Church control: education should "promote the everyday interests of society rather than the welfare of the church" (Artz 1966, 67). Critics felt "the stress placed on Latin rhetoric seemed particularly absurd" (Artz 1966, 66–67).

Change came slowly; as late as 1802, matriculation at Harvard University demanded proficiency in Latin but not in mathematics. But by the century's end, the emphasis on mathematical requirements had increased markedly (U.S. Bureau of Education 1911b, 15). In continental Europe and England, as in the United States, mathematics became the chief reliance for measuring educational success through self-discipline (or repression, as Davis would have it). Mathematics superseded not only Latin and theology, but also moral philosophy and logic (Cardwell 1957). As Tobias (1978) remarks, "Quantitative method, if not math itself, has become the Latin of the modern era" (p. 42).

Belief in the antagonism of mind and body is as old as civilized society (Rothschild 1981). Medieval religion associated passion with women and the devil. Seeking to hold the passionate body in check, the Church promoted abstraction against empiricism, or learning through the senses (Ehrenreich and English 1973). By the eighteenth century, reason had replaced faith as the dominant ideology (Artz 1966). In the nineteenth century—the century wherein "the sense of limitation [was] the common sense" (Hodgkin 1981, 67)—reason, morality, and self-discipline joined to control the unruly passions.

Samuel Smiles wrote his famous mid-nineteenth century *Lives of the Engineers* to prescribe the good and productive life, and his readers welcomed his prescriptions. "The Smiles engineer . . . cultivated first the world within and then externalized the forces of his [self-disciplined] character" (Hughes 1966, 12–13). Smiles believed an engineer could not fulfill his major task, bringing order from chaos, if he were sensuous, self-indulgent, reckless, untidy, or emotional. A time of rapid social change promoted an ideal vision of nature under disciplined control, a control that encompassed the unbridled nature of man himself. "Science . . . is the habit [of mind] recognizing that there is a rational way of doing things as over against a passionate, impulsive, instinctive or partisan way of doing things" (F. J. E. Woodbridge, quoted in Finch 1948, 43). Another scholar spoke of the "solid and certain reasoning" induced by the study of mathematics, which prevents "youthful conceits and presumptuousness" (Finch 1948, 43).

Mathematics, especially in technical education, would teach a rational mode of thought. The 1793 national plan of education for France stressed mathematics because, according to Magistrate La Chalotais, "It is very possible and very common to reason badly in theology, in politics; it is impossible in arithmetic and geometry. The rules will supply accuracy and intelligence for those who follow them" (Artz 1966, 68). A nineteenth-century British cleric argued that mathematics "induces habits of industry" even if later cast aside; such study would be beneficial for nontechnical professionals such as lawyers as well (Cardwell 1957, 44).

Then as now, however, doubters wondered whether science and mathematics education could quench the fires of youth. As one British professor of philosophy and opponent of increasing mathematics and science in the curriculum questioned: "Should young men, at an age when their passions should be restrained, be introduced to the study of such a subject as 'the reproductive functions'?" Doing so might, he felt, "corrupt the youthful mind. It would make all students medical students" (Cardwell 1957, 38). (I asked a friend, a mathematics professor, if indeed his study "cooled the passions." "Hell, no," he said, "but it allows you to sidestep them.")

To others, science and mathematics showed as little promise in teaching reason as in cooling passion. In an 1826 issue of the *Edinburgh Review*, a writer asked of the mathematician, "He can reason?" and answered himself: "But no one reasons so ill as the mathematicians!" Another critic questioned the most important presumed value of mathematical study, disciplined thought: "To say that discipline is the object of a place in education, is much the same thing as to say that the object of an army is to be drilled" (Hugh Wyatt, quoted in Cardwell 1957, 77). And yet another critic cited the mistake of "teachers who value grammar higher than literature itself," and science teachers who value "mathematics preliminary to a knowledge of the laws of nature . . . higher than the knowledge itself" (Clarke 1875, 257). Clarke also claimed:

> Much time is wasted in our colleges and technological schools over the higher mathematics. Every engineer here will agree with me that the times where the use of the higher calculus is indispensable are so few in our practice, that its study is not worth the time expended upon it. (p. 257)

Controversy surrounded both the value of mathematics and how best to teach it; both remained subjects of continuing debate. In the United States, it emerged most strongly in the "shop culture" versus "school culture" struggle to control engineering education. Like England, the United States in the nineteenth century relied on the shop floor for most engineers. Training through apprenticeship still characterizes the British approach to engineering education. Engineering status and pay are notably lower there than here, largely because a greater degree of professional muscle in the United States keeps salaries high and limits access to the field.[2] Relatively early in the nineteenth century, however, American engineering diverged toward the French model, beginning with education in the military academies (Calvert 1967). The American transition was not an easy one, as Noble's brilliant 1977 book illustrates. Corporate capitalism demanded control over the new, dynamic, and often unruly technical elite. With the help of the military, engineering/management in powerful science-based industries came to direct engineering education. Eventually, this extended even to the minutiae of preferred character traits (see Noble 1977, 176ff., for this "boy scout" list), and the personality tests to discern them.

In the mid-nineteenth-century beginnings of the movement for engineering professionalism, entrepreneurs and other "practical men" preferred what Calvert (1967) calls "shop culture." They handpicked young men to learn technical and social skills, work with machines and get their hands dirty, meet future clients, get to know future subordinates. Support for shop culture also came from other sources—elite educators, for one, or naval officers who complained that school graduates might know mathematics but had never touched a machine. These proponents of shop culture, according to Calvert, represented the cream of mechanical engineering located or trained in elite institutions. They selected young men most like themselves to be the next generation of engineers. Their arguments for the shop approach were couched in terms of work quality and democratic principle. Hands-on experience produced better engineers, and mathematical requirements for engineering degrees might exclude many young men without previous mathematical experience. (And too many degreed engineers would raise the cost of labor.)

The representatives of "school culture"—largely land-grant college engineering educators—also argued for quality and democracy. They claimed that mathematics skills had become necessary for good engineering, given the increasing fusion of science and technology (Merritt 1969). Mathematics criteria, they hoped, would also open engineering to the average middle-class young man, making it no longer a field restricted to those handpicked by entrepreneurs. School culture triumphed over shop culture. This was not, however, a product merely of more persuasive argument. Behind the demise of the shop approach lay several factors. Educators themselves campaigned successfully for schooling credentials. Perhaps more decisive, shop training could not readily accommodate the process requirements of large-scale, science-based industries, notably electrical and chemical. Processes of mass production also increased demand for cheaper technical workers educationally "inferior" to engineers. Mathematics became a means of differentiating shop workers from engineers, as shown, for example, in the pages of *American Machinist* at the turn of the century (1899–1900; see especially the works of Halsey).

Supply did not long exceed demand. Perceived overcrowding in the engineering field quickly brought raised admissions standards to limit and reduce the number of entering students. As critics had foreseen, the result disadvantaged those young men whose education had not earlier emphasized mathematical skills. Neither shop nor school culture very closely matched professed democratic ideals. The mismatch scarcely aroused great concern when the emergent profession took stock of itself early in the twentieth century. The Society for the Promotion of Engineering Education commissioned reports from Charles Mann, W. E. Wickenden, and other prominent science and engineering educators. A significant issue was the growing number of young men seeking engineering degrees and threatening to "overcrowd" the field. The midwestern land-grant colleges, funded under the provisions of the 1892 Morrill Act, became the major source of the rapid influx of degreed engineers into the work force. By the 1920s, it seemed that "every technical student wants a degree" and that "a prestige hunger sought to claim a prairie college 'the same as Cornell' or a YMCA school a university" (Wickenden 1930–1934, 1078, 1112–13).

The younger states seemed particularly pushy, seeking to "telescope the entire span of social evolution from sod-breaking to a system of complex economic interchange into fifty years or less" (Wickenden 1930–1934, 1079). They often required nothing more than a high school diploma for entrance to college engineering. In 1926, the engineering profession proposed enrollment limits "to protect and elevate professional standards rather than to increase the number of engineering colleges"; the "excess" students might attend technical or trade schools (Wickenden 1930–1934, 94). "Many who ought not to try to become engineers are permitted to undertake a course of study for which they have little natural ability" (Mann 1918, 47). That ability proved to be primarily mathematical test taking.

Engineers, in fact, viewed education as "the most important branch of the engineer profession in that the development of the profession depends upon it more than any other branch" (Wadell, quoted in Stine, 1980, 15–16). The profession watched over the status and pay of its members, staked out a body of knowledge it could call its own, controlled access, and measured merit on its own terms. (The issues of concern have not, in fact, changed much; then as now they centered on status and money. Within education, the clear problem was attracting high-quality men to teaching, when professorial salaries fell far below industrial, and even a new graduate might expect to receive more than the professor who had trained him.)

Engineers were aware that engineering differed from "one- level" professions such as law and medicine. No linear route leads from nurse to doctor, or from legal secretary to attorney. Engineering support workers, however, were male; the path from craftsman, technician, or mechanic to engineer lay open. This might help prevent technicians from unionizing, but such mobility also "lessens their [engineers'] chance of public recognition as members of a professional aristocracy" (Wickenden 1930–1934, 1109–10; see also Calhoun 1960). This is the contradiction between democracy and merit inherent in professional-ism. Educators had hoped that school culture, using mathematics as filter, would be more democratic than shop culture. Their concern, however, centered on young, middle-class, white Protestant males alone. Women were excluded, non-Anglo-Saxon men unwelcome. In the 1920s, the profession wondered if the infusion of Eastern and Southern European immigrants might account for failure rates in mathematics. Research laid this concern to rest; mathematics courses also weeded out those of "sound extraction" (Wickenden 1930–1934, 168).[3]

In the United States, requirements varying from school to school provoked demands for standardization (see, for example, U.S. Bureau of Education 1911c). The Joint Council on Engineering Education commissioned Charles R. Mann to assess the status of engineering education. The so-called Mann Report of 1918 was but the first such effort. From the beginning, engineering educators preferred to claim scientific and mathematical expertise, in contrast to practical skills. Mathematics, physical science, and English formed the essential core of engineering preparation. So the high schools were told in 1930: "The misconception that preparation for engineering should be based chiefly on . . . manual training . . . should be dispelled" (Wickenden 1930–1934, 175) The profession, as a result, was more than once challenged to show how it differed from the other sciences.[4]

The standardized curricula began to reflect this image cleaning. In one early study, engineering teachers and graduates ranked mathemat-ics, physics, chemistry, and graphics (largely descriptive geometry) as the four most important courses. The first three waxed, while graphics declined (Mann 1918, 35–36). Wickenden (1930–1934, 549) summarized engineering curriculum trends from the late nineteenth century to 1930 as follows:

1. a gradual transfer of mathematics from requirement for gradua-tion to requirement for entry;
2. gains in physical science with losses in graphics;
3. less emphasis on foreign language; and
4. increased emphasis on the need for economics and manage-ment.

Mathematics and science remained in the curriculum; graphics did not. Graphics was siphoned off for less highly trained and less well-paid people, eventually emerging as a separate field called drafting, or drawing. Increasingly, women entered this occupation. Much of this work is currently automated, while engineering has retained the abstract skills. Baynes and Pugh (1978, 1981) describe both how women entered such jobs as engineering-drawing copiers in the 1880s and how a century later copying machines have replaced the women.[5]

How mathematics was to be taught and how performance was to be evaluated concerned practitioners as well as educators. A "mania" for examination had swept British institutions in the mid-nineteenth century in a reform movement to eliminate patronage in the professions, and in response to the clamor for admittance from middle-class men. There was considerable criticism of the attempt to replace such means of student evaluation as research projects, reports, displays, or fieldwork with rationalized, specialized, and expert examinations. Opponents noted the injurious consequences of relying on something as useless as a test in assessing talent. Examination addressed professional rather than industrial needs (Cardwell 1957, 119–20). The best suffered most in testing, while only the lazy majority benefited; examinations were the "poison of education" (Cardwell 1957, 13). They would never give "a love of things of the mind" (Cardwell 1957, 114). Yet the 1850s and 1860s saw a heightened enthusiasm for examination (Cardwell 1957, 112). The overwhelming appeal of an examination system lay both in its claims to eliminate personal bias in evaluation, thus promoting democracy, and in its "efficiency." In British science education, mathematics examinations were the first to be subject to rationalization (Cardwell 1957, 114).

During the first decades of the twentieth century, freshman-sophomore engineering college curricula in the United States were largely limited to basics—calculus, mechanics, higher algebra, coordinate geometry. From 1899 through the 1920s, varying little from year to year, 60 percent of students flunked out, with calculus and science courses weeding out the most (Wickenden 1930–1934, 200). Some voices called for efforts to reduce the rate of failure, and perhaps enhance understanding, by integrating theory with practice. Students might benefit from modeling, visualizing, drawing, building, testing pieces of technology. Others wondered whether measuring a student's ability to pass mathematics tests really served the best interests of engineering education. "Is the ability to pass current school and college examinations a valid criterion of engineering ability?" Mann asked (1918, 48).

In 1913 he approached General Electric for help in attacking the question empirically. Mann asked the actual employers of engineering graduates to rate them on technical ability, accuracy, industry, ability to get things done, and personality. Granted, a high rating in such traits may seem particularly useful to those seeking a profit in a competitive system while enjoying a trouble-free work force (Noble 1977). Yet, to the extent that engineering skills could be defined, Mann's list fairly represented then-current views of what they were. Subsequent studies included evaluations of the graduates' work by foremen and peers as well. Mann found *no correlation* between grades and job performance. A similar study of 40 graduates employed by Westinghouse produced the same results.

Mann, Thorndyke, and others also undertook extensive research on engineering skills tests. At least eight components failed to correlate with grade-getting ability within engineering education as it was (and is). Some of these skills were verbal; most were visual or manual—matching or completing diagrams, solving laboratory problems, constructing devices from unassembled parts. These skills, they suggested, were not so much unimportant as simply not measured in college (Mann 1918, 50–62). For all that, however, Mann favored retaining mathematics requirements and tests—students "will 'soldier' just like workers" unless forced to study for an exam; they "know as well as anybody that college grades are very ineffective measures of the type of abilities that win recognition in the world's work" (Mann 1918, 69). A decade later, Wickenden found nothing amiss in this pattern either; he urged maintaining the system as it was, and even raising admission standards. Once again, the perception of overcrowding controlled. To those whose concerns centered on building and protecting professional status, and on preserving engineering against industry's drive for cheaper, nonprofessional help, nothing else served the purpose as well as mathematics examinations.

Such abilities as visualizing physical phenomena, drawing them, or manipulating physical objects presented problems of evaluation. They may not, in fact, best be learned in the classroom. Mathematics tests, on the other hand, fitted smoothly and easily into the newly bureaucratized way of becoming an engineer—mass professional education in large bureaucratic institutions. High school grades and entrance examination scores predicted a student's ability to win good grades in the early years of college. Grades in the first two years in turn predicted grades in later years. But such measurements—grades—do not predict how well one performs as an engineer. Large classes and limited time still encourage teachers to rationalize grading and record keeping as much as possible. A set of calculus problems I submitted in one course, for example, received a grade reduced by 10 percent because the pages had not been stapled together. A statistics professor, asked why students could not have two hours instead of one for an examination, responded: "If we gave people more time, anyone could do it. The secretaries could even pass it." (Tobias 1978 suggests that timed tests are one of the strongest barriers to understanding and appreciating mathematics.)

This problem—the value of test scores for predicting a good engineer—plagues researchers today, largely because the definition of a good engineer remains obscure. Mann acknowledged the absence of such a definition. Income, he noted, might identify the most successful, but not necessarily the best. The dean of engineering at an eastern university recently told me much the same thing: defining a good engineer remains the crux, and income makes a poor gauge; it perhaps reflects less quality of engineering than quality of contacts derived from proper family background and matriculation at the proper school.[6]

Engineering faculty members, when interviewed, admitted that calculus and other forms of higher mathematics may have little relevance to job performance. But they insisted on the importance of such courses, often echoing arguments current for a century or more. Passing calculus, they felt, was important "to show that you can do it," or to "develop a proper frame of mind." But others saw mathematics as not only irrelevant but harmful. Engineering, they argue, not only can but should avoid higher mathematics, which "separates you from the physical reality," or gets in the way of knowing "what is happening, physically." Interviews with mathematicians who teach "weeder" courses such as engineering calculus show they find the chore as distasteful as do the students. Many mathematics and engineering teachers, no less than their students, continue to question the justice or wisdom of allowing mathematics tests and similar criteria to decide who succeeds and who fails in engineering.

However, an interesting new development is occurring in mathematical criteria. In the summer of 1982, an elite, invitation-only conference of educators and mathematicians met at the Sloan Institute for Management in New York to explore the displacement of calculus—the mathematics of continuous change—by forms of discrete mathematics more appropriate to digital computers. Discrete mathematics concerns itself with individual on-off, yes-no functions, more suitable to the study of probability than the analysis of continuous functions. Many educators feel "calculus . . . may be going the way of Latin—more honored than taught." According to science writer Lee Dembart (1982), "The pending eclipse of calculus, which has been the handmaiden of science and technology practically since the Renaissance, is one more example of the pervasive influence of computers on the way society works and on the ways in which we interpret reality" (p. 3). Citing scholars pro and con, Dembart nonetheless found spokespersons from such institutions as Berkeley and Dartmouth strongly supporting the Sloan Foundation and discrete mathematics. As it happens, discrete math is "easier for many students than calculus . . . an easy way to satisfy a requirement."

As women struggle to overcome their inexperience in such forms of mathematics as calculus, computer-related substitutes can gain in importance for them. Less prestigious institutions, with women and minorities increasingly seeking admission, may persist in stressing calculus much longer than elite institutions. Professional/technical positions may also begin to require other skills—skills now important at the cutting edge of technology, but not yet integrated into the bureaucratized engineering curriculum.[7]

Technical fields today offer opportunities far superior to traditional options for women and minorities. Not surprisingly, according to community college counselors, women and minorities express high satisfaction with the programs, jobs, and salaries. While this is a welcome development and we should seek to overcome remaining barriers, such progress should be viewed within a larger context. As Joan Acker (1980) remarks in her recent review of the literature on sex stratification: "The interesting and useful questions are not how individuals get into certain slots, but how the structure itself is formed and what its changing contours are." The ongoing question must be how mathematics testing helps form the new contours and composition of the technical work force and affects the barriers faced particularly by women in engineering education. Applying what we know about the role of education in maintaining social stratification (Bowles and Gintis 1976; Collins 1979; Pincus 1980) and about the processes of stratification within engineering education (Brittain and McMath 1977; Noble 1977) to career training generally (Grubb and Lazerson 1975), we can ask with Karabel (1972) if career education in community colleges may be a device to keep women and minorities in low-status occupations. DeVore (1975) observes that the case of occupationally linked education is proliberal and prodemocratic, but the results are too often illiberal and undemocratic.

In emphasizing abstract mathematical criteria for professional engineering education, educators eliminate other criteria—the hands-on and visual skills. These choices reflect tastes and skills of men at the top and the boundary maintenance needs of the profession. But overemphasis on abstract criteria may warp the practice of engineering, an effect that will be explored in the next section.

THE IMPACT OF THE
MATHEMATIZATION OF ENGINEERING

When systems of stratification emerge, those near the top of the pyramid generally establish the standards for success. Although they tend to justify such standards on rational or technical grounds, they may well have other reasons for their choices, perhaps covert, perhaps unconscious, but in any case notably less objective. Rosabeth Moss Kanter (1975) tells us that several decades ago the tough, aggressive, competitive, independent people who held management positions unconsciously elevated just such characteristics to criteria of excellence.

Only later did much of the business community begin to recognize the dysfunctions of overemphasizing these qualities at the expense of others, such as cooperation and sensitivity. Something similar marks the structure of engineering and engineering education: too great an emphasis on mathematical criteria may adversely affect the field and its products.

Some engineering faculty have judged that overattention to mathematics at the expense of visual and manual skills threatened good engineering. Cooley (1982), a British engineer, traces the impact of automation and abstraction on creativity in engineering design. Rosenbrock (1977) argues that mathematics in general, and calculus in particular, represents only one aspect of engineering: engineering as algorithmic, mathematical, scientific technique. Indispensable and intellectually appealing as that fact may be, Rosenbrock warns, it is not the whole of engineering, nor does technical expertise encompass everything the engineer must possess. Such important qualities as judgment, experience, and understanding of social complexity, to name a few, must not be neglected.

Ferguson (1977) carries this argument a step further. Large systems failures, he suggests, may stem from the engineer's decreased contact with physical reality. He is particularly concerned that engineers no longer receive the extensive training in visual and drawing skills they once did:

> Two results of the abandonment of nonverbal knowledge in engineering colleges can be predicted; indeed, one is already evident. The movement towards a 4-year technician's degree reflects a demand for persons who can deal with the complexities of real machines and materials and who have the nonverbal reasoning ability that used to be common among graduates of engineering colleges. In the longer run, engineers in charge of projects will lose their flexibility of approach to solving problems as they adhere to the doctrine that every problem must be treated as an exercise in numerical systems analysis. The technician, lower in status than the systems engineer, will have the ability but not the authority to make the "big" decisions, while the systems engineer in charge will be unaware that this nonverbal imagination and sense of fitness have been atrophied by the rules of a systematic but intellectually impoverished engineering approach. (p. 835)

Noble (1979) also notices the problems engineers face when they are several layers of workers removed from the sounds and smells, the sensual input of the shop floor. Out of touch with the real machines and materials, the engineer is left with too little "feel" for what he designs. Ida Hoos (1972) offers a witty and cogent study of systems thinking applied to social problems, and Lilienfeld's (1978) analysis of its ideological role also addresses these issues. These works provide a healthy balance for Tobias's (1978) uncritical acceptance of the increasing use of systems analysis in many fields (pp. 35ff.).

As engineering tends toward abstraction and managerial tasks, mental labor departs still further from physical labor. Engineers and scholars alike note the adverse effects, not only on the profession and its practitioners but on the organization of technology itself. Mathematical skills receive even greater stress as engineering strives to protect the field from challenges verging on crisis. For example, mathematics may serve to distinguish the technician and the technologist from the engineer; it may serve to prevent industry's potentially inappropriate use of lesser trained workers; and it may select the students for contracting numbers of places in colleges of engineering.

The process has its ironies. More elite institutions, for example, seem least likely to adopt the most extreme division of labor, formally separating mind and hand work. Published and private correspondence stimulated by Ferguson's (1977) remarks on the damage engineering suffers from deemphasized visual skills tells much the same story as interviews with engineering faculty members (see "Leonardo" 1978 and Chapter 4). Elite institutions such as MIT are more likely than others to retain such training, to stress hands-on experience and laboratory contact with expert craftspeople (see also U.S. Bureau of Education 1911b, 37, for interdisciplinary efforts in elite schools). Asked why such institutions might place less emphasis than others on separating mind from eye or hand, Professor Ferguson thought they might be more secure in their status. It should be added they may also feel less enrollment pressure.

SUMMARY AND CONCLUSION

Now, as in the late nineteenth century, both the structure of technology and the institutions that provide its work force are changing. Failing to recognize this fundamental fact, we are all too likely to misinterpret what we see—women once again breaking into male-dominated areas of engineering and technology, especially in technical support of engineers. But, if women are to take advantage of contradictions between capital and patriarchy—patriarchy here structured in professionalism (Brown 1979; Hartmann 1977; Sokoloff 1980)—we must bear in mind Acker's call to understand how new structures form, and what their changing contours are. Because capitalism needs cheap labor and the system can routinize and cheapen engineering tasks, women benefit in the short run as new technical jobs open to them. The more patriarchal profession (that is, engineering) appears to be declining—again, in the short run—unless technicians can be persuaded to view themselves as professionals. This may not prove difficult. Paraprofessional status offers prestige, all the more attractive given the newcomers' otherwise disadvantaged place in the labor market; the "real" professions virtually exclude women, chiefly through the peculiar manipulation of mathematics as a standard. The result is that women are channeled toward the lower range of the job market, while men enjoy less competition for the better jobs (Sokoloff 1980).

As their work becomes more routinized, engineers begin to complain about its "factorylike" quality (Cooley 1982). Less costly technical workers take over routine engineering as automation looms. A U.S. Bureau of Labor Statistics (1966) report called for a long-term (through 1975) increase in the ratio of technicians to scientists and engineers, in part due to "rising salaries of . . . engineers" (p. 48). This plan did not include raising the ratio of drafting positions (the area attracting may women today) to engineering ones because of greater projected use of photoreproduction, mechanized drafting equipment, and automation. Women assume the role of technician, and the gap between the pay of technician and engineer begins to approximate that between female and male workers in society generally. If technicians identify with other workers in unions, rather than with their own paraprofessional technical societies, they may in fact become better technical workers. Not only may they thus increase their income, they may also prevent further degradation of nonverbal and nonmathematical skills, the otherwise vanishing essence of good engineering.

Tensions between business and the profession of engineering have waxed and waned over the past century. The early twentieth century saw such tensions alleviated (Layton 1969), but now we may again see contradictions emerging (see, for example, Gouldner 1976). This chapter suggests the need to alter the structure of engineering in ways that might benefit us all. Professional criteria, especially for access to the field, developed as the product of a small, technically trained elite. In particular, special kinds of testing have allowed engineering to maintain its homogeneous positions. Mathematical examinations become the powerful filters of entry to engineering.

In stressing nontechnical or nonrational reasons for this use of mathematics, my intention is not so much to imply that such reasons are necessarily the most important (although they may be). Rather, I wish to draw attention to the unexpected: seemingly technical standards for a technical field that are imposed for reasons having little to do with the field's technical demands. This suggests one way to desegregate and improve engineering: remove scores on mathematics tests as the major standard of success in engineering education. Though small, given the vested interests of the educational gatekeepers, such change will not likely be easy. Further, as suggested by Benet and Daniels (1976) in a special issue of *Social Problems*, the smallest adjustments in the direction of greater equity in education may ultimately require basic changes in the institutional fabric of society. The efforts of women to enter male-dominated professions such as engineering must be joined with a struggle for structural change in the field, especially given the power of engineering to shape the direction of technology, and thus our lives (Ferguson 1977).

NOTES

1. Feminist attorney Marlene Drescher of Eugene, Oregon, and others have filed creative legal actions to eliminate discrimination in apprentice training programs (*Cormier v. Central Electrical JATC et al.*, Civil No. 82-607E, U.S. District Court for the District of Oregon 1983; *Judy Marlene Parks and Deborah Marlye Grossberg v. San Mateo County JATC for the Electrical Construction Industry*, Case No. C-81-3389 WHO, U.S. District Court for the Northern District of California).

2. It may also slow the proletarianization of engineering, which appears to be moving much more quickly in England than in the United States (Cooley 1982).

3. Tables report percentage of students whose parents and grandparents were born in the United States, and industry urged schools to note graduates' "heredity," "parent's occupation, education and nationality" (Wickenden 1930–1934, 251).

4. Layton (1969) has suggested that the distinction may be chiefly point of view—engineering seeks to do, science to understand.

5. Eugene Ferguson, an engineer and historian, notes the continuation of this process today: "The sad fact is that the status of non-verbal knowledge is lower than the verbal-mathematical in the powerful councils of the New Mandarins of scientific technology" ("Leonardo" 1978, 350).

6. Someone else at that college of engineering, trying to discover whether good grades promised a good engineer, took income—measured in the amount of alumni contributions—as the index of engineering success, equating success with quality. Size of donation proved to be correlated significantly with former grade point average, but negatively—the larger the donation, the poorer the grades.

7. For example, a technical job notice in the *Los Angeles Times* in July 1982 ended: "Prefer someone good at video games."

Part III

Technological Change and the Changing Stratification of Engineering

DOROTHY: Joan [Acker] suggested we should talk about the kind of difference that coming to Corvallis [Oregon] made. You mentioned, I think, that you'd had more time, were less involved politically. . . . Since you couldn't find . . . couldn't make the context with working women you had had before that you gradually shifted toward asking yourself, "What could you do in relationship to the kids in university?" for example. And were there other changes?

SALLY: Hmmm. That's an interesting question because . . . and I didn't create much, that would satisfy my desire, you know, to work with women on the lower end of the occupational structure. The working women that I hung out with—my drinking buddies and so on—were very individualistic and going to move up into management. With the same working-class toughness—you know, "management is full of shit" and so on. But it is a different part of the country—it's a small university town. . . . For all those reasons, it just didn't happen. So it was easier to do these studies that weren't so closely tied to social action. It was fruitful too. So I think it was helpful to both the historical and the ethnographic studies. I think those are both worthwhile. I might have done them in Boston, who knows? I was beginning to do something like that in any case. But probably I would not have done as thorough a job if I'd had meetings to go to twice a week, or three times a week, or a bulletin to get out, or a leaflet to write or whatever.

So I did have time to do the ethnographic work on learning mathematics. Then I thought a study of *all* graduates by race and sex of *all* technical and craft schools in Oregon—it's a real small state, so that wouldn't be hard to do at all—would be useful to people. You get that structural knowledge—you know I think "counting" is important. How many are there? How many are getting jobs as engineers? What race? What sex? What class background? What education? How many have had calculus? So you can lay bare the system and people can *see*. Maybe parents will get off the backs of children who are trying to get their engineering degree and all of a sudden it's a little more difficult. Maybe the engineers will see enough to figure that maybe it's better to join with the technicians rather than put them off in their own paraprofessional society. Maybe even with women . . . I thought women need a larger view of how the world of work is changing so as not to fight merely for a place in things "as they are."

What we were learning was that engineering itself was changing. Work was being routinized—drafting and much design work is done by computer. So engineers who usually design systems for others are suffering the effects of automation themselves. Two-year technicians, more and more of them women, are hired to do some of the work engineers did, and the profession is mightily upset by these developments. It cuts turf and lowers salaries. But once again, women are encouraged to enter work like drafting that is already being automated and to go into fields like technicians and engineers that are being "degraded" with technological change [Braverman 1974].

157

Who knows, but there could have been action-oriented components from a study of that. But that's the one that didn't get funded.

DOROTHY: And when you talk about this work, in part in the context of teaching, do you view teaching, in some ways, as a political process?

SALLY: Ohhh. Almost entirely! To take a bazooka to even the balance of power between me and what they are learning from everywhere else. So I don't feel very badly about coming on very strongly, politically. For one thing I tell them what I am doing. And I will tell them about alternatives. "So this is the way we study things like stratification. This is the way Marx studies"—he puts it together a little differently, a different way of looking at class. And symbolic interactionist and so on. I might give examples of each. And then I will tell them my own work, which might be a combination of methods that I think gets you . . . not closer to the truth, but gives you a fuller, richer picture/story to tell. Doing it that way, it doesn't hit them over the head—or their minds close. Yeah, it's an entire . . . it's a very political act.

DOROTHY: Hmm. So that these papers, or this work was sort of inserted into the political process of a somewhat different kind and in a different way, but nonetheless had their part in what you were, then, able to say. Like in the class—when you are teaching students.

SALLY: Yeah, yes. It's not bad. You know you get a thousand students a year and . . .

DOROTHY: That's incredible. I can't even imagine that.

SALLY: Oh . . .

DOROTHY: When you say, "It's not bad." I find it staggering.

SALLY: It is staggering. And it's stressful because my style is real personal and open, which gives the *appearance* of a personal relationship, which is real nice for teaching, but it is real hard on you. You know, because you've got a thousand new friends a year. So it is political. But not in the same way as working with unemployed women and migrant workers or the telephone operators . . . I mean it's such a different—they all want to grow up to be corporate executives. You can talk about the poor, and for them the poor are out there somewhere, and certainly not something they are going to have to worry about. The "unemployed," you know, "That's those old guys." So I use this research on the "degradation of work" to try to let them see how we are all caught in this same thing, and that there are larger forces operating, that they are helping by simply taking part, even just by believing in the grade. And then I will tell them about taking engineering. I will do the stories and then I will say, "We call this process 'degradation.'" And then just go on. So they've got a word that's attached to it. But it is more the *stories* that you've got to fight over. All that comes in different parts in a large Intro class. It can't hurt. How much help? You know, sometimes you get the impression maybe 5 percent of them will hear and maybe they already knew to begin with.

DOROTHY: And maybe if they remember 10 years later, you are still . . .

SALLY: In this kind of society if you've got the engineers on your side it is a little different kind of struggle. The union people were forever telling me, "If we could just figure out how to get the engineers in the bargaining. . . ." There was a group of radical engineers in the sixties. About the time we [Charles Starnes and Sally] were writing this [the "Computers in the Workplace" paper, now Chapter 8], the engineers of Western Electric, which belongs to AT&T, finally joined the bargaining unit. But again, you are working with white males.

DOROTHY: Yeah. Yes, and if they join the union it's, in part, to protect that situation.

SALLY: Yeah. So, I think the research I did and writing it was a result of trying to enter the discourse, as it was. I applied for funding to study these processes. I wanted to see where and how male and female technicians and engineers made their living, and for what price, during this period of rapid technological change. Most financial support is for research on how to get more women *into* these fields. In fact the funding was approved, but the funds were cut by Reagan administration action. Under these folks, proposals to study race and sex discrimination were targeted for rejection or cuts by appointed grant "evaluators," many with no research experience at all. One appointee also said he couldn't find much value in proposals which didn't mention God. So I called a large electronics association that funds research on education, technology, and employment. The guy I talked to asked a few questions, said that yes, they did have about $6 million in a fund for research, but they tended to fund studies which would come to different conclusions than I seemed to be proposing.

And that's when I quit and went to L.A. for a year to try and get a job as a technician. I'd decided to do the study a different way. I took a year's leave of absence from teaching, without pay, and went to L.A. to work in the aerospace industry as a technician or production worker. I was trying to get *inside* so that you could see and feel what was happening. I wanted to see how much engineering work was being performed by other workers, and where women were being placed. And couldn't get hired as a technician. And couldn't get hired as a production worker, either.

DOROTHY: So what happened when you went to L.A.?

SALLY: Yah. I had $2,000 saved. I put my tent, sleeping bag, cooler, et cetera in the back of the VW squareback, and took off with little money, no job, and no place to stay. One is not put up at the local Hilton by government or business for this type of research, but I did find that you can live in a tent, on Malibu beach, for a few dollars a night—if you move your campsite every now and then. Even cheaper, a KOA on the outskirts of L.A. only collected from the rows of heavy metal in the RV section and didn't bother to collect rent from tenters. Later I shared a room with a friend. Community college campuses had typewriters you could rent for 20 cents for 20 minutes to write job applications. A friend with an answering service let me use it for taking calls.

My daily routine was: wash up in the public toilets, read the *L.A. Times* want ads. Dress for production work application; dress for clerical work, when the factories don't hire. Eat lots of beans and lentil soup. Try to find a room closer to the jobs (first and last month plus deposit took it all). All of this takes hours a day in L.A., and I had a car and quarters for phone calls. And my old job waiting for me in Oregon the next year. It was rough. I thought more about the old poor and the new poor than I had recently. I wondered how you could do this with no car, no money, no phone, and maybe a couple of kids. This sort of ethnographic works does get you out of familiar daily routines. It brings you together with people that your usual pattern never makes contact with.

When I couldn't get hired in production, I took a job as executive secretary in an engineering firm for three months. I learned more about the structure of the electronics industry, but I learned even more about being poor. And remembered all those years I'd typed for a living before. And how you have to dress, and sit, and move and how difficult it is—jokes were real difficult. Because they were joking about working people. And . . . you know, that's like joking about your family. And so you don't laugh right—you don't laugh on cue. And again I could see management's divide-and-conquer tactics and management's use of misinformation for control. I learned again how workers appear busy when there's no work and layoffs looming; about managing impressions—particularly laughing and facial expressions and the incredible intellectual and social skills a clerical worker has to have. I found out about the effect on one's spirit of doing a good clerical job on a weapon system proposal or—you know, seeing this messy file and whipping it into fine shape because you know you can do it—it's hard not to do a good job. And it turns out to be their "defense" file.

DOROTHY: So you could see a lot that was going on.

SALLY: Yeah. Not only that, but you've made it easier for them. Because you just can't stop yourself from doing a good job. It's real difficult to do work poorly. "Well, there's a job to be done. I'll do a good job." Bah humbug. But there wasn't too much fruitful . . . except ways in which the engineering firm itself was so connected to defense money and right-wing politics in L.A. You know you could see this in the meetings the boss went to. The people who called. How sleazy he was—how they would change records and put new dates on things. Oh . . . always on the wrong side in court testimony. But nothing relevant . . . as relevant as I had hoped for my project.

Then I got fired . . .

DOROTHY: Why were you fired?

SALLY: I don't know. It was a strange place—this big barn of a company with four people in it, these two strange women, one older and one younger, a Chinese engineering tech and this very strange engineer who owned the company. I was going to be executive secretary. One reason for getting fired might be that they had a reputation for hiring into the executive secretary position for three months and then firing people before the benefits come on; another could be that they found out who I was; another would be that my man friend would come around, and he was pretty sleazy looking. But the ostensible reason was that I had misplaced mail. And I knew the other secretary had done it. I remembered where she'd put it and I said, "Oh, I know where it is. You put it down in . . ." and she says, "No, no, I didn't put it anywhere," starting to cover up like that. We opened the drawer and there it was, just where she'd put it. The next day the boss called me in. He said, "We're going to have to let you go. That was just an unforgivable lapse." I said, "Well, you know it wasn't me who did it," and he said, "That's beside the point." So I asked, "What is it really?" and he said, "We just can't afford to have that kind of attitude." So it was my "attitude," at least ostensibly.

Then I went through the endless routine of application and rejection to qualify for unemployment. The line at the employment office took an hour—not a busy day and not downtown L.A. The form on top said "press hard," so I did, and ruined all the carbon forms below. So I waited again for a new stack of forms to fill out. I heard the supervisor chastising my "helper" for not explaining to "these people" how to fill out forms. "*These people* have to be told how"; "You have to watch *these people* at every step," and on and on. But it gave me the "unemployment" to do the interviewing that I did for half of that work on computers in the workplace [Chapter 8].

Even with all the advantages I had—some money to start with, a job to go back to, education, all these daily experiences, the habits of everyday life get to you, affect your self-concept. Feminist and worker meetings after hours were the best support group. Sharing experiences, ideas, analysis, and putting what we had learned to use—to change the system, not just grab a piece of it—that is to me the best counter to alienation on the job and in the community.

If you're in a professional job, ethnographic research of this sort is only one way to keep in touch with women at the lower levels of employment/unemployment. Taking part in action-oriented groups is another. This kind of effort is important. Our daily lives do affect what we see and how we think about problems and our style of research. And in professional work, it's all too easy to begin to drift away from the problems faced by most women.

Chapter 7

Automated and Automators: Human and Social Effects of Technological Change

*A*utomation and mechanization create and eliminate work. Given that a social division of labor based on sex gives rise to a sex-segregated modern work force, automation and mechanization do not affect men and women alike. Further, their effects are not restricted to those whose jobs are directly automated. Technological change has implications for the automators as well as for the automated.

In this chapter, I examine stratification based on sex among the automated and the automators, first looking at the role of women workers during periods of technological change in U.S. corporations representing three industries—agribusiness, printing and publishing, and especially telecommunications. Data and observations are presented here from a firm in each of the three industries: the telephone company, a newspaper, and a poultry plant, where in a broader societal rather than a narrow organizational context, the human and social costs appear to outweigh the benefits. Second, the profession most closely related to the implementation of automated systems—engineering—is analyzed while it is in a process of vertical differentiation related to automation. Here too I explore how stratification based on sex differs at different levels of the professional and technical work force. I also examine the overall effects as the nature of engineering work changes, and as sex stratification and other uncertain criteria are employed to introduce order into the processes of social and technological differentiation. In conclusion, I note the need to look for overall effects beyond particular industrial settings to the complex of institutions to which they are connected.

THE AUTOMATED:
DISPLACEMENT OF WORKERS BY
TECHNOLOGICAL CHANGE AND ITS HUMAN COSTS

The U.S. literature on technological and organizational change rarely considers displacement or unemployment as a problem. Literature on automation and displacement tends to focus on overall employment patterns by a company, or examines the impact on management versus workers. Such research may gloss over processes that irritate existing social divisions in a society, such as divisions based on older hierarchies of race and sex. If these divisions are heightened by automation, even inadvertently, the social problem becomes more complex than a matter of unemployment alone.

One cannot generalize about the impact of automation in terms of the effects on management versus nonmanagement employees, female versus male workers, or white versus nonwhite workers in these case studies. Automation takes place at different levels within one firm, and between industries—affecting craft work at one time, clerical, unskilled, or management at another. But at this point in time, females and people of color seem most adversely affected by automation in labor-intensive industries. Automation in industries with a more sophisticated technological core affects white male craft workers and lower-level (female) management, and women workers in clerical positions.

Informal discussions with workers in urban and rural areas suggest that people react to job loss or perception of declining opportunity in various ways. White male craft workers direct anger toward groups of lower status who are "moving in." Most female workers, however, tend to individualize the experience as their "own fault," or to accept the processes of change as inevitable in the name of progress. In either case, the loss of self-esteem is severe.

Telecommunications

The U.S. system of telephone communication provides an impressive model both for reliability of service and for change—research, development, and incorporation of technological innovation. AT&T, the major corporation in telecommunications, integrates technologies on several levels of sophistication at once, and moves relatively smoothly through what could be disruptive changes in its occupational structure due to automation.

Even in the best of technical systems, however, with vast resources available for social problems attending automation, the costs absorbed by the labor force and the society are high. AT&T represents 2 percent of the employed U.S. labor force. The operating companies and Long

Lines division, which furnished most of the data for this paper, employ close to a million people.

In the mid-twentieth century, the telephone company adopted technologies that reduced the need for workers at the lowest levels of its occupational structure. Systems such as automated message accounting, direct distance dialing, customer records and billings, and the traffic service position allowed cutbacks of tens of thousands of operator and clerical worker jobs. The customer records billing system, according to a Bell Labs engineer, has made for people savings up to 50 percent in some areas. These systems continue to reduce employment during the seventies. Data from the operating companies and Long Lines for the period 1972 through 1975 show a net loss of only 8,506 workers. The cost of automation was borne by management and workers, cutting across the traditional boundaries of groups usually affected adversely by the technological change. In addition to a loss of over 36,000 operators and lower-level clerical workers, there was a decrease of 1,535 lower-level supervisors—those who formerly supervised workers displaced by automation.[1]

However, closer examination shows that women, whether management or nonmanagement employees, were far more adversely affected than men. Men gained 13,767 jobs over their 1972 level, while women lost 22,273 jobs during the same time. Part of this process was due to affirmative action taken by the company to encourage men into traditionally women's work, and women into traditionally men's work.[2] Men were more successful at breaking nontraditional barriers than were women; at the nonmanagement level, 9,400 women moved into men's jobs, while 16,300 men moved into women's jobs.[3]

It is also apparent, however, that the electronic switching system and related systems in installation, repair, and maintenance will reduce the need for skilled and semiskilled craft workers, jobs traditionally held by white men. As this work is simplified prior to automation, women and nonwhite men are moved into craft work. There are thousands fewer white male skilled craft workers than there were in 1972, and thousands more women and nonwhite men.[4] There are also far fewer men (both white and nonwhite) in semiskilled craft positions, many of which are now filled by women. Fibre-optics transmission is another innovation that promises more reduction in traditionally male construction and repair work.

Most women with whom I spoke worked at the lower occupational levels in the telephone company. Some reported not being able to "keep up with" the faster pace of work preceding automation, or more stringent requirements regarding punctuality or absences. They reported that low-level supervisors were increasingly "strict" about personal movement (being away from one's desk, drinking coffee, yawning or stretching on the job). They felt they were treated "like kindergartners," in the words of one, with their physical movement and their attitudes under constant surveillance and criticism. Older workers, those near retirement, were more reluctant to complain about the organization of work during automation than were younger workers. Rural and small-town women, generally older, resented the choice of early retirement or "tearing up roots" to transfer to the cities as smaller telephone offices closed. White male craft workers said that "a white man can't get a job at Bell these days," and usually blamed legislation for equal employment for the problem. A company social worker reported resentment among colleagues. They perceived that the organization of work led to anger, frustration, drinking problems, depression, anxiety, and tension among workers. Social workers were then expected to alleviate these problems through counseling and other clinical services.

Printing and Publishing

In the newspaper firm, cold-type and other processes decreased the amount of craft work. In other areas of the United States, secretaries could be hired to type camera-ready copy, formerly a job for craftsmen—typesetters. In this case, however, a largely white male union protected craft jobs from greater access by women and nonwhite men, even though this work was routinized in the transition to computer or cold-type processes. Projected displacement of typographers was set at 35 percent.

The experience in the newspaper corporation reflected U.S. patterns in general, where reduction in employment affected linotypists, copy cutters, proofers, makeup workers, mat molders, stackers, bundlers, tiers, delivery and type luggers, typists, and perforators. Due to automation of other systems of work at the newspaper, employment was also reduced in mailing, circulation, and billing. Employment gains came in electronic editing, systems analysis, and sales—primarily sources of male employment.

Male craft workers who managed to retain their work after reduction and simplification referred to it as "junk" work. While these workers strongly resisted such changes, many women workers scheduled for displacement—for example, those who took want ads—were described by management as apathetic.

Agribusiness

In the poultry plant, technological innovation reduced the work force—primarily female—by about half. White female workers gave way to Mexican-American female workers and to youths, with future plans on the part of the company to employ American Indian labor and move to further automation. Mechanization of field harvesting brought a 15 percent decline in field labor in one year in a three-county area of a midwestern state. Here, Mexican-American males and females were affected equally. Middle-sized farming operators faced increased cost of farming related to more sophisticated technology (Hacker 1977a).

Farm owners considered such processes as vertical integration, mechanization, agrochemical use, and attendant increased cost of farming as inevitable. These processes were necessary, in the words of an Iowa farm woman, "If this country is going to feed the world." The most negative result of higher technology from their point of view was the impact on family relations. The high cost of farming meant few if any of their children would be able to raise their own families among rural traditions. Sons and daughters would migrate to urban areas for work. Farm women, in addition, felt they would be unable to continue family farming if their husbands died, due to the structure of inheritance taxes and negative attitudes toward women in agribusiness industries (supplies, equipment, financing, and so on).

In the migrant camps, community health workers sought alternatives to field work for migrants as harvesting was mechanized—helping migrants "settle out" in the canneries and meat-packing plants in the area. In this instance, prejudice toward Mexican-Americans on the part of Anglo city dwellers made such settling out difficult. One could observe semiorganized efforts among small businessmen and white workers to resist the intrusion of a "different" people into the already tight job market in this small midwestern town.

The human and social costs of automation extend beyond the boundaries of the corporation, and are difficult to perceive if those boundaries are accepted as a legitimate parameter for analysis. As modernization draws women into the work force, for example, it weakens traditional family ties but provides few new institutional support systems. Child care needs and care of the elderly are prime examples. Female-headed households account for an increasing proportion of families in this highly industrialized country. Where automation primarily displaces female workers, they, and the young and the old who are not in the labor force, are adversely affected.

Thus, in addition to the personal and psychological effects of displacement or simplified and repetitive work, technological change such as automation has interinstitutional ramifications, particularly in this intersection of work and family. Ideology suggests strengthening the older family patterns compatible with an agricultural society (where women perform unpaid domestic labor), while the contradictory process of development draws women into the paid labor force. Further, this research on automation in selected industries shows a pattern of interaction with existing social divisions based on race

and sex. This exacerbates social tensions during a volatile period in
U.S. history.

THE AUTOMATORS:
VERTICAL DIFFERENTIATION IN ENGINEERING

In the process of this study of the social costs of automation,
I became interested in the people who designed and implemented
the technologies in question. Most of those with whom I talked were
managers with engineering backgrounds. It seemed equally important
to assess the social, political, and economic forces affecting those who
research, develop, and apply automated systems as it was to assess
those forces as they affect workers who are displaced. I was also
challenged by the disparity in worldview and in the universe of
discourse—the different "languages" we spoke.[5]

Many had not thought of the problem of new workers, young
people facing a more difficult job market. Many felt that automation
would increase employment, for example, in other sectors such as food
services, but had not thought about the lower income level in those
sectors. Those who recognized some difficulty with displacement had
not thought of the differential displacement by race and sex. Most
thought of women as wives and mothers, a flexible pool of labor
that could be reabsorbed relatively easily into the home. This is a
special problem in developed countries such as the United States,
where three quarters of women workers either do not have husbands
or are married to men earning less than $10,000 per year. These are
not unsophisticated reactions, however, since social science literature
itself has until recently stemmed from a similar conceptual orientation.
It may seem unreasonable to expect engineering/management to be
more sensitive and aware of these problems than are academic
social scientists. But the significance of decisions—especially in an
international context—made by those who direct technological change
might argue the reverse.

Also relatively poorly researched is the impact of automation on
engineering itself, and the quality of the engineering/technical work
force. Specialization and stratification accompanying automation do not
stop at the boundaries of this profession, but affect its very organization
as well (Chestnut and Mayer 1963; Rosenbrock 1977).

Vertical Differentiation in Theory and Practice

Automation spurs the development of new occupational groups
providing technical support to engineering. Engineering is now faced
with finding ways to prevent management from the inappropriate

use of cheaper technical labor. Skills of abstraction, such as calculus and other techniques easily quantified, become even more heavily emphasized as the important ingredient of engineering. As Rosenbrock (1977) suggests, this may have unintended effects on the nature of work remaining in the profession. This may provide work opportunities of limited creativity and autonomy "at the bottom," while engineers may be further removed from the tinkering, or hands-on, experience that draws many young people to the field.

Engineering education literature and career education literature indicate complexities surrounding the development of new occupations and paraprofessions related to engineering—demand, definitions, training, curricula, accrediting bodies, and criteria. Of concern also are the status and pay appropriate for such skills. This literature allows insight into the attempts to direct vertical differentiation within emerging technical/scientific occupations. New levels are added to a hierarchy of occupations and paraprofessions; these new groups, by definition of accrediting bodies, are to work under the supervision of a professional engineer. An intricate pattern of relationships develops among training programs, educational institutions, professional societies, and industry needs.

In theory, the lowest level of new occupations is made up of industrial technicians, who may have some minimal technical/educational training in community colleges, military, trade, or technical schools (public or proprietary), but most often receive training on the job, or in formal short courses offered by corporations. A local electronics firm reports that this training offers one route toward upward mobility for women on the production line. Career educators Harris and Grede (1977) suggest that no theoretical knowledge or general education is necessary at this level; they cite "industrial technician" as an excellent occupational opportunity for women. Harris and Grede also describe the next level, "engineering technician," which usually demands a two-year associate degree from a community college, and entails minimal theoretical knowledge and general education, as an ideal opportunity for women.

Newest and next highest on the scale—in theoretical and general education, status, pay, and autonomy on the job—is the engineering technologist, a graduate of a four-year program generally offered through colleges, universities, or technical institutes. The literature does not encourage women at this level.

All of these occupational groups are in theory to work under the supervision—direct or indirect—of an engineer, for the most part a graduate of a B.S., M.S., or Ph.D. engineering program. In theory, accreditation occupies a significant role in maintaining orderly development of these emerging occupations.

But, not surprisingly, the operating reality reveals some slippage. Recently, when the supply of engineers dwindled, technicians were hired in their place (Mingle 1979), and those holding a bachelor of engineering technology (BET) degree have been hired as engineers.[6] Corporations and engineers may disagree about the practical difference between a B.Sc. in engineering and a BET, but in fact the BET share of the technical human resources pool shows a small but steady increase over the past 10 years. In fact, differences in the response rates from engineering and technician/technology schools mean that the latter are underrepresented in the studies (Doigan 1979), and the engineering share of this labor pool might well show a more marked decline.[7]

While the engineering profession has recognized that automation creates a need for technical workers below the level of engineers, it may be caught in the tension between economic factors and traditional ties to management on the one hand and values internal to the profession on the other—values such as quality of product and fulfilling work. For example, educators in two-year programs report that many of their students are former engineering students. Some left engineering because of its "difficulty"; others left in search of the hands-on, "tinkering" work they prefer to management or paperwork. In a recent discussion with a group of engineers in industry, they expressed some resentment that technologists were getting the "fun" work, while engineers were increasingly shifted to management and paperwork. At the same time, some engineers, both on and off campus, question the quality of work produced by technicians or technologists hired as engineers, ascribing large system disruptions to mistakes by those with less engineering background.

Internal strain may result within the profession as it is charged with ordering the process that produces the potential competitors. The very selection of criteria may have a further effect on the content of engineering. In distinguishing between engineer and technologist, for example, much weight appears given to what Rosenbrock (1977) argues is only one aspect of engineering—algorithmic, mathematical, scientific techniques. While accepting that these techniques are indispensable and have great intellectual appeal, he emphasizes that other skills—judgment, experience, understanding of social complexity—are also necessary for a full development of engineering. There is more than an echo here. Competition affects the basic sciences as well. Restivo and Collins (1980) trace the impact of competition and prestige on historical developments in mathematics itself. Further, stronger emphasis on mathematics as a criterion for good engineering has operated as a filter restricting women's and minorities' access to the upper levels of the field.[8]

Harris and Grede (1977) insist that community college technical programs live up to their promises to provide two-year graduates with employable skills and to provide industry with qualified employees. They note a tendency for the community college programs to alter curricula in order to make transfer easier for the student. The Engineering Council on Professional Development (ECPD) (1976) also discovered the inclusion of general education courses or theoretical courses at the two-year (technology, not preentry) level. In Volume 2 of the ECPD's *44th Annual Report*, the council viewed such alteration of two-year curricula as "in conflict with ECPD accreditation criteria." Thus concerns for the community college's adherence to vocational goals, for employability of students, and for greater clarity in demarcations between emerging technical occupations through educational criteria may work against the desire of some students for cheaper education and smoother transition to four-year institutions.

At present, transfers may be even more difficult for students to obtain, as economic factors curtail engineering education. Patterns of funding education now allow expansion of educational programs at the lower levels (for example, the community colleges and the military as a training institution), while requiring cutbacks at the state university level. These factors perhaps foretell a settling down—fewer engineers and many more technicians. Since over half the graduates of BET programs are hired as engineers, the BET may be perceived as a competitor by engineering and a threat to the quality of engineering work. Management may perceive the BET as a cost-saver, representing 10 percent lower average salaries. Management may also view the BET favorably for other reasons, including the BET holder's probable preference for professional identification and association over trade union membership (see Chapter 8).

Similar misgivings about the effect of extreme division of labor on quality and productivity in industry have been expressed by others (for example, Sandkull 1980). As Alvin Gouldner (1976) suggests, dissatisfaction and desire for higher quality of work in engineering may foretell a fragmentation of traditional loyalties of engineers to government or industrial leadership.

CONCLUSION

The effects of automation and mechanization on women and men and on stratification based on sex differ at different levels of industrial organization. I have described above how automation in labor-intensive industries tends to displace women and minority workers. In the technologically more sophisticated industries, such as telecommunications, management, clerical, and craft workers are most affected. The overall effect, however, is a disproportionate displacement of women workers.

Automation also affects those who are responsible for its design, planning, and implementation—that is, engineers. It increases the division of labor and also produces greater vertical differentiation in engineering. As in the telecommunications industry, this new division of labor builds on the existing divisions of sex and race. At the lower levels of vertical differentiation on which some of the work formerly done by fully qualified engineers has devolved, women are seen as appropriate recruits. At the upper levels, there is a displacement of male engineers toward more strictly managerial functions, a move that also has its human costs, attracting those in the more abstract or scientific fields of engineering, but repelling those who like the more "hands-on" aspects of engineering.

I am suggesting that automation is having fairly major effects on the division of labor and the sex stratification of the labor force across the board. In labor-intensive industries, women and minorities are displaced from the work force without clear prospects of alternative employment. The human costs are very great, with major effects on women's family lives. At the same time, management, professions, and crafts, the stronghold of white males, are being transformed; in some cases, some types of work are eliminated altogether. As we have seen in the telecommunications industry, automation at first opens up new levels of employment to women and minorities. Women move into craft jobs formerly the exclusive prerogative of men. But these are not the same jobs as they were; they have already been "degraded." Automation has already reduced the skills required. A parallel process can be seen in engineering, as women are given access to the new "technical" levels at the lower end of the emerging hierarchy within engineering.

The older hierarchies of sex, with white males commanding the technological heights both as engineers and as craftsmen, are built into a division of labor that is now being undermined, affecting some of the traditional bases of sex stratification. At the same time, preexisting stratification based on sex and race is exploited in the processes of vertical differentiation, degradation of work, and technological displacement.

It is important not to limit our research to the overall effects of industrial policies of technological change on unemployment, or to restrict it to the impact on management versus workers. The effects are wide ranging within and beyond the industrial setting. Changes in the educational system at all levels are also part of this reshaping of the scientific and technical work force. As students are transformed into a work force, an intricate pattern of interaction emerges among industry, various educational institutions and their funding sources, accrediting societies, and professional organizations. The extraorganizational and interorganizational aspects of this changing division of labor need more attention from researchers. Policies of technological change also have effects for the sex stratification system, providing new opportunities in technologically advanced industries, while, in general, displacing women at the lower levels of labor-intensive industries and resulting overall in lower levels of women's employment. Displacement and the degradation of skilled labor irritate further existing social divisions based on sex and racial stratification. There are major human costs in terms of men's and women's lives on and off the job.

NOTES

1. See Chapter 1, Table 1.1, for details.

2. *Affirmative action* is the phrase normally used for the effort required by U.S. law and regulation to assure equal employment opportunities for women and certain ethnic minorities.

3. For further details, see Chapter 1, Table 1.2.

4. See Chapter 1, Table 1.3.

5. The significance of mathematical abstractions in the culture of engineering is explored in Part II of this volume.

6. See Chapter 8 for a fuller discussion of this issue.

7. Assumptions underlying this line of reasoning must be tested—to what extent do engineers, technologists, and technicians compete for similar positions? Also, the ratio of engineer to technical support personnel varies widely from field to field.

8. Special training programs, however, such as those sponsored in recent years by the National Science Foundation, enable the groups to develop mathematical ability equal to that of men.

Computers in the Workplace: Stratification and Labor Process among Engineers and Technicians

coauthored by Charles E. Starnes

O ur aim in this chapter is to consider current transformations in the stratification of the technical work force related
to microprocessors and other factors. We explore the degree to which
the degradation hypothesis of Braverman (1974)—the deskilling of
work accompanied by the replacement of skilled labor with lesser
skilled labor or machine—fits what we know of the organization
of the engineering and technical work force. We shall discuss the
"middle layers" of technical management through the interaction of
industry and the career education movement; some criteria for vertical
differentiation in the technical/engineering profession, and interactions
with race, sex, and class; and tensions between professional engineering
and corporate needs.

Many of us—parents, faculty, advisers, and others—subscribe to
the view that an engineering degree is a "ticket" to immediate and
secure employment at relatively high pay for interesting and prestigious
work. The thesis of this chapter is that several forces, including but not
limited to microprocessor technology, must moderate this optimistic
view, depending on actions of various forms—deskilling, replacement
by technicians or technologists, automation through computer-aided
design and computer-aided manufacturing (CAD/CAM). This desire for
secure, well-paid, and interesting employment is countered by diverse
groups, each offering its own form of resistance. The engineering
profession strives to maintain its boundaries. Engineers join in collective
bargaining, or challenge the effect of automation on the quality of work.
Technical workers organize, and could challenge certain educational
criteria for success—calculus, for example (see Chapter 6). Given that
the work of some technologists or even technicians is of comparable
worth to that of many engineers in their workplace, pay equity may
become a legal issue.

Management itself, depending on the specific conditions of time and place, may prefer to keep the loyalty of its engineers, thus moderating the drive for labor savings (Whalley 1985). On the basis of our research, we perceive a decline in employment opportunities of engineers and a short-term energetic role for technicians and technologists. We expand Braverman's framework, limited to the marketplace, to include attention to nonmarketplace phenomena such as professional societies in interaction with the state, educational institutions, and the role of a technical ideology. The future depends on the mosaic created by these forms of resistance to automation.

Braverman (1974) notes, "Marx has pointed out that unlike generals, who win their wars by recruiting armies, captains of industry win their wars by discharging armies" (p. 236). In winning their wars the captains of industry often enlist machines designed by management engineers. Braverman tells a story of how "the capitalist, the manager, and the industrial engineer" have abstracted from the concrete situations of human labor its general and dehumanized form. They thereby mold it as a machine tool over which they possess all creative control, and which they then employ in pursuit of the accumulation of capital (Braverman 1974, 181). In this process there has been a thin line, at best, between the engineer as a servant to the capitalist and manager and the engineer as partner.

The irony of this, as Braverman hints but does not develop, is that engineering, as a category in the detailed division of labor, is itself undergoing a breakdown and rationalization. Even Florman (1976), who waxes poetic about the pleasure of engineering, acknowledges that "thousands" now work in detailed, repetitive, and boring tasks. (He suggests optimistically that each of these workers experiences "the satisfaction of having participated in a great undertaking.") Beginning in the 1950s and proceeding at a quickening pace, there has been a rapid development of para-engineering occupations commonly referred to by the general term of *technician*. In 1966 the U.S. Bureau of Labor called for a long-term increase (to 1975) in the ratio of technicians to scientists and engineers, in part due to "rising salaries of . . . engineers." Drafting—the area currently attracting many women in community college courses—was not, however, included in this plan due to the projected use of photoreproduction, mechanized equipment, and computer automation. More recently, even the term *technician* has undergone fractionation, and various grades of "technologists," "associates," or "aides" are offered as subcategories that capture aspects of the further rationalization of engineering labor. Sex and race interact with this process of stratification, as Braverman notes.

DEGRADATION OF ENGINEERING:
SEX, RACE, AND THE
TECHNICAL DIVISION OF LABOR

Deskilling of labor and automation are key elements in the process of degradation. The engineering profession has long acknowledged the need for technicians and technologists, for example, through standing committees in professional bodies and through publication of guidance materials for technicians and technology students. They see that an increasingly complex organization of industry creates a need for the production of technical workers with various levels of skills below the level of engineer. Automation is cited as a prime force driving this need. According to *The Technician Education Yearbook, 1978–79*, "Automation of industrial processes and growth of new areas of work such as environmental protections and urban development, will add to the demand for technical personnel."

This raises the question of whether or not automation "deskills" the worker—in this case, the engineer. The worker him- or herself may become deskilled by having to perform simpler, more routinized tasks than before.

U.S. engineers do report deskilling in progress (Katz 1977; Dubin 1977). They report that the majority of their work can be performed by people with less education than themselves; they increasingly work at repetitive tasks under pressure of time, which limits creativity; they are subject to replacement after five to eight years by younger (and cheaper) engineering graduates. Degradation or proletarianization of engineering is countered by others. Whalley (1985), for example, disagrees that such processes are taking place. He, however, focuses on the British experience. Braverman himself noted that the organization of engineering differed greatly between the United States and other nations. Thus, in 1970, the ratio of technicians to professional engineers in the United Kingdom was 4:1, in France and West Germany roughly 2.5:1, and in the United States a mere .62:1.

Architect or Bee?, written by British aerospace senior development engineer, Mike Cooley (1982), describes with energy and passion the effect of computer-aided design (CAD) on the creative process within the work of design engineers. He notes that as capital-intensive equipment "aids" this process there is an increasing tendency to "Taylorize" the work force, emphasizing the speed of response, rotating shifts, and other facets of proletarianization. Not even the work that was once an intimate part of design itself is exempt:

Up to the 1940s the draughtsman was the center of the design activity. He could design a component, draw it, stress it out, specify the material for it and the lubrication required. Nowadays, each of these is fragmented down to isolated functions. The designer designs, the draughtsman draws, the metallurgist specifies the material, the stress analyst analyses the structure and the tribologist specifies the lubrication. Each of these fragmented parts can be taken over by equipment such as this automatic draughting equipment. (p. 2)

Fragmentation allows automation and transfers the creative element to those who design and control the computer. But that is not the full story, by any means. Cooley's description of degradation within "what engineers do" and, hence, within the community of engineering, is paralleled by the work of Greenbaum (1976) and Kraft (1977) for the field of computer programming. The introduction of structured programming may limit not only the creative decisions about resources of materials, as in the degradation of traditional crafts, but choices about allowable modes of thought. Control over machines and work flow is transferred to upper management, and now thinking itself comes under such control.

Deskilling often interacts with both the technical division of labor and social stratification on the basis of class, race, and sex. First, the complex task is routinized. Abstraction and skills are separated from the detail work, which is then assigned to a new layer of lower-paid workers. These workers are usually recruited from the relatively more disadvantaged segments of the social division of labor, but not from the most disadvantaged alone. The new workers are generally willing to work at wages lower than those paid for labor prior to routinization. They are also more tractable. If this new detailed labor proves too costly from management's point of view, the next step will generally be automation (assuming technical problems are solved). Detailed labor may be judged "too costly" and thus automated either because labor costs are generally higher than elsewhere (for example, as between nations) or because increasing scale of organization relative to competitors makes automation a cost-effective method of increasing profits and shares of the market. The fact that automation often follows upon the transition from "traditional" labor pools to "marginal workers" (for example, female and minority workers) suggests that deskilling may sometimes be a conscious policy in preparation for the elimination of whole segments of labor.

On occasion, this process is articulated explicitly. As AT&T simplified and automated craft jobs such as switching, framework, or installation, the work was transferred from white male skilled workers to minority male and female semiskilled workers, then to women clerical workers, then to machines. This pattern is not consistent, however. In other industries, printing and publishing, for example, craft worker employment in a firm was protected by a strong union throughout the transition from hot to cold typesetting (see Chapter 7). Thus, under these conditions, the social composition of the work force showed no dramatic change.

In the history of engineering, women have performed routine tasks that were later absorbed by machine. Women copied drawings until copy machines became cost-effective (Baynes and Pugh 1978, 1981). They entered drafting just as much of this work began to be performed by computer. Now career educators suggest women can find excellent opportunities as community college-degreed engineering technicians, work that itself may be automated in the near future.

Engineering and career education literature indicates some of the complexities associated with newly developing occupations and paraprofessions related to engineering. This literature cites problems of labor demand, occupational titles and definitions, modes of training, curricular content, accreditation bodies and criteria, status, and pay. Professional engineers attempt to assert authority over emerging technical occupations via accrediting bodies and definitions that assure supervision through a chain descending from the professional engineer at the top.

STRATIFICATION

The Presumed Process

At the "lowest" level of these new occupations are "industrial technicians," who may have some minimal technical/educational training in community colleges, military, trade, or technical schools (public or proprietary), but, most often, receive training on the job or in formal short courses run by corporations. Career educators Harris and Grede (1977) suggest that no theoretical knowledge or general education is necessary at this level. They cite "industrial technician" as an excellent occupational opportunity for women. A local electronics firm also reports that this type of on-the-job training as a technician offers one route toward upward mobility for women on their production line.

The next higher level, "engineering technician," usually demands a two-year "associate" degree from a community college, a degree entailing minimal theoretical and general knowledge. Harris and Grede (1977) also describe engineering technician as an "ideal opportunity" for women. The ECPD, in 1953, defined a "technician" (one, two, or four year) as "one who could carry out in a reasonable manner either proven techniques which are common knowledge among those who are technically expert in this branch of engineering, or those specially prescribed by engineers."

Newest and next on the scale of theoretical and general education, status, pay, and job autonomy, is the "bachelor of engineering technology," the BET. The technologist is presumed to be a graduate of a four-year program generally offered only through colleges, universities, and technical institutes. This middle-level technical program shows less participation by women and minorities than do either engineering or industrial technician levels.

Workers in these newer occupations are intended to work under the supervision—direct or indirect—of an engineer who is presumed to possess a B.S., M.S., or Ph.D. in engineering. Accreditation occupies a major role in maintaining the orderly development of these occupations. During the early years, there were battles over whether technical education funds should be directed to vocational or higher educational systems and over the appropriate accrediting body. This history is traced in the *Technician Education Yearbook, 1963–64*. The postsecondary technical education programs and the ECPD (now ABET—the Accreditation for Bachelors of Engineering and Technology) won out.

Over the years, the engineering profession has struggled with curricula and with definitions of the new middle layers of workers. Descriptions in the 1970s suggest the "TECHnician/TECHnologist" sets up and does experiments, draws, sketches, does routine design work, gives advice that is more limited and practical than that given by scientists and engineers, writes manuals, checks specifications, and supervises production workers. The tech/tech follows plans set by scientists and/or engineers, but "often without close supervision." In 1976, the ECPD's *44th Annual Report* stated:

> Engineering technology is part of a continuum extending from craftsman to the engineer. Located nearest the engineer, it requires the application of scientific and engineering principles in support of engineering activities. The support is given whether or not the engineer technologist or engineering technician is working under the immediate supervision of an engineer. The "engineering technician" is applied to the graduates of the associate degree programs. Graduates of baccalaureate programs are termed "engineering technologists."

The Process in Practice

The above description indicates how the process is assumed to work. Not surprisingly, the actual practice reveals some slippage (Middleton 1980). For example, when the supply of engineers recently dwindled, technicians were hired in their place (Mingle 1979). Another study indicates that four-year BETs are also hired as engineers (Moore and Will 1973). As carefully as educators and accreditors have been in distinguishing BET degrees from B.S. degrees in engineering, a survey of 45 BET programs showed that, on average, 51 percent of their graduates are hired by industry as "engineers" (the range was from 0 to 98 percent). In 1982, 69 percent of BET graduates were hired as engineers (O'Hair 1984). Representatives from electronics and aerospace firms in Oregon and California reported to us that they will hire BETs and technicians should the supply of engineering graduates fall short of demand. Underfunding of four-year engineering B.S. programs assures such a shortage. Current demand for BET graduates appears quite high, especially in California's electronics industry; BET programs report roughly 10 job offers for every graduate in some specialties. Not all agree, however; faculty from two-year technical programs have argued that the four-year BET degree produces a "misfit," someone who aspires to be but is not an engineer. They predict the ultimate decline and demise of the BET. (One BET administrator countered by remarking that his graduates were "laughing all the way to the bank.")

Even "engineering technology" educators may be disturbed by the lack of clear distinction between engineering and engineering tech/tech fields. Williams (1980/1981), in two recent issues of *Engineering Education*, asks the "rhetorical questions":

> Which is the broader term: engineering or technology? Professional Engineering (Professional Engineer), Engineering (Engineer), Engineering Technology (Engineering Technician and Engineering Technologist), Technology (Industrial Technician and Technologist). WHERE ARE WE GOING? How long can we stand the fracturing?

Pay

The profession of engineering is concerned that proper dollar distance be maintained between employees in the various levels of scientific and technical work. Calculations from data in the *Engineering Manpower Bulletin, Engineering Education*, and *Professional Income of Engineers* yield the premiums for more advanced degrees shown in Table 8.1.

B.S. and BET salaries began to draw closer together in 1975. One study indicated as little as 6 percent difference (Smoot and King 1981). A Brigham Young University study showed that their own BET and B.S. graduate starting salary differences hovered under 4 percent for the previous four years, with some fields of BETs earning higher starting salaries than graduates in some fields of engineering (Holt 1983). Holt notes, however, that bulletins continued, at that time, to report the general "10 percent" starting salary difference for the two groups of graduates. One large aerospace corporation in Los Angeles paid its BETs only 8 percent less than its engineers, to start. Even though the salaries began to approximate each other in the mid-seventies, savings

TABLE 8.1
Average Monthly Starting Salaries: Premium for Higher Degrees (in percentages)

	1964	1977	1978	1979	1982
BET > Associate	X	28	29	40	33
B.S. > Associate	47	48	53	55	54
B.S. > BET	X	10 est.[a]	10 est.[a]	11	17
M.S. > B.S.	22	11	11	12	11
Ph.D. > M.S.	42	28	30	28	11[b]

[a] Estimated in the literature.
[b] Data from 1982 Ph.D. starting salaries were not considered "realistic." This comparison is based on salaries two years after the Ph.D., the first period for which these data were provided in *Professional Income of Engineers: 1983*.

could still be realized through the "flatter" lifetime salary curve of the BET, beginning roughly six years after graduation (Smoot and King 1981). The most recent data from the eighties show perhaps the power of the engineering professional societies to bring the BET programs and processes in line. At any rate, industry can now "buy" a BET at a considerable savings, compared to a B.S.

Lower salaries are only one of several important factors that make technicians and technologists attractive to industry, but this threat of lower-salaried substitution is a volatile issue. Kramer Associates Inc.'s (1978) report, *Manpower for Energy Research*, rhetorically asks, "Do employers substitute one specialty for another [technicians for engineers, for example] when relative salaries make it attractive, or are occupational demands relatively stable regardless of relative salaries?" Fazio et al. (1978), themselves engineers, seem to have little doubt that management would make such substitutions:

> A major problem facing engineers today is management's concept of them as a labor input rather than as professionals. This problem manifests itself in terms of low salary and status. . . . An associated and often neglected point is the question of what group is to control admission to a given profession. To propose an absurd example, imagine the bright, ambitious nurse who is rewarded for ten or twelve years of dedicated service with promotion to the position of "doctor" by the hospital's management. It is not uncommon, however, for management to promote a seasoned draftsman or designer to "engineer." It is, of course, management's prerogative to bestow the title of "engineer" on anyone they please. A prime example is the railroad industry which abounds with various so-called engineers, for example, Division Engineers, Office Engineers, Production Engineers, Material Engineers, etc., etc. For none of these positions is an engineering degree necessarily a prerequisite. It is farcical

to consider these nondegreed people as colleagues in the engineering profession. (pp. 162–63)

These authors conclude that unionizing engineering would not solve the problem but only add to it; the only solution they see is to gain control of admissions to the practice of engineering and to define and enforce rigorous and restrictive definitions of the term *engineer*.

Before leaving the topic of relative pay, however, we should note that the salaries for two-year associate technicians compared to B.S.-degreed engineers are roughly equivalent to the average differential pay between male labor and female labor. Further, this parallels a time when career educators are counseling "technician" positions as very appropriate for women and ethnic minorities. The January 1981 issue of *Engineering Education* speaks favorably of the prospects for minorities and women to increase or maintain enrollments in "engineering technology" education. Thus, as Braverman (1974) notes, the technical division of labor builds on older social divisions of labor.

FUTURE EMPLOYMENT OF
ENGINEERS AND TECHNICIANS:
THE ROLE OF COMPUTER-AIDED DESIGN
AND MANUFACTURING EQUIPMENT

Computer-aided design (CAD), one of the largest growth industries for the eighties (Anderson 1980), is of special relevance to employment in the field of engineering and related occupations. Microprocessors allow the generation and manipulation (including 3-D rotation) of engineering and architectural drawings, design of integrated circuits and printed circuit boards, designs and drawings for equipment, for mapping, site planning, highway design, and so on. This markedly increases productivity. Educators suggest that CAD can enable a technician or technologist (some say upgraded production workers) to do much of the work formerly performed by engineers.

Not only does CAD promise to alter the shape of the occupational structure, but economies of scope rather than scale imply that organizational and management forms will also be affected by CAD. New forms will emerge as integration of design and manufacturing functions proceeds. The time and pacing of innovation is often closely linked to cost factors; the strength of impact may increase with the fluidity of the system at any one point in time.

Knowledge of supply and demand in scientific and engineering occupations is a national priority issue (American Association for the

Advancement of Science [AAAS] 1984), as is the impact of high technology on employment of college graduates (Levin and Rumberger 1983). The 1980 "College Recruiting Report" issued by Abbott, Langer, and Associates (1980) projected a higher rate of increase (5 percent) in demand for technical graduates than for engineering graduates (2 percent). Further, "demand" figures for engineers are often inflated, since they rest in part on requirements found in proposals for contracts. When contracts are given, technicians, rather than engineers, may be hired.

The American Association of Engineering Societies' (1983) survey of employed engineers reports more than twice the proportion of engineers in 1983 as in 1981 expect a decline in employment opportunities for engineers (20 percent versus 9 percent). In-mobility of workers from technical and scientific fields to engineering raises issues of quality—whether or not those with baccalaureate (or lesser) degrees in fields other than engineering can indeed perform the work (Daufenbach 1984). Using these arguments, professional engineering societies now argue for holding the line on in-mobility to engineering, for example, through the process of preventive licensing (Institute for Electrical and Electronic Engineers [IEEE] 1980). The profession of engineering actively seeks state help in its crisis competition with industry. The recent "Engineering Technology Report" of the IEEE (1982), supports preventive licensing of tech/techs. The job market is sufficient for engineers now, but due to the expected decline, the IEEE must formulate a strong position on licensure, "if in fact the state boards are going to be able to hold the line" (IEEE 1982, 15). These then are some sources predicting less favorable employment opportunities for engineers, in engineering.

Most professional literature and statistical models, however, predict increasing need for engineers in the future (Daufenbach 1984). But as the Office of Technology Assessment (1984) points out, these predictions are often made on the basis of ambiguous data. The state of the predictive modeling arts is best described as "basic research" (Daufenbach and Fiorito 1983).

Williams (1980), a spokesman for engineering technology educators, points out that employment data are based upon the *Dictionary of Occupational Titles* (DOT), and even the latest edition does not include a number of occupations, for example, "engineering technician" and "engineering technologist"—though it does include several specialty technicians. Other data sets on scientific and technical labor classify as an engineer anyone working in the job title "engineer"; some restrict this to anyone with a scientific/technical baccalaureate working in the job title "engineer." Data on degrees conferred do not account for considerable nondegreed technical employment or entry into employment with other than these degrees (for example, a chemist who takes a job as "environmental technologist" in a water treatment plant). Even data on lifetime salaries of engineers assume the engineer obtained a B.S. at the age of 22, if degree information is absent. Researchers and authors compiling data sets often bemoan the fact that the organization of data does not allow answers to questions about changing employment patterns for engineers and technicians, or the share of jobs held by women and minorities. (Confidence is not strengthened by statements such as a concern over the "decrease" in minority technical enrollees from 13 percent in 1982 to 14 percent in 1983, or by information as asterisked in Table 8.1.) In conversation, frustration is apparent in such remarks as "flakiest data sets," "unintelligible data," and "Be skeptical of results." In print, one is more likely simply to read that the data are not organized "to examine the point," for example, of differential placement. (We may seem to belabor this point, but the field after all rests a good deal of its legitimacy on dealing with facts, accuracy, and precision. We merely register surprise here at the remarkable state of its own data regarding the field.) Finally, information from educational placement offices regarding employment of graduates is less than thorough, resting on voluntary reporting of graduates.

The Vanski (1984) and Fechter (1984) reports are straightforward: data are not available or organized to answer these questions on supply and demand, input/output, or deskilling. Fechter calls for disaggregated data, for finer analysis, and especially for attention to technicians—overlooked by NSF, for example. Case studies of skill requirements, given new technologies, are particularly timely. We simply do not know enough about these requirements to model the future with any degree of precision.

While admitting such data weaknesses, we can gain some insight into changes in stratification in the technical work force and linkages to the credentialing process, by using a combination of aggregate data, interviews (1980–84), primary documents, participant observations, and the literature. The following interpretations are based in part on interviews with more than 40 people in upper and middle management in industry (electronics, aerospace), some of whom sit on educational advisory boards; deans, chairs, faculty, counselors, and placement officers in schools of engineering, in four-year BET programs, in two-year community college technical programs, and in vocational education and industrial arts educational programs; organized engineers; and administrators of new high-tech programs for training or retraining. They are also based on participant observation as a "student" in university mechanical engineering courses and in community college technical education courses, from 1978 to 1982.

Given the state of employment data in the engineering and technical work force and the strong connection between engineering and technical education and employment in this country (Whalley 1985; Noble 1977; Brittain and McMath 1977; Grubb and Lazerson 1975; Bowles and Gintis 1976; Karabel 1972; Pincus 1980), we have chosen first to examine aggregate data on degrees awarded to engineers, to technologists graduating from BET programs, and to technicians graduating from engineering technician programs at the community college or two-year level for the past ten years (see Table 8.2).

TABLE 8.2
Share of Eng/Tech Degrees Awarded, 1974–1983

Year	Percentage B.S.	Percentage BET	Percentage Associate Degreed Technician	Total N
1974	63	11	26	67,823
1975	62	12	26	63,830
1976	61	13	26	63,016
1977	65	10	24	61,555
1978	66	10	23	69,354
1979	71	9	20	73,829
1980	71	9	19	81,501
1981	70	9	20	89,379
1982	72	9	18	92,513
1983	72	9	18	101,021

Source: Obtained from relevant issues of *Engineering Education*.

From these data, it appears that the share of all such degrees going to BETs, compared to engineering, increased up to 1976. One can observe, however, the strength of the engineering profession's counterattack through licensing, accrediting, and so on, from the mid-seventies to the early eighties. During that period, the ECPD, the professional accrediting society, reorganized to include oversight of BETs, and changed its name to ABET.

It would appear, counter to our hypothesis, that technicians' share of the technical-degreed work force has steadily declined. Caution is advised in reaching this conclusion, however, especially with respect to the number of two-year degreed technicians reported. The survey of engineering schools is far more thorough than that of tech/tech schools (Doigan 1979). It covers "virtually all" engineering schools, but only accredited tech/tech programs, and "some of those nonaccredited who 'choose' to reply" (Sheridan 1980). (The latter accounted for about half the reported tech/tech graduates.) In the May 1984 issue of *Engineering Education*, we learn that the number of two-year degrees increased 12 percent despite a decrease that year of 13.3 percent in the number of schools reporting. Further, these data do not account for the recent proliferation of unaccredited programs, corporate programs, or military training. The last, military training, is quite significant. Current patterns of funding allow some expansion or at least maintenance of technical educational programs at the lower levels, for example, the community colleges, but increasingly the military is a training institution. These data do not reflect the fact that the military is the largest vocational skill training program in the nation; its educational budget for 1983 was over $12 billion (Gilmore 1983). The military also retains its fairly low ceiling on the proportion of women admitted to the armed services, in this case, largely by classifying most jobs for which significant technical training is given as "combat related," and therefore off limits to women. This is of considerable importance to those working for equity in scientific and technical opportunities for women (Betty Vetter, *Scientific Manpower Commission*, August 8, 1984, personal communication). If data on degrees awarded were adjusted to reflect these factors, the engineering share would likely show a more marked decline rather than a holding pattern for the last several years.

Universities respond to economic crisis with stiffer admission, retention, and transfer requirements. For example, some engineering schools have raised entrance requirements for grade point average, and require a B rather than a C in all core courses. The usual 70 percent flunk-out rate before the third year may be raised if enrollments continue too high. Similar effects are seen in computer science. In one institution, the administration allowed more lower-division students into upper-division courses than the faculty and equipment could handle. Faculty opposed this process; it meant arbitrary or random selection of those who had earned the right to upper-division status. An easier process is simply to raise the criteria at the freshman or sophomore level. Faculty reported the reason so many were allowed to move beyond the sophomore level is that administration estimated the "excess" students would shift fields and courses (into something "easy," such as sociology, according to one informant) when they couldn't get into their own major classes. The university thereby maintained its number of students.

Long-range planning is less successful than planners might hope, but the effort is substantial. Pincus (1980) analyzes longer-term trends, noting that there were warnings in the sixties of an oversupply of engineers by the 1980s. A pattern of underfunding of undergraduate engineering education followed such warnings. Underfunding continues today. At that time, the literature called for reversing the 4:1 ratio of engineers to technicians. We are well on our way with today's ratio of less than 3:1.

The Bureau of Labor Statistics now predicts that 20 percent of college graduates, through the 1980s, will work at jobs for which their degrees are not necessary. The College Placement Council cites a cutback by one-half of jobs offered to graduate students since last year (McMillan 1983). These patterns hold for scientific and engineering graduates as well.

To bolster the information on degrees awarded, we turn to observation and interviews with industry and educational leaders. Interviews with leaders in industry and engineering/technical educators support the inferences drawn from data on degrees awarded. Touring a sophisticated research and development division of a large aerospace firm, I asked if technicians were replacing engineers. "Engineers? Technicians?" the manager asked. "Do you see any engineers out there?" I saw men sitting in front of terminals. Waving around the room, my guide explained: "We've automated them all, here. All we need are mathematicians at the top, and data entry people at the bottom."

A graduate adviser for a large university computer science department reports that demand is down from five offers per graduate in 1982 to one offer per graduate in 1983. In another large university, the head of the placement office in the school of engineering reports that many entry-level positions for the B.S. are flooded, and discusses some sources of the problem: "Five years ago, we said computers are it" (and encouraged four-year degrees in computer science). "Now, generally that's not the case." National data, as well, indicate a glut of four-year degreed programmers (Treadwell and Redburn 1983). He feels that industry does not plan ahead sufficiently; it tends to react to technological change after the fact. When planning does take place, information on related labor force projections is considered "proprietary information." "We're in a capitalist system trying to understand a world system which can compete with us."

Educators' outcry for funding yields little for undergraduate education. Resources go to the graduate level, training ground for the "super-engineer" of the future. Even NSF has "gotten out of providing undergraduate education" needs for the mass of engineering students at that level (McDermott 1982). BET graduates may ride the crest of a wave of enthusiasm—a four-year trained "near" engineer, with more practical experience and lower expectations for salary and the like than the B.S. But in the late seventies, their jobs, tasks, and salaries approached those of engineers, and their programs fell under the organization of the engineering professional societies. Their faculty now report they feel unfairly treated, compared to engineering faculty, their labs are not as well equipped as before, and less weight seems given to the "hands-on" experience than five years ago (O'Hair 1984).

According to administrators of BET programs, the four-year BET's success over the four-year B.S. engineering graduate can be attributed in part to computer-aided design and manufacturing (CAD/CAM, or CADAM). While computer-aided manufacturing has replaced assembly line workers, computer-aided design affects the need for engineers. Young men, primarily from the lower middle class, can obtain their BET degrees and work as engineers. "With CADAM," a BET administrator (1983 personal communication) told me, "technicians can do a lot of the work of engineers." A head of a community college technical program suggested further that in five years, there would be little difference between the tasks performed by the two-year technician, the BET, and many four-year degreed engineers. Corporations take this a step further yet; they find their employees can be upgraded from production to CADAM technicians without even the two-year degree (director, community colleges/industry high-tech program, 1983). This same director also provided figures for sex and race enrollment comparisons between the traditional community college technical program (90 percent male, 76 percent white) and the new short-term courses provided with the help of industry (up to 80 percent female and 65 percent minority). Thus, new economic development programs can hasten the transformation of some technical work from white males to women and minorities. The opportunities for women and minorities are vastly better than those on the line, or in clerical work. But, as with the telecommunications industry (Chapter 1), the stage may be set for some serious difficulties of racial tension and exacerbated tensions between men and women.

Pincus (1980) cited 1960s educators and studies warning of the crises that can occur given unemployment among college graduates, and the proposed solution—to view the two-year degree as the safety valve for radicalism in the 1970s. The problem for the 1990s may be an oversupply of the two-year graduates as well, including those with technical degrees. The head of another community college technical program said—in 1983—that two-year programmers and computer technicians have already "peaked out." He said the two-year program was not necessary for much of today's technical work. When asked why students continue to enroll, he leaned forward and replied confidentially, "Because we're not telling them." (We found that such cynicism was quite exceptional, rather than the rule.) Otherwise, people seemed to believe that their particular program was riding the crest of the future, whether B.S. in engineering, BET in technology, community college technicians' program in short term, or high-tech programs to upgrade production workers to the status of CADAM technician.

There are political issues of great significance involved in this process of vertical differentiation within and beneath the profession of engineering. For example, Harris and Grede (1977) list "union membership" as one of the likely characteristics of the industrial technician, while the engineering technician and engineering technologist, as paraprofessionals, will instead choose membership in their respective professional societies. The intermediary technologist degree may soften the distance between engineering and technicians, strengthening the likelihood of professional identification on the part of all.

The loyalties and political power of the new middle- and lower-level management personnel entering the technical work force, however, may not conform to expectations. If the proletarianization of engineering proceeds, we may expect more degreed engineers as well as technical support workers to join collective bargaining. Only half of the 55,000 member Engineers' and Scientists' Guild members are degreed; this organization and others resist further fractionation of engineering and technical work, as in the recent attempt (Los Angeles, aerospace) to fractionate the position of CADAM technician itself. Organized (Seattle and California) engineers and technicians in aerospace have been most active, especially since the late 1970s, and engineers in the significant telecommunications industry today show increased propensity for unionizing, as at Western Electric.

COMPARABLE WORTH

Technicians, their educators, and often their employers object that technicians' skills are equally as valuable as those of the engineers. For example, educators in two-year and some BET programs report that many of their students are former engineering students. Some left engineering because of the difficulty of mathematical tests, but many others searched for the visual, hands-on "tinkering" work they prefer to management or paperwork. Some employers value this combination of mind/hand skills in addition to the more sophisticated abstract skills of theory and math. Some engineers also echo these sentiments. In a recent discussion with Portland engineers in industry, they spoke of the intrinsic value of hands-on work; they expressed some resentment that technologists were getting to do the "fun" work, while engineers were increasingly shifted to management and paperwork. They did not consider their higher pay worth the loss of interesting things to do. Strong unionizing efforts among technicians and technologists may, further, protect the dollar measure of worth (leading one industry representative—in 1980—to state that if this continues, it may no longer be cost-effective to hire a technician rather than an engineer).

This leads us to the question of legitimate criteria for the division between engineers and their technical support occupations. Volume

1 of the ECPD's *44th Annual Report* (1976) shows that organization's increasing concern with curricula, especially the depth of coverage of concepts of calculus. A three-year report reaffirmed the need for calculus for the technician and the technologist, but suggested that "approved alternatives" be allowed as a calculus substitute for the associate-degree technician. Differentiation between the engineer and the technologist by educational criteria is more difficult. Some insight into the difficulty is outlined in a report from a local dean of engineering concerning the State Board of Engineering Examiner's review of engineering education. At issue is the fact that some graduates of technology programs have been able to pass the engineering examination and claim status, therefore, as "engineers." This dean points out that a local four-year program for the BET does include a three-course calculus sequence in its curriculum, but that the last course in this sequence approaches the level of difficulty only of the first course required in the engineering calculus sequence. This is particularly ironic, as elite institutions move to replace the study of calculus with that of discrete mathematics (Chapter 6). One professional response (referred to as the Oregon Solution), is legislation that prohibits BETs from access to the professional engineering examination. At the same time, recent interviews with engineering faculty reveal that the use of calculus is often seen as being for its "ability to develop a proper frame of mind," or to "show that you can do it," rather than its necessity for job performance. Some go so far as to suggest that calculus and more abstract forms of higher mathematics may interfere with a sense of "what is happening, physically"; "it separates you from the physical reality" in certain fields of engineering. For civil engineering, for example, one suggested that geometry and other forms of mathematics of this level more than suffice; they enhance awareness of the problem to be solved. And finally, Eugene Ferguson (1977), long an advocate of restoring visual skills (for example, graphics) to a central place in engineering education, warns of the consequences for engineering products and systems.

Thus, another nonmarketplace factor affecting labor process is technological ideology, an ideology that long predates capitalism (Aronowitz 1978). This ideology helps reshape the field of engineering and technical work, especially through what some would see as the misuse of mathematics. Students or workers have yet to launch a serious challenge to these practices. While sophisticated, science-based industry indeed required more mathematical sophistication, awareness grows that math tests may be a poor way to measure such an ability. These tests often provide an easy and "universalistic" way to demarcate the technician and technologist clearly from the engineer, to prevent what some see as industry's sometimes inappropriate use of lesser trained and less expensive workers, and to make selections from ever contracting numbers of places in schools and colleges of engineering, as discussed in Chapter 6. Stronger emphasis on math *tests* as a criteria for good engineering also serves, inadvertently, as a filter restricting women and minorities access to upper levels of the field. (Note that this process parallels Kanter's 1970 suggestion that some characteristics of managers—such as a masculine aggressive style—were often elevated to criteria of good management, regardless of their relationship to performance.)

From these reports, the labor process of engineering is changing so that most any worker can perform many engineering functions. At the same time, math test scores—although there is no correlation between these and performance as an engineer (Chapter 6)—are increasingly used to divide jobs and training into more and more levels. This "limitless division of work with the abolition of division among workers" (O'Connor 1980) is part of the ideological control system in modern industry. Student and worker challenge—for example, job validation of such criteria—is one form of resistance to ideological control.

SUMMARY

Microprocessor-based systems such as CADAM transform industrial processes today as did mass production and science-based industries earlier. We have focused on related changes in one profession, and conclude that engineering faces proletarianization or degradation, following the analytic framework of Harry Braverman (1974). The thrust of this chapter, however, has been to explore some avenues of existing or potential resistance to changes in the labor process of engineering and related technical work.

The overall picture is one of declining employment opportunities for the B.S. graduate in engineering—a situation perhaps grasped last by the engineering student him- or herself, or by that individual's parents. We venture some predictions of our own. Engineering/technical employment will increase steadily only for a few at the top—for applied mathematicians, systems analysts, and engineers with graduate training. Degrees raise aspirations, especially for salary. Given industry's desire for lower labor costs, employment and places in degree-granting programs will decline first for four-year engineers. In the short run, the BET will flourish, as does the technician now. Later, two-year degreed engineering technicians and then four-year BETs may also face declining opportunities. They are likely to be replaced by upgraded production workers or data-entry workers.

These new opportunities are indeed bright, especially for the minority, female, or working-class male who might never be able to purchase an engineering education. These opportunities are not to be disparaged, in the least. (Such low-level technical work, however, is perceived as less of an opportunity for displaced craft workers, or more highly paid production workers from unionized industries. High-tech retraining programs for these displaced workers do not have a reputation for great success.) The task for sociologists, as Joan Acker (1980) says, is to keep our eye not only on how individuals get into certain slots in the stratification system, but to understand what factors shape its contours, as well.

Corporations and government will help modernize some lab equipment on two- and four-year campuses, but most gains will come at the graduate level. Corporations, in conjunction with community colleges, will further socialize labor costs through high-tech short courses that do not lead to a degree, nor will they include general or liberal education. The courses will, to some extent, substitute business, industry, and military personnel for campus faculty. Campuses will also be encouraged to purchase computer-aided educational equipment, resulting in yet higher student/faculty ratios. Needless to say, faculty already object.

The short-term high-tech courses will increase participation of women and minorities in technical occupations. Affirmative action ideology and effort will aid entry of women and minorities at B.S. and lower levels of the technical work force, as work at these levels is routinized. Thus, again, as proletarianization proceeds, the social and technical divisions of labor interact.

Campus educators, wittingly or not, join industry and the professions in the production of ideology—a belief in job security and high pay through a technical or engineering degree. Unfortunately, students, counseled through educators' cynicism, ignorance, or merely confusion in the context of the rapid rate of change, may be the last to learn the reality of their long-term employment possibilities—perceiving security, if not a rosy dawn of increased opportunity. As the reality falls into place, one might expect many alienated responses, such as hostility based on race and sex of worker.

This is the way the story usually goes. In this chapter, we have presented our understanding of changing labor processes in engineering, using Braverman's powerful analytic framework. We have modified the emphasis, however, to allow for the impact of resistance and reaction. We call attention to the interaction of professional societies in engineering, with the state, for example, through licensing and accrediting procedures, to maintain the boundaries of the profession. This effort is aided by our general adherence to a technological ideology, and the prestige associated with skills of mathematical test taking. Strains between capital and the state, then, can slow the replacement of existing engineers by technicians or technologists. Engineers' concern for job security (but also for quality of work life and for product) may stem rationalization or fracturing of tasks. New forms of cooperative, collective behavior among engineers and technicians may present stronger barriers to proletarianization. Civil rights movements have the potential to weaken links between social divisions of labor (based on sex or race) and emerging technical divisions of labor, for example, through traditional affirmative action, *if* joined with issues of equal pay for work of comparable worth.

Students' and workers' early awareness of these trends and possibilities can enhance any of these current modes of resistance to the changes summarized above. And certainly our first criterion for a democratically organized society is an informed citizenry. We perceive a major problem, not one of a conspiracy of silence or distortion, however, but of confusion among groups unfamiliar with the social context of technological change. A comprehensive and cooperative approach would certainly make the task easier, but that does not reflect the current conditions among and between institutions and actors described herein. One thing does seem clear, and that is that no one has a sure grasp of the outcome. Here, various respondents presented views in some contradiction to those of others, depending in part on their locations in competing institutions and groups. The strength of each group or institution will affect the shape of things to come.

Part IV

Sexuality and Technology: Feminist/Left Debates

SALLY: So I went off to L.A., in part because I missed a city. There is less color . . . variety here, and there's a conservatism that is chilling to the soul. And in L.A., I was working with groups of people who were concerned with "issues." [laughter] You know these issues. But I wanted to find out what was going on—I listened to some of the old radicals from the sixties who would give talks at the community college; I would go and see how they were talking to people these days. It was much more moderated. There was much more common sense; it was more practical. About "you" and "your jobs" and "your home"—linking those to broader issues. So I was learning. As I told you, I really didn't get the kind of job that would let me see differences between engineers and technicians. So mostly what I learned was the ethnography of being a secretary in an engineering firm. But then this one night, there was this bulletin that says "Feminist Debate" between Susan Griffin and . . . I think it was Carol Vance, I'm not sure . . . on pornography. I thought, "I haven't seen Susan Griffin in a long time." So I went to this debate and then I happened to think, "*Debate?—feminist* debate? That means there has to be two positions." You know, they must've worded it wrong. So I got up there and whoever it was was doing the propornography side, looked just physically gross and kind of snarly and had on pink tights and a short skirt. [laughter] And Susan Griffin was looking healthy and decent, as always. I couldn't get my mind around this debate. I couldn't understand why . . . but then through the course of the afternoon, the arguments in favor of sadomasochism as a way of exploring your sexuality between women emerged (sex with children didn't emerge at that one). They would use a Marxist language of women workers in the sex industry. I thought, "Well, Jesus!"

I have always been disturbed between the split between feminism and the Left, which I think is one of the most dangerous. So I would hang out with different groups—one called "Leather and Lace" was a kind of umbrella group for different groups of women in the L.A. area. People would talk about their feelings on sadomasochism—in fairly rough terms—these are not academic people—"Boy, is this great" and I would say, "Where did you get started?" "I don't know but let's keep it going." And, "All this soft erotic stuff doesn't do a thing for my clit." You know a very rough approach. "Who are you to define my sexuality?" There was a black woman who was the head of Black Women for Wages for Housework, U.S.A. (I think this group is based in London). She was talking about prostitution. People were asking her, "How do you feel when you get home at night? Does it do something to your relationships?" trying to find some moral claim *against* prostitution. And she would say, "I feel tired, how do you feel?" Then someone said, "Yes, but you're selling . . . " And she said, "We all *sell*." She said, "What part of your body do you sell? Do you sell your hands?" "Do you sell your minds?" she says. [laughter] The rest of us are sitting there realizing that we're selling some part. Knowing that there is *something* wrong with this argument, but not being able to get a handle on it. Inevitably somebody will say, "What about the children? What about kiddie porn?" And she

would say, "Those kids are the vanguard movement." Oh . . . and she
would say, "They are escaping battering homes," and "It's far past the
time we should suppress adolescent sexuality anyway."

DOROTHY: Strong stuff!

SALLY: So you can kind of see that they are talking *past* each other, the
one group thinking about the 2-year-olds and the other group thinking
about teenagers relating to teenagers. So I was trying to figure out just
from looking around at the folks who are one side or the other of the
pornography controversy, and the people I knew who are antiporn,
who look a little puritanical and who tended to have backgrounds like
my own, working-class backgrounds with this kind of "decency" that
Reagan can play off so easily—you know people getting status or money
but you are a decent person—especially for women.

And then my other friends on the Left are a little more blasé,
sophisticated. Again there's that tension between the Left and feminism
not only on this issue but from times past. The Left will end up calling
the women's movement "middle class." Where the backgrounds are just
the opposite.

Probably I would not have thought about it if I had not gone to L.A.
I was encountering the same debates afterwards when I got back here.
We started having potlucks to discuss this. I was telling people this thing
was going on and they said, "Where have you been?" It turned out
that four or five of the women I knew fairly well were experimenting
with dominance and submission. Then came the more sophisticated
arguments as in Ann Snitow's collection, *Powers of Desire* [Snitow et al.
1983]. There are some fairly sophisticated justifications there. But I still
think that it's the playground of the better-off. I asked one of the women
in our group among the people who were experimenting with bondage;
I said, "How did you feel?" She said, "I felt like a turkey." [laughter]
Then we'd get down to basics and we would all say, "Well, we can all
at least agree about children." But then somebody would say, "Well,
when I was 10 and my uncle Joe did thus and so, I didn't experience it as
exploitation." So we would just go round and round and round. It wasn't
ever settled. We all had very different views and experiences. We were in
different locations, almost across the whole spectrum of class, but having
thought lots and talking it out. This was one way of maintaining lines of
communication between the Left which is more or less middle-class and
professional and the working-class woman who is, more or less, against
all that stuff. Again it seemed to me that most of the women who were
more concerned with decency were women who now have professional
jobs—middle-class jobs—but come from a working-class background.
So we've got that decency attitude towards sexuality which makes
us vulnerable to manipulation in all kinds of ways. On the other
hand, the folks who had the more liberal approach—propornography
or anticensorship, or whatever, even those who become part of the
proletariat—had middle- or upper-middle-class backgrounds.

So I tested it out in my "Intro" class. This was not the kind of
scientific research we were talking about before—there were violations all

over the place. I started by explaining both positions, trying to give what I saw as good points of view on either side. Then I'd ask the students what their folks did for a living when they were growing up—when they were 16 or 17. But "class" did not have nearly the effect that "sex" did. The propornography, the more liberal stance, among the students was almost an exclusively male position. Within men and women, however, "class" did make a difference. A working-class guy is not nearly as likely as the middle-class guy to favor the more liberal position. Not one working-class woman suggested that it was a good idea that there should be more liberalization or that prostitution or pornography were legitimate jobs just like any other. *No* working-class woman made those choices and very few of the middle-class women. But among those who did make those choices, *all* the women were middle-class. I had asked them also, "Well, if it's a legitimate job, how about your kids? Would it be okay? What would you think if they went into the trade?" The middle-class kids tended to say, "Well, I wouldn't like it, I mean that's for other people's children." [laughter] The working-class kids were much more concerned. They would be angry; they'd feel betrayed; they would reject the kids; they would do one thing or another, but it was universally bad.

DOROTHY: So your thinking on pornography and technology came partly out of these debates and your experience of this division?

SALLY: You need somehow to do these things at the same time. I was trying to talk about the erotic component of technology and at the same time trying to figure what's going on with this new split in the women's movement and then realizing some pretty strong connections between the two. I wanted to get it on paper, somehow, so people might explore some class-based differences. The "two" being technology and eroticism. Because the other stuff I had done . . . you can talk about technology and the organizational work and deskilling and reserve labor armies and you know something is being left out. Then you can do the other sort of thing, like I did at MIT, and try to figure out how they put together the ideology that justifies what they do and their privileges. How do they get the desire to do what they do in a workplace like AT&T? What would make even it aesthetically appealing?

The radical women's movement turned me off because they look like such a dead end. That's a "victim" position. You look at these patriarchical, military institutions—"Look how evil they are; look what they've done to the men"—all of which is true. Then, "Look what the men do to the women." That way of looking at technology and sexuality leaves something out; it leaves out the other way that you want to talk about things, which is "Ohh . . . this is great!" The kind of exhilaration that largely white middle-class males are allowed and encouraged to enjoy in a distorted way. We don't get to do that. When men are describing technology there is an erotic component there. I think women do the same for the kinds of technology that are supposed to be ours—weaving, child care, or whatever. I wanted to make that explicit and prevent the folks who are into hierarchical arrangements from capturing that word!

DOROTHY: I'm wondering about your use of the term *erotic* here and whether *sensual* wouldn't be closer. In your chapter "The Eye of the Beholder" [Chapter 9] you cite Mumford and Stanley and your quote from [Stanley] talks about gardens. So I remember back to your account of your childhood garden at the beginning of the book on Mondragon [Hacker 1989], and I'm reminded that in Sally's childhood garden there was this wonderful technology.

SALLY: Yeeeaah.

DOROTHY: You know, a delight and joy and somehow these two go together.

SALLY: Yes, that's true. And the essential freedom . . . in one sense there was always an eye to make sure none of the funny business was going on. I don't mean that there was that degree of freedom. It was a typical southern, lower-middle-class, working-class town. But to run and play and move and climb and fly and, God! This book I was reviewing on the science and technology programs in England is concerned about young girls about 11 years old getting into both craft and science—both levels. In the last chapter, they were summing up and I read that the most effective programs had to have, or could have, the following components: girls only was one of them—because the boys will take over—but that there must be some physical and graphic interaction and representation, particularly for women. I was thinking that was true for blacks, for working-class. It's true *because* of the way in which we've used abstractions to weed people out. But I think that just that sheer delight—physics and astronomy were my first loves in school beyond third grade. I was fascinated. Then I got into Freud because I found what people did to each other most peculiar and fascinating. So I decided I would be a psychiatrist because you could be both scientific and . . .

DOROTHY: Yeah. So you thought? [laughter]

SALLY: So I thought. Yeah, right. But I think that Jacoby, also in her longitudinal study of girls, claims this tomboy-like existence very good for developing what comes out on I.Q. tests—whatever that means—that test-taking ability which will carry you pretty far in school. In pleasure and in deviance—the backyard was just a place where we would lay on our backs and look at the stars and tell stories. Almost all male, in my age group. Almost all female in my sister's.

DOROTHY: So would *sensual* be better when you're talking about this? Because it's like a total sensual experience. You can see how the technology you describe in your backyard enhanced this joy—this passion. Then you can see how those guys sitting on top of this great machine of subjugation or machinery of dominance—what an incredible experience of power that is!

SALLY: I think I want to hang on to *erotic*. If we managed to live in such a way that our lives were more pervaded with sensual experience, that would be great. We need to do that. That to me sounds like revolutionary behavior, the kind of behavior you engage in, in revolutionary periods—parties and building and stuff like that. But *erotic*—sexuality, orgasms, connection with, fusion with another person, that intensely new creation that happens between two people—to me that is different from sensual experience.

DOROTHY: So you see this intense creation, this fusion, getting built into the engineers' relationship to the technological process?

SALLY: To machines, I think. And to projects, to physical projects.

DOROTHY: So that rather than fusion with another person the engineer experiences fusion . . .

SALLY: Yeah, yeah.

DOROTHY: With a machine process through which others are subjugated rather than . . .

SALLY: Yes, yes. And reading things like Tracy Kidder's *The Soul of a New Machine* [1981], you can feel that intensity. I think it's either erotic or a similar kind of energy. But there's always "control." You've got control over the machine. Or you want it and you know you can have it if you are just smart enough—good enough. I think that takes the place, replaces, substitutes for this other kind of thing that would be reciprocal between two people. When I was in Spain we visited various technological sites, as you might have imagined—history and sociology, technology. One had these Franco-like, Fascist statues that go on for miles. The projects themselves are staggering in their size. You sit and look at them and you know what these guys are talking about—those quotes from Florman where they get all excited and passionate. How are you going to express passion and feeling—through religion? And they do that. Glory and God and Rome! But there is also that erotic component that I think they get because the tracks are there, the dominance/submission, the power/the powerless, the feeling of being in control over these huge, huge projects.

DOROTHY: Heavy.

SALLY: Very heavy stuff. Not real playful. But that's how many of us are with eroticism, not very playful. It does get constructed with a very heavy element of dominance/submission.

Maybe this is the project: starting from having so much fun in the backyard, thinking that was what technology was and discovering that somebody had done something rather rotten to this whole enterprise. Realizing that, somewhere, that fun, enjoyment, sensual experience that should be part of every job—could be part of every job—wasn't that way. That's background to this. Then working for equal opportunity for women in the women's movement and finding simultaneously that the women were complaining about being treated in very humiliating ways because of their gender; also that the shape of the technology had a lot to do with why women were treated as they were treated; that the shape of technology shaped their daily life. *And* if the technology was to change, they were expendable. And all of that—the horrible stuff that you can do to this human project that could be very lovely.

Now who would do a thing like that? Why? What is the percentage in it? They'd have to give up so much, for so little. Those were the

questions which led to the MIT and historical research and the problems
of discipline and how the eroticism of men gets shaped around those
dominance and submission modes we were talking about. [sigh]

    I would like to call all of that "work." You know that one definition
by Marx that makes so much sense, that work could be an act of human
freedom and expression of human creativity. Because work then sounds
like play and it sounds like having block parties and it sounds like people
getting together and enjoying—doesn't matter if they're building a house
or damming a river, maybe. And technology is the way we organize
energy and materials to get work done. I don't have a feeling that people
ought to "hands off" nature. But it's the "gentle touch" that would be
more pleasurable, I think, for both.

DOROTHY: I hadn't really thought of technology in that way before. I
suppose technology has come to have a thoroughly bad name.

SALLY: Yeah, yeah.

DOROTHY: So to see technology as it could be, as embedded in really
human relations is kind of surprising. And as enhancing people's
capacities to . . .

SALLY: To be playful!

DOROTHY: To be playful.

SALLY: Yeah. Like firecrackers as opposed to gunpowder. And certainly,
the guys see it. I'm reading this interesting little book—I haven't finished
it yet and I don't know the political framework. It's written by this guy
who's a big honcho contractor and a spokesman for engineers and
how they are going to lead us out of our existential morass. But
in the early part of the book, he describes how much we know
innately about engineering "innately" through kinesthetic experience
with your environment, your experience of lifting, turning, picking
up a child, walking down the street, opening a door—like levers, and
cranes and pulleys and forces and also the forces on bodies and he
does it in a playful way. He is looking at engineering failure, bridges
falling down and walkways collapsing and what that teaches us. His
approach, at least in the early parts of the book, bridges in a way
that gap between one's body and the physical world that is usually
exacerbated by engineering.

DOROTHY: So there's been a whole perversion of work in which people
have been subjugated to the disciplines of technology and they've been
separated from it. Rather than adding to pleasures and capacities.

SALLY: Yes. And so the contradictions—and the tensions in my own
thinking. The notion of technology—you can define it so broadly as to
describe any organization of material and energy to accomplish work as
a piece of technology.

    So when you define it that way you can see how it could be
experienced differently. But generally what is commonly understood
as "technology," technology as we know it, does leave most people
cold. To a woman friend, for example, I said, "Okay, you want to
move to management? Take yourself some computer courses; take a
course in engineering—you know you can pass it. Go to the community

college, take a craft course of some kind." But "Ba, ba" just in distaste, disinterest. You can see this contradiction though—some of the women I talk to liked electrical engineering a lot—they liked math. But the ones that didn't, said, "Well, you can't see or feel electrons moving around." It was the absence of that essential stimulus in one area or another that bothered them. You can't hear it, you can't see it, you can't smell it. There are those different approaches. The women in Denmark who describe different approaches of young boys and girls to learning—girls are much more likely to do it cooperatively—"Hey, try this!" "What do you think of this?" "Shall I do this?" And the boys just driving in. So there are different kinds of pleasure. And they don't have to be "gendered." There are certainly times when we [women] might want to do that singly, "Leave me alone, I want to do it myself"—that kind of pleasure.

Things may be shifting such that we can do a better balance, or have a wider variety of erotic kinds of choices. That's going to take "degendering." I think most everything hinges on degendering. And getting rid of social hierarchy—which amounts to the same thing, from my point of view, where I'm coming from. You and I would not enjoy erotic relations with someone who is not directly equal in power. We wouldn't want relations with a big daddy or someone who is dependent on you. Both would be very troublesome and perhaps, if not impossible—unless you felt wildly in love—at least very unlikely. It just wouldn't be appealing. So what eroticism would look like without dominance and submission may be the essential question. Life would sure as hell be a lot more sensual than it is now. You know, Stanley and Mumford in the backyard[1] and so on! Maybe this is the "space" that we are negotiating now.

NOTES

1. See references to Stanley and Mumford in Chapter 9.

Chapter 9

The Eye of the Beholder:
An Essay on Technology and Eroticism

*E*roticism excites the mind and body; so can technology. Technology and eroticism arise from similar wellsprings of pleasure learned in cultural context. As Foucault (1978, 1979) suggests for the discourse on sexuality, that on technology is also about power and alliances (1979). Inequality takes many forms: here I am concerned with that based on gender. Current social patterns favor men's dominance over women; the social constructions of both technology and eroticism reflect that underlying structure.

The larger framework for this essay is as follows:[1] I suggest that technology and eroticism were once fused, as with reason and passion (Valverde 1987), and referred to the same set of activities. These activities began to be differentiated, gendered—technology masculine, eroticism feminine—and hierarchically ordered with the emergence some 5,000 years ago of patriarchal societies, whose core institutions are military institutions. Not the only institutions to shape both eroticism and technology, they have, however, a significant and largely overlooked influence on these activities; hence the emphasis upon them here. Military institutions arose and survive on gender subordination and the accompanying distortion of technology and eroticism. Military institutions perhaps more than most, even more so than religious institutions, must control erotic and technological activities to accomplish their ends. With many variations over time and place, military institutions lock both gender and technology, including eroticism and labor process, on an authoritarian dimension. Within them, we find women's structured subordination; specialization and hierarchy in the organization of work; the separation of mind from hand in the labor process and the detailed division of labor; forms of discipline that mold the passions of men (Hacker and Hacker 1987).

Mumford (1966, 1967) and Stanley (1981, 1983) describe the life-centered biotechnics of the Neolithic age, wherein technology and eroticism were one set of activities, not yet differentiated and gendered. The garden, for example, was a sensual feast of food, perfume,

205

color, texture, and spiciness; the domestication of plants and animals

> owes much to an intense subjective concentration on sexuality in all its manifestations. . . . Plant selection, hybridization, fertilization, manuring, seeding, castration were the products of an imaginative cultivation of sexuality, whose first evidence one finds tens of thousands of years earlier. . . . The Neolithic garden, like gardens in many simpler cultures today, was probably a mixture of flood plants, dye plants, medicinals and ornamentals—all treated as equally essential for life. (Mumford 1967, 81)

Mumford's and Stanley's thesis is that social technologies, symbols shared in play, song, and dance, were likely as important to the life of the Neolithic community as any machine or tool technology. Both Mumford and Stanley describe the Neolithic as an "age of woman," suggesting egalitarian relationships rather than an earlier matriarchy. They contrast technologies of this period with what Mumford calls "megatechnics," the shape of technology in a hierarchically organized, patriarchal society. Mumford describes the first great tasks accomplished by patriarchal societies. Not surprisingly, these were the building of tombs, pyramids; the first great machines to accomplish these tasks were composed of human parts organized in a hierarchical and finely differentiated division of labor.

Mumford implies, but feminist scholars explicate, the active agency of women in the Neolithic period. Stanley seeks to understand and explain what she refers to as the "takeover"—how changing conditions, both social and physical, and particularly those surrounding increased childbirth and technological change, transformed societies unmarked by gendered domination and submission to patriarchal forms.

This chapter has a related but far more limited goal, however, than tracing the historical and materialist origins of patriarchy. It explores relationships between technology and eroticism/pornography today, by comparing the usually discrete discourses on these two issues, primarily in the United States, Canada, and England. The two sets of activities appear to be highly gender segregated. Technical skills and knowledge are viewed as a masculine sphere. As Mariana Valverde's (1987) sensitive analysis of today's "sexual liberation" shows, the burden of sexual performance still rests with women because sex (and relationships) continue to be regarded as women's specialty. I begin by arguing my point that in spite of this appearance, the two sets of activities, technical and erotic, are in fact closely intertwined. I then compare the passionate aspects of technology and the rational aspects of eroticism in order to explore the common ground of contemporary practices of both machine and social technics. I will then proceed by examining similarities and contradictions in concepts and strategies for social action toward degendering those practices of technology and eroticism, and suggest how these strategies may vary by social class.

TECHNOLOGY AND EROTICISM

The Erotic in Technology

Let us consider the field of engineering, foregrounding the passionate context of this occupation. This field, the apparent epitome of cool rationality, is shot through with desire and excitement. Much of this excitement stirs the mind. It is as though an intricately shaped erotic expression finds its most creative outlet today in the design of technology. The contemporary images of eroticism and of machines and systems reflect the imagination of the designer. How could it be otherwise in any human venture?

As with any human and social activity, some care a lot and some don't give a damn. Technical skills and activities and erotic skills and activities leave some cold, but fire the imagination of many. The latter, rightly or wrongly, view the disinterested as alienated, pathological, or deficient in some way. The disinterested may view the aficionado as obsessed, either with sexuality or with technology (like Weizenbaum's programmer in *Computer Power and Human Reason* [1976]). When some men describe their feelings about technology, they often talk about God, glory, honor, and other noble sentiments. These are acceptable channels through which men can express transcendent desire. There is also, however, a lot of sexy, gendered talk about technology. This talk is heterosexual and male dominant. Gender discourse is yet another approved mode of expression for passionate feelings. The phallic and reproductive imagery of weapons systems has escaped no one (see Chapter 4 and Hacker 1982; Easlea 1983; Cohn 1987; Edwards, forthcoming), including cartoonists in most any progressive publication. But that is hardly all there is. Both these modes of expression signal "off limits" to most women, and to many men and women with their own, different form of passion for science, technology, and eroticism. Relations of dominance and submission are also eroticized in gender-stratified societies (Valverde 1987), and shape the design of technological products and systems. Many note the grim connections between these phenomena under Fascism as men suppress the feared and envied feminine within themselves (Millett 1970; Griffin 1981; Theweleit 1987).

Samuel Florman (1976), the oft-cited apologist for technology as it is currently organized, a wealthy contractor, conveys his excitement with technology, the passionate relations between men and machine.

Engineers, he says, have yet to express their own powerful feelings about technology. He gives examples, quoting from literature, the Bible, and so on, describing structures and fabrics and machines and tools with sensual delight:

> From Frank's "Panama Canal slashing its way through the tropical jungle: its gray sobriety is apart from the luxuriance of nature. Its willfulness is victor over a voluptuary world that will lift no vessels, that would bar all vessels;" from Kipling, on how the "Feed pump sobs and heaves;" Spender's airliner, "more beautiful and soft than any moth, with burring furred antennae . . . gently, broadly she falls;" McKenna's description of engineer meeting engine. " 'Hello engine. I'm Jake Holman' he said under his breath. Jake Holman loved machinery in the way some other men love God, women and their country;" Longfellow's ship which "Feels the thrill of life along her keel" as she "leaps into the Ocean's arms!" Platonov's engineer who enters "into the very essence of the abstruse, inanimate mechanisms . . . actually feeling the degree of intensity of an electrical current as if it were a secret passion of his own;" the pilot who "Passed his fingers along a steep rib and felt the stream of life that flowed in it. . . . The engine's gentle current fraying its ice-cold rind into a velvety bloom." (pp. 133–39)

This is steamy stuff! But what about real live women? Florman cites the engineer who says, "I'm in love, Chief." He hears from his boss, "So was I once, but I shut myself up for three weeks and worked at an air machine. Grew so excited I forgot the girl. You try it" (p. 38). Florman explicitly acknowledges the safety and comfort of technology, the world of things and machines, compared with the confusion and conflict of the social world of human interaction. As above, the passion culturally ascribed to the erotic or sexual sphere often drives that of the technical. The technical is coyly eroticized, and, with it, the relations of dominance and submission, sometimes driven by violence and fear.

Some spoof this phenomenon and its trappings, as in Norman Spinrad's brilliant satire on Fascism and eroticism, the science fiction novel *The Iron Dream* (1972; compare Le Guin 1975). The novel contains no women, but is chock full of detailed descriptions of heel clicking and truncheon wielding, outrageous perceptions of the world and others, technologies as exaggerated extensions of the human form, and the peculiar intense interest in uniforms, never complete without the ubiquitous "bright shiny metal work." [2]

Valverde (1987) describes milder forms of the eroticization of domination, in which one simply desires to be overwhelmed by the erotic force and power of the other, not necessarily experiencing pain or humiliation in the process. These and other forms of eroticized power relations seem apparent in many older men/younger men scientific and technological scenarios, as in the frenzied social relations of high-tech production systems and products (Edwards 1985, 1986). Many young men in the field experience a special high in being driven to inhuman intensity and competition with their brothers by the older men of the tribe (Kidder 1981). (This of course may be characteristic of all, not merely technical disciplines.)

Inmates of various institutions—schools, prisons, monasteries, madhouses, and barracks—order themselves in proper space, time and motion, to prescribed muscle movement, posture, and attitude. These culturally approved techniques of control do the job more efficiently than any external authority. I have suggested elsewhere that these techniques, this "microphysics of power" (Foucault 1979, 139), may be easily observed today in the structure of the engineering classroom and curriculum (as I've described in Chapters 3 and 6). What I failed to note was the extent to which the techniques of constant examination and grading controlled professor more than student.

In that experience I learned how it felt, day by day, sometimes minute by minute, to encounter a subtle control, largely self-imposed, that affects both mind and body. I learned that many of the faculty were as turned off by the hidden curriculum as I, and felt it impaired the students' ability to learn to do good engineering. The overall impression was one of intense discipline—particularly over pleasures and the use of time. I also came to appreciate the special privileges, delights, and fascinations of the field and to understand the faculty I had interviewed earlier a little better. I saw how others reacted as well, friends and colleagues holding back from demands on my time now that they saw me as engaged in "important" work. Above all, I learned how engineering education is embedded in a context of rational criteria for the practice of engineering that is essential to leadership in bureaucratic organization—control of sensuality, emotions, passion, one's very physical rhythms. Dominance in such rationally ordered institutions is indeed inscribed on the body (Foucault 1979).

It is no surprise to find relations of dominance and submission an important part of the curriculum in our engineering classrooms (Snyder 1971). Bart Hacker (1987) shows the origins of engineering education in military institutions of the eighteenth century. Max Weber (1968) suggests that military institutions provide the model for discipline in all major social institutions. He notes that "military discipline gives birth to all discipline" and it has always in some way affected the structure of the state, the economy, and possibly the family. As Fatima Mernissi (1975) observes, without the control of men's eroticism, armies would be impossible.

Eighteenth- and nineteenth-century debates over the form of training of a new military and administrative leadership reveal many motives for the teaching of mathematics and science (Chapter 6). These subjects would "cool the passions," "calm the fires of youth." "Math was used to educate gentlemen, not to train mathematicians" (Enroe 1981). The way these subjects were taught was also important. Rationalized examinations in mathematics and science, by which students were to be rejected or accepted, ranked, and placed, provided a filter against all but the most disciplined, or repressed, as Davis (1980) would have it (see Chapter 6).

Noble's *America by Design* (1977) shows the predominance of military institutions in the forming of engineering education, and the men in it, at the turn of this century. Public and vocational education soon followed. Military forms of discipline, standardization of "parts" (men), hierarchy and order pervaded university engineering and then spread to secondary education through programs such as vocational education. This process further strengthened that arid technical rationality built on suppressed emotion decried earlier by critical theorists and radical feminists.

Thus control of passion, particularly among men, shapes the organization of technology and technical education in fascinating form. It is but one note in the important theme (Kandiyoti 1984) that the first purpose of patriarchy is the control of most men by a few older men with power. And it is in our interest to continue to learn how we persuade and are persuaded to give up so much for so little. Some of us are seduced by gendered, stratified, and eroticized technologies—both machine and social technics of dominance.

The Technical in the Erotic

As men specialize in technology and its disciplines and relations of dominance, women are also specialized. As erotic passion may influence technology, so may technological exhilaration inform erotic activity. Eugene Ferguson (cited in Hounshell 1984) calls attention to the exhilaration technologists feel for their work, an intense pleasure and arousal at the core of technological development and innovation, captured most recently by Kidder (1981). Ferguson warns against too economistic an analysis of technology, and says we ignore the role of exhilaration in the organization of technology at our peril. I agree. Above, I have suggested ways in which gendered eroticism shapes its technology to fit. Here, I want to explore the masculine nature of technological exhilaration for its influence on the shape of eroticism.

Some may merely delight in the exercise of technique or skill, while remaining distant from passionate involvement in process or goals of others.[3] Homey examples of technological excitement as it influences erotic activities may be found in extensive directions for use of fashion, cosmetics, or sex toys; or in explicit suggestions for women to please their men, through techniques and technologies of clothing, scents, postures, or numerous social and physical accoutrements. Manuals for service workers in the sex industry (see Delacoste and Alexander 1987; McLeod 1982) and related service industries (Hochschild 1982) or prescriptive books for fundamentalist housewives, provide fascinating analyses of the technology of eroticism (see MacCannell and MacCannell 1987; Brownmiller 1984; Banner 1983). Comparative research would be rewarding (as well as fun) with the antierotic sex and hygiene manuals issued by the U.S. military, the first form of sex education for several generations of young men. These technologies of eroticism have been exchanged among women for centuries (Jones 1987). Erasmus in 1523 warned young men not to let their women gossip with married women, who would share these valuable skills of manipulation (Thompson 1965).

Rita Sabagh's (1983) ethnographic study of the "sex goddesses" in an L.A. mafia strip joint seems to provide a contemporary explication of the technologies of sexual power. One can tease, throw out a jerk, allow measured familiarities depending on tips, place one's cigarette near a favorite at the bar to indicate one's intent to return. However, in such a situation, the participant's attention is rarely captured by the overwhelmingly male-defined political and economic setting. One is more impressed by the moment-to-moment interpersonal power of women over the men who enter as customers.

Similarly, Valverde (1987, 40–41) describes the sexiest women in society, those who most skillfully maximize "feminine wiles," the passive power to grant and withhold. Such wily women exercise skills of timing and manipulation with such expertise that these politics of powerlessness, this passive power, "almost looks and feels like active power." Within a situation defined by others, it sometimes works.

Machine as well as social technics are seductive. In the passion to control desire, or shape it through technologies of discipline, one can become intrigued with transforming the body itself into a machine (see Chapter 4). The vulnerability of being human, especially female, in a world that increasingly prefers the flawless and mechanical (Noble 1984), is expressed in Haraway's (1985) brilliant essay on cyborgs. Perhaps the fear of punishment for freely expressing erotic capability encourages us, particularly men, to channel the energy safely toward the machine.[4]

In its most obvious and fetishistic mode, perhaps, technological exhilaration may fasten on the loving care and maintenance of S/M equipment and tools (Samois 1987). Intense concern for erotic skill and technique can be observed in conversations with managers in the sex industry (for example, the 1982 film *Not a Love Story*) or in the discourse of sex therapists (see English et al. 1982; Rubin 1984, 1987). The fascination with measurement appears in the practice of sex researchers who attach electrodes and rings to the penises of sex offenders viewing erotic material (Griffitt 1987), as if these objective data could give access to human thought and emotion.

There are, then, some striking interpenetrations of erotic and technological spheres. Examining one in light of the other can be both interesting and illuminating. We can explore in greater detail points of contact in debates over definitions and concepts, parallel theoretical concerns and related conclusions, and the strategies we adopt toward whatever it is we define as the social problems (Schneider 1985; Woolgar and Pawluch 1985a, 1985b; Pfohl 1985; Hazelrigg 1985) of technology and pornography/eroticism. The problems of one—technology or pornography—will not be alleviated in isolation from the other. The two are only apparently ideologically separated, and it is one of our most pleasurable tasks to degender and reunite technology and eroticism openly. Finally, I suggest that unexplored class differences among proponents of various arguments cloud the debates, and inhibit unified action necessary to deal effectively with antifeminist forces.

CONCEPTS AND DEFINITIONS IN THE
DEBATES ON TECHNOLOGY AND PORNOGRAPHY

For the last several years, in the United States and elsewhere, feminists have debated and discussed and struggled to define sexuality, particularly eroticism, and a particular kind of eroticism, pornography (see Valverde 1987; Smith and Waisburg 1985, for annotated bibliography; Vance 1984; also Hacker et al. 1984).

Some feminists would eliminate pornography as it is produced, or as it is consumed. This view of pornography emphasizes women's and children's relative powerlessness in patriarchal society. Women's image in sexual material affects both men and women viewers, and is an instrument of gender domination socially constructed by men to maintain women's subordination to men's desires. From this perspective, less against sex than against violence, sex can be playful, gentle, rough, hetero- or homosexual, but should exclude relations of dominance and violence. Sexuality is best expressed in relationships of egalitarian community, or long-term relationships of mutual trust and commitment. Female imagery in pornography subverts the possibility of such egalitarian relationships. Pornography rouses prurient interest, demeans women or sexuality in general, eroticizes domination, and is morally offensive (Linden et al. 1982). As Andrea Dworkin (1979, 1983) says of the definitions: in patriarchal society, pornography is women; women are pornography.

A few, sometimes called sex radicals, say all of that is true, and they like it that way. They emphasize a person's right to choose her own type of hetero- or homosexual behavior, to work in or consume the products of the sex industry as any other, as a path to liberation from older, more puritanical stereotypes. Some activists oppose censorship and boycotts, speak to women workers in the sex industry, and demand greater protection of civil liberties of sex radicals. Efforts to block the production and consumption of pornography may undermine civil rights (Burstyn 1985). Any regulation of pornography may be extended to feminist and lesbian material, and women to workers in the sex industry. Still others say it is impossible to differentiate pornography from eroticism, except in the eye of each beholder. They argue against censorship and for increasing dialogue on sexuality. Sex can be playful, gentle, or violent, can include relations of dominance and submission, and can take place in superficial, temporary relations. For some, this is the only kind that is exciting, and feminism should also liberate our right to choose our own sexuality. They argue that antipornographer feminists went "over the heads of the [sex] workers," threatening their employment and dignity at work. Sex radicals answer arguments against the exploitation and brutalization of women and children by noting that any waged work is exploitive, that children's sexuality should not be repressed, and that the sex industry often offers the only escape route from even more violent and brutalizing families (Ruben 1984, 1987; Califia 1987; Delacoste and Alexander 1987; Constantine and Martinson 1981).

To sex radicals, antipornography feminists appear puritanical, antimale, and antisex, wanting to define a sanitized feminist sexuality for all. "Vanilla sex," the "missionary position of the women's movement" (Ruben 1987), soft, gentle sex in relationships of long-term commitment to others, "doesn't do a thing for my clit," as one puts it at a meeting of Leather and Lace (Los Angeles, 1983). Another asks why women get stuck with eroticism while "men get to do the interesting things, like violence and aggression." Games of domination, sadomasochistic role playing, are experienced as exciting. These practices provide a route out of restrictive, passive, erotic roles for women. Sex radicals themselves threaten to degender eroticism, claiming for women a participation, a style, formerly appropriate for men only. And interestingly, sex radical texts display something of the technocrats' compulsion for technique, with prescriptions for the proper care and use of sadomasochistic toys and tools (Samois 1987).

Interestingly, in a debate less familiar in feminist circles, similar questions surround the definition of technology. Some think technology refers merely to machinery (as sexuality might refer to genitals), while others insist it means the entire set of social relations within which the machinery is designed, developed, and used (Staudenmaier 1985). Some argue that technology is shaped by historical and material relations, even if totally socially constructed. The machine has no meaning outside that which we give it through interaction. Similarly, feminist scholars argue that all sexuality is socially constructed; there is no absolute, really "natural" sexuality other than that which is in our minds (Stimpson and Person 1980; Rich 1980; Ferguson et al. 1981).   .

Some define technology broadly as the organization of material and energy to accomplish work; the research has recently been extended by women studies scholars to include household technology and the work of homemaking (Bose et al. 1984; Cowan 1983). It could be extended as well to work performed in the sex industry. Others say that this definition is much too broad and thus includes everything—a similar argument against defining sexuality as pleasure.

Occasionally, the legitimacy of the concepts themselves is called into question. As some suggest that the very concept of technology takes our attention off real power relations of class and productive forces (Noble 1984), so others suggest the concepts of pornography (Ehrenreich et al. 1986) and eroticism (Foucault 1979) do the same. The concepts themselves are diversions, distracting attention from the real issues: alliances, relationships of power and control. Some go so far as to say that technology studies may have been created for this purpose. Likewise, the pornography debate takes our minds off the economic and political subordination of women, and how difficult these conditions are to resist.

There is no single, parallel, negative term for a kind of technology that rouses prurient interest, demeans the powerless, eroticizes domination, or offends along a moral dimension. We could all think of technologies that fill this bill, such as the short hoe recently outlawed for migrant field workers, nuclear energy, or the fat American car; tools of torture, or weapons systems; chemical technologies for the exciting and often eroticized domination and control of nature (Hacker 1985). Many do describe such technologies as pornographic.

As with the sex radicals, there are those who agree, but like it that way. Some have described to me the beauties of napalm, difficult to understand without "being there": "You really have to see it in action to appreciate it." Or the excitement of watching weeds "grow themselves to death" in the search for chemical defoliants; the challenge to implant the embryo of a calf into the womb of a rabbit for cheaper transportation to a Third World country; or the curiosity to see whether a bioengineered calf will be too large for live birthing (see Chapter 3).

The only terms we have for technologies embodying hierarchical social relations are Lewis Mumford's (1967) "megamachine," or Langdon Winner's (1977) "autonomous technology." These seem somewhat bland terms for the technologies and social relations described above, which so specifically eroticize domination, as in tools and training designed to inflict pain on a helpless prisoner, perhaps for the erotic gratification of the captor. Bart Hacker has suggested coining another term, "pornotechnics," with which we could analyze, comparatively, "pornographics."

Similar political implications surround the definition of porno-technics as of pornographics. For example, some of us may find our favorite forms of technological excitement classified as politically incorrect—the rides we love to scare ourselves with at the carnival, the fast cars and motorcycles of our young (and not so young) adulthood, the risks we willingly share with others in outdoor adventure, the chemicals we freely consume. Finally, it is not difficult to imagine who might be morally offended at the control by the working class, or by the enlisted soldiers, of certain "command" technologies (Noble 1985).[5]

In the debate over technology, too, one side addresses power held among those who research, design, implement, and distribute new technologies. People, even the earth itself, may often be the victim of such innovations. Activists argue for the elimination of industries from and for which these destructive technologies emerge. Technology can be playful, exciting, but not violent or set in social relations of dominance; it should emerge from democratic communities, within long-term relationships of mutual trust and commitment, in relations of caring for others and the natural world (Cooley 1980). The other side argues that a free expression of technological imagination benefits all. If everyone is allowed his or her free expression to invent, to create, to consume the technology of his or her choice, the wellsprings of human creativity will be unleashed, perhaps providing a way out of much of the existential alienation of the modern world. Activists oppose attempts to curb research and development, and argue greater freedom for the free play of invention (Florman 1981; Rybczynski 1983).

The parallels in these debates over strategy raise interesting questions for us, which return us to the issues of community and power. Do those in the environmental movement, for example, argue for a "vanilla technology"? Do they want a sanitized technology, cleansed of the excitement of danger and risk? Are they really antitechnology, modern Luddites, as their opponents claim, similar to the antisex, puritanical members of the antiporn feminists? Do they want to lead us back to the closed societies of the past, characterized by stagnation and informal moral and social control?

On the other hand, are those who argue for laissez-faire technology or eroticism really blind to the relations of power within which both are designed, developed, and distributed? Do they really believe that entry to the field is democratic and open to all? Will more women in engineering change the organization of technology? Will more women playing masculine games of eroticized dominance change the organization of eroticism? Are most of these arguments actually self-serving (to those who make their living through the Department of Defense, or the sex industry, or are dependent on others who do)?

CLASS CONTRADICTIONS IN THE DEBATES ON TECHNOLOGY AND EROTICISM

In the case of both technology and pornography, some of the debate, then, turns around the definitions: What is it? Who gets to define it? And, perhaps most important, who gets to define what as a social problem? But problems of class as well as gender are relevant.

Those who rule truly fear a working class in control of its own technology, or its own eroticism. The voluminous literature on the labor process documents the former. And here is a military example. Susan Douglas (1985) analyzes the U.S. Navy's adoption of radio communication, an adoption not welcomed by the previously independent heads of bureaus, and captains of ships, who were now in communication with central control while out to sea, coerced, coordinated, cajoled by the powers that be, helped by the disaster of the *Titanic*, to adopt this new technology. Among points of contention was whether or not enlisted men were to be trained as operators and allowed free, unmonitored use of the equipment. The strategy for adoption would be more successful if officers could be involved. The winning argument for officers came with the observation that unenlisted men used the equipment for irreverent comments about their work and supervisors, and to chat up their girlfriends back in port.

Studies of early twentieth-century working-class leisure (Peiss 1983) and sexuality (Bullough 1987; Money 1985) show excessive concern over urban youth pleasure in general, and masturbation in particular. Thus, the docile worker or woman is good; that worker or woman is dangerous who messes with his or her own equipment, one way or the other. Such fears led not only to the various youth club movements in the twenties, to control the troublesome energy of the immigrant youth (Pivar 1972; DuBois and Gordon 1984; Woloch 1984), but to such bizarre inventions as J. H. Kellogg's (as in cornflakes) "birdcage" device to be worn around the waist by young girls, to prevent masturbation (Kellogg 1882).

Unfortunately, within the working class itself, as Cockburn (1983, 1985) demonstrates, control over technology and technical skill is a core element of masculinity, defining one male worker against another and stratifying male workers. Control over technical skills is also a painful source of contradiction and division between men and women, as the working-class man and his union fail to include women in the technological enterprise. Feminine control by some over the exercise of erotic skills is equally potentially divisive among working-class women (Walker 1982) and is certainly a key to the division of man from woman.

The working-class man may gender eroticism and technology to the detriment of solidarity among working-class people. Realizing the problematics of defining class among women (Acker 1988), I want to focus on ways in which women's class background may encourage us to work against each other on these dimensions of technology and eroticism.

Middle-class and working-class men are seriously divided on the current organization of technology, its apparent threat to health and safety, its ability to provide the comfortable living we have come to expect, its implications for a democratic society. Middle-class and working-class women may be divided on eroticism for analogous reasons. Within the debate on pornography/eroticism, in my experience theoretical support for the sex radical position is often offered by socialist feminists, speaking for and to the working class. Such analyses oppose censorship or limits, in part because those limits would likely come down hard on feminist and homosexual/lesbian material, and on women workers in the sex industry. But most socialist feminists I know, even those working in laundries, factories, and restaurants, are upper-middle-class in origin.

On the other hand, though most of the radical feminists I know are indeed middle-class or professional, their origins are working-class. Many argue against pornography and violence against women, and are termed middle-class "cultural feminists" by their opposition. In the early 1980s, a legitimate concern for sexual violence and abuse of women and children led feminists (called "cultural feminists" by the Left opposition, to indicate a lack of material analysis) to a somewhat overdrawn picture of woman as victim and male sexuality as aggressive and dangerous. One strategy is to eliminate the pornographic stimulus for this. The practice following from such perspectives tends toward the politics of the powerless, seeking protectors.

Thus, an upper-middle-class socialist analysis of eroticism argues greater freedom and less restriction on sexual behavior, arguments that many working-class women may find appalling. On the other hand, the "middle-class feminist" fighting pornography and violence against women may speak more directly to the way in which working-class women construct sexual reality (Dworkin 1983).

This informal observation about the class origins of friends on either side of the debate led me to test the notion by questionnaire among 120 of my undergraduate students—a fair cross section of a large land-grant university, mostly but not entirely white and protestant,

Pacific Northwest and therefore somewhat more socially conservative than East Coast or Midwest, half working-class in origin (plywood mills, food packing plants, clerical worker parents, with moderate to low income), and half middle- or upper-middle-class (professional, entrepreneurial with high incomes).

For several days, we discussed the two sides of the debate—sex radical and radical feminist, as I had experienced it during an ethnographic study in Los Angeles, in 1982 and 1983. In addition, five of us, feminists with different positions on these issues, met over potluck once a month to hash it out (Hacker et al. 1984) and try for as balanced a presentation as possible.

In response, the majority of students rejected both positions as too extreme, or wanted a position that incorporated what they considered to be the best of both. Of the 30 to 40 percent who did make a choice, the major difference was not by class, but by sex. Almost all those who chose the sex radical position were males. After sex, class did matter. Most of the young men and all of the women who chose this position were middle- and upper-class in origin. Working-class kids, and all working-class young women who chose one or the other position, chose the antipornography stance of the radical feminists.

In one question, I asked those who saw the sex industry as providing jobs like any other how they would react if their sons or daughters chose the profession, as managers or workers. Most of those who chose the sex radical position, the middle- or upper-class college young people, made it clear they had no prejudice against these professions—for other people's children. They stated it was unlikely their own would make such a choice.

Thus, socialist feminists who argue the sex radical position, and usually in the name of or for the benefit of the working-class woman, have missed the mark. Ideologies of decency and romance may be strongest among the working class (Snitow 1983; Vance 1983), accounting for the otherwise most puzzling support of antiwomen policies and politicians (see Dworkin 1983; the literature on romance novels, the literature on ideologies of working-class women).

CONTRADICTIONS AND QUESTIONS

We find ourselves caught in peculiar contradictions in the debates over pornography/eroticism and over technology. It is, of course, at these painful moments, when we find ourselves "of two minds" that we may withdraw, hang on to old comforts, familiar problems and discourses. Or possibly we may be able to break out of older habits and see the problem afresh. Are there any two spheres as greatly gendered as eroticism and technology? I suggest we ask the questions we are familiar with in one area of the other. Some examples:

- Some wonder whether either technology or eroticism/pornography is inherently good or evil, or whether the value merely lies in the eye of the beholder. Does the Buddha, as Robert Pirsig (1975) claims, rest as easily in the transistors of a computer as in the petals of the lotus? What, then, do we do with the knowledge that both computer and transistor but not lotus were designed and shaped by military needs? (See Smith 1985; Edwards 1985, Tirman 1984; Misa 1985.) If the artifacts of technology contain a politics, as Langdon Winner (1980) suggests, what about the technologies and practices of eroticism?
- Do we substitute violent for erotic imagery, and are the two fused in our culture at this moment? Do we substitute violent for playful technology, and are those activities confounded? How does the common person experience technology or eroticism?
- Should there be limits on the creative expression of either technology or eroticism? Set by whom? What would technology or eroticism look like, if freed from the context of domination and exploitation? How much of contemporary alienation is cause or effect of existing pornotechnic or pornographic relations? How much of the analysis flows directly from the writer's (including this one's) concrete experiences?
- What is our active, participative role as subjects in the construction of technology and eroticism in the activities of daily life? Even given that both are defined, designed, and shaped by a few for the many, how are we encouraged, seduced, to support these constrained meanings by taking part in technological or erotic activities so defined in the round of everyday activities? Is resistance on this level sufficient?

Both technology and eroticism show signs of a degendering transformation. Women do enter the crafts and engineering. This entry of women into new technologies threatens the masculinity of some craftsmen, while other men enter traditionally women's fields such as nursing (Cockburn 1983, 1985). A new eroticism legitimates a pouting, "feminine" style for men, and a tougher, teasing, "masculine" stance for women.[6]

Today, as engineering undergoes the deskilling and degradation familiar to older crafts (described in Chapter 8), working-class women are encouraged to enter those aspects of engineering and computer science next most likely to suffer automation, such as drafting and design

(Kraft and Dubroff 1983). In erotic activity, women are encouraged to be independent and aggressive, to depend less and less on men.

As Dworkin notes in *Right-Wing Women* (1983), women are not stupid. Even knowing that the old protections, economic and physical, do not work, there is at this point no alternative, short of a revolution in all major social institutions. And no revolutionary force at the moment is also feminist. The few support systems for women's economic and political independence dwindle, particularly in the working class. Thus it is especially important to explicate various ideologies, to see wherein we are confused about class perhaps, to examine closely those points at which we may be most easily manipulated by those with vested interests in maintaining hierarchical and patriarchal relations.[7]

CONCLUSION

A marvel of our experience is found in the different ways in which we delight each other and ourselves. The pleasures and delights of technology and eroticism do not need to be gendered. Men and women can enjoy the activities of either. The problem is neither technology nor pornography, but the deep and pervasive difference in power between, and limits on spheres appropriate for, men and women. But this means foregrounding, not burying the connections between technology and eroticism, for these are the processes most successful in mystifying the relations of power.

"Where there is strong eroticism, there is power," as Mariana Valverde (1987, 47) notes. But equality, not gendered power, can be eroticized without enveloping everything "in the soft mists of tenderness and harmony" (p. 43). An imbalance of power is woven into the social fabric of all civilized societies and is expressed in the social control of both technology and eroticism. We are born into a society with traditional and enduring institutions. In this chapter, I have tried to show how we also support these institutions by taking part in them in our everyday lives.

Most of us find at least some technology sexy, erotic, engendering some passion, strong feeling, comfort or pleasure. For some this will be the technology of dazzling weapons systems, with their speed, elegance, complexity, and power, or the high- science technologies of scientific, or even social scientific, research; for others, automobiles, motorcycles, or our own personal computers. Then there are the areas of traditional "women's technologies," perhaps called "women's" because of the absence of the elements of risk and danger, or the relatively small number of people influenced at once—cooking, language, photography, basket weaving, pottery, gardening, the technology of fashion or cosmetics. The contemporary images of eroticism and of machine and system reflect the imagination and desires of the designer. How could it or should it be otherwise in any human venture?

An imbalance of power and resources means, however, that the designs of both technology and eroticism primarily reflect the desires of a certain class of men. These designs will at times reflect the hostility and suspicion this dominant group has, for us, the subordinated group, and possibly for the natural world as well.

Ann Kaplan (1983) describes the "male gaze" in the construction of pornography. Men see, view, point, photograph, write. That gaze may idealize women or watch us with suspicion and hostility. Kaplan suggests that filmmakers, photographers, and authors could imagine both male and female gazes, which can lead to an unconscious delight in mutual gazing.

The fusion of eroticism and technical exhilaration need not be expressed in relations of dominance—firecrackers as opposed to fire-arms, for example; the Golden Gate Bridge's cables plucked like a harp; as in Henry Petroski's *To Engineer Is Human* (1985), playfully comparing the human body walking, turning, lifting a child, to the cranes, scaffolding, pulleys, and mechanics of building and engineering, to explain how much each of us knows "by nature." Sensual delights with texture, light, sound, taste, and smell inform the world of the infant as well as the sexual delights of one's own and others' flesh and form and energy.

But given our humanness, there are also the abuses of power of which we are capable. We have to figure out the best arrangements, structures, and processes to minimize such excess, those that bring out the best in us without expecting ever to eliminate the worst. This is what continuing revolution is all about.

Neither eroticism nor technology should be defined and shaped by a few. Neither should be difficult or expensive to experience for the many. An appropriate technology or eroticism, a democratic technics, could allow the vision and imagination of all to shape a new society. But these fine sentiments are not enough. Those in power do not of their own volition offer to share it with the powerless. And it will take more than willing and wishing our own way of constructing reality in our circumscribed areas of direct face-to-face contact. And so I return to the notion that to change relations in gender and technology, we will have to work together, often with people we don't like a lot, to change the relations of power in the community.

More has been suggested on appropriate technology communities than on appropriate erotic communities. One problem was and is that by choice we live in one of the three most highly mobile societies in the world. It appears that communities, cities, societies in rapid social change are those wherein we need most of all to build strong local and neighborly affinity groups, to develop our own technology and eroticism—this time not so cozy and intolerant of difference, not so class/taste/race based, more open. The same principles that we found could create community in the midst of rapid change before, and that often led to sharing of skills and techniques, to a more democratic technics, could also lead to greater freedom and creativity in erotic expression. These were not easy efforts, nor were they free of conflict.

I am not sure we have the luxury of returning to individual solutions. People in such communities making open decisions with each other, and openly helping children of the community to make decisions as they mature, should be able to approximate communities wherein work, as Marx puts it, is an act of freedom and a source of human creativity (see Street 1983). In that case, the organization of material and energy to accomplish work, embedded in relationships of democratic technics, might once again unite technology and eroticism, freed of the authoritarian dimension that has distorted both since military institutions emerged some 5,000 years ago.

NOTES

1. This chapter was originally presented as a paper at the Third International Interdisciplinary Congress on Women, Session on Technology, Religion and the Status of Women, Trinity College, University of Dublin, July 6–10, 1987.

2. Those unfamiliar with military history museums may be amazed at the amount of space—most, in my recollection of museums in several different countries—devoted to fashion: case after case of jackets with ribbons and braids, hats with feathers and ornaments, boots, leather, much of it studded with some version of Spinrad's bright, shiny metal work, and all of it taken quite seriously, indeed. Spinrad was truly a man ahead of his time in the fashion world of S/M.

3. As Tom Lehrer (1981) suggests for Werner Von Braun, Georg Simmel (1984) claims for the flirt.

4. There is no denying that for many of us, such channeling is most pleasurable. I explored the seduction of the abstract and the mathematical in my ethnographic study of the engineering students (see Chapter 4). The pleasures are not unlike those of the empirical social sciences, or the abstraction of any professional discipline or calling, which offers a buffer against the demands of "women's work," unrewarded work in the community.

5. Some radio and film technologies are now possessed solely by the military. Twenty years ago, in Houston, we tried to buy infrared, heat-sensitive film equipment for our son to play with. He was fascinated by film and its related technology. Whether true or not, we were told such equipment could

be purchased only by police or the military. I still experience a sense of rage at this incident. As a HAM operator, I am sensitive too, to the increasing military possession of frequencies and other technologies of communication.

6. As always there is greater freedom, less punishment for such cross-sex behavior in the upper middle class than in the working class. Analyses of causes of high school dropouts, or arrest rates, may well indicate these tendencies. Donald Black in *The Behavior of Law* (1976) notes such effects on children with one—insufficiently patriarchal family—parent.

7. Truly ethnic and urban experience will make a difference; Peiss (1983) observes that New York ethnic migrants have greatly varied traditions of heterosociality, Germans and Italians holding polar positions. Working-class women in those times and places may have played out a different, gutsier sexuality than today. But as Gordon notes, the working class in England has been extremely sexually conservative for decades. The picture that emerges from the histories of sexuality portray sex radicals in two lights. One picture shows us well-heeled men and opportunistic women of any class. Others, working- and middle-class radicals, organized around the sexual freedom of themselves and others, linked these to other struggles and issues and landed in jail for their efforts (Kansas City, nineteenth century). By and large today, evidence such as we have would suggest more sexual conservatism among the working class.

On the other issue the working class may be less likely to be critical of technology and technologists, suspicious in fact of environmental movements that show little concern for employment. I have been struck over and again by the strong beliefs in "progress" and positive attitudes toward technological change even among those whose jobs are most likely to be threatened.

Bibliography

Abbott, Langer, and Associates. 1980. "College Recruiting Report." *Enginering Times*, Dec., 21.

Acker, Joan. 1973. "Women and Social Stratification: A Case of Intellectual Sexism." *American Journal of Sociology* 78: 936–45.

———. 1980. "Women and Stratification: A Review of Recent Literature." *Contemporary Sociology* 9: 25–39.

———. 1988. "Class, Gender, and the Relations of Distribution." *Signs* 13: 473–97.

Acker, Joan, and Donald R. Van Houten. 1974. "Differential Recruitment and Control: The Sex Structuring of Organizations." *Administrative Science Quarterly* 19: 152–63.

Adamson, Lesley. 1980. "More to Lose Than Their Chains." *New Internationalist* 89: 7–9.

Airman, John, ed. 1984. *The Militarization of High Technology*. Cambridge, Mass.: Ballinger.

al-Hibri, Azizah. 1981. "Capitalism Is an Advanced State of Patriarchy: But Marxism Is Not Feminism." In *Women and Revolution*, ed. Lydia Sargent. Boston, Mass.: South End.

Allen, Robert. 1977. "The Bakke Case and Affirmative Action." *Black Scholar* 9: 14.

American Association for the Advancement of Science (AAAS). 1984. "Reassessing Personnel Supply and Demand in Scientific and Technical Occupations." Session, May.

American Association of Engineering Societies. 1983. Figure 1 in *Engineering Manpower Bulletin* 66 (June): 2.

American Telephone and Telegraph Corporation (AT&T). 1976. "Non-Traditional Male and Female Job Changes." *AT&T Bulletin*.

Anderson, B. 1980. "CAD/CAM: Big Markets for Factory Systems." *High Technology* 2(1): 99.

Arner, Paul. 1966. "Computer Aspects of Technological Change." In *Employment Problems of Automation and Advanced Technology: An International Perspective*, ed. Jack Steiber. New York: Macmillan and St. Martin's Press.

Aronowitz, Stanley. 1978. "Marx, Braverman and the Logic of Capital." *Insurgent Sociologist* 8(2–3): 126–48.

Artz, Frederick B. 1966. *The Development of Technical Education in France, 1500-1800*. Cambridge: MIT Press.

Baker, Elizabeth Faulkner. 1964. *Technology and Women's Work*. New York: Columbia University Press.

Banner, Lois W. 1983. *American Beauty*. New York: Alfred A. Knopf.

Baran, Paul A., and Paul M. Sweezy. 1966. *Monopoly Capital: An Essay on the American Economy and Social Order*. New York: Monthly Review Press.

Barnet, Richard J., and Ronald E. Mueller. 1979. "Engines of Development?" In *Crisis in American Institutions*, ed. Jerome Skolnick and Elliott Currie. Boston:

225

Little, Brown. Excerpted from chapter 7 of Barnet and Mueller, *Global Reach: The Power of the Multinational Corporations* (New York: Simon & Schuster, 1974).

Baxandall, Rosalyn, Elizabeth Ewen, and Linda Gordon. 1976. "The Working Class Has Two Sexes." *Monthly Review* 28: 1–9.

Baynes, Ken, and Francis Pugh. 1978. "Engineering Drawing: Origins and Development." *The Art of the Engineer*, ed. Welsh Arts Council. Cardiff: The Council.

———. 1981. *The Art of the Engineer*. Woodstock, N.Y.: Overlook.

Beirne, Joseph A. 1965. "Automation: Impact and Implications: With a Focus on Developments in the Communications Industry." Report prepared for the Communications Workers of America by the Diebold Group, April.

Benet, James, and Arlene Kaplan Daniels. 1976. "Education: Straitjacket or Opportunity?" *Social Problems* 24: 143–47.

Bernstein, Harry. 1973. "Duel in the Sun: Union Busting, Teamster Style." *The Progressive*, July. (Reprinted by American Friends Service Committee, Des Moines, Iowa.)

Black, Donald J. 1976. *The Behavior of Law*. New York: Academic Press.

Blau, Peter M., Cecilia McHugh Falbe, William McKinley, and Phelps K. Tracy. 1976. "Technology and Organization in Manufacturing." *Administrative Science Quarterly* 21: 20–40.

Bose, Christine E. 1978. "Technology and Changes in the Division of Labor in the American Home." Paper presented at annual meetings of the American Sociological Association, San Francisco.

Bose, Christine E., Philip L. Bereano, and Mary Malloy. 1984. "Household Technology and the Social Construction of Housework." *Technology and Culture* 25: 53–82.

Boserup, Ester. 1970. *Women's Role in Economic Development*. New York: St. Martin's Press.

Boulding, Elise. 1976. "Familial Constraints on Women's Work Roles." *Signs* 1: 95–118.

Bowles, Samuel, and Herbert Gintis. 1976. *Schooling in Capitalist America: Educational Reform and the Contradictions of Economic Life*. New York: Basic Books.

Braverman, Harry. 1974. *Labor and Monopoly Capitol: The Degradation of Work in the Twentieth Century*. New York: Monthly Review Press.

Brittain, James E., and Robert C. McMath. 1977. "Engineers and the New South Creed: The Formation and Early Development of Georgia Tech." *Technology and Culture* 18: 175–201.

Brown, Carol. 1979. "The Political Economy of Sexual Inequality." Paper presented at annual meeting of the Society for the Study of Social Problems, Boston.

Brownmiller, Susan. 1984. *Femininity*. New York: Linden Press/Simon & Schuster.

Brunhild, Gordon, and Robert H. Burton. 1967. "A Theory of 'Technical Unemployment—One Aspect of Structural Unemployment." *American Journal of Economics and Sociology* 26: 265–77.

Bullough, Vern. 1987. "Technology for the Prevention of 'Les Maladies Produites par la Masturbation.' " *Technology and Culture* 28: 828–32.

Burstyn, Varda, ed. 1985. *Women Against Censorship*. Vancouver, BC: Douglas & McIntyre.

Calhoun, Daniel H. 1960. *The American Civil Engineer: Origins and Conflicts*. Cambridge: Technology Press, MIT.

Califia, Pat. 1987. "A Personal View of the History of the Lesbian S/M Community and Movement in San Francisco." *Coming to Power: Writings and Graphics in Lesbian S/M*, ed. members of Samois, 245–83. Boston: Alyson.

Calvert, Monte. 1967. *The Mechanical Engineer in America, 1830–1910: Professional Cultures in Conflict*. Baltimore: Johns Hopkins University Press.

Cardwell, Donald S. L. 1957. *The Organisation of Science in England: A Retrospect*. London: Heinemann.

Center for United Labor Action (CULA). 1972. *Center for United Labor Action Newsletter*, Dec. 4.

Chestnut, Harold, and Robert W. Mayer. 1963. *Servomechanisms and Regulating System Design*. New York: John Wiley.

Chodorow, Nancy. 1974. "Family Structure and Feminine Personality." In *Women, Culture and Society*. eds. Michelle Zimbalist Rosaldo and Louise Lamphere. Stanford, Calif.: Stanford University Press.

Christoffel, Tom, and Katherine Kaufer. 1970. "The Political Economy of Male Chauvinism." In *Up Against the American Myth*, eds. Tom Christoffel, David Finkelhor, and Dan Gilbarg. New York: Holt, Rinehart & Winston.

Clarke, Thomas C. 1875. "The Education of Civil Engineers" (and discussions). *Transactions of the American Society of Civil Engineers* 3: 255–66.

Cockburn, Cynthia (1983). *Brothers: Male Brothers and Technological Change*. London: Pluto.

———. 1985. *Machinery of Dominance: Women, Men and Technical Know-How*. London: Pluto.

Cohn, Carol. 1987. "Sex and Death in the Rational World of Defense Intellectuals." *Signs* 12: 687–718.

Collins, Randall. 1979. *The Credentialled Society: An Historical Sociology of Education and Stratification*. New York: Academic Press.

Conlin, Roxanne. 1974. "Women and the Law: Protected or Neglected." Address to the Iowa Farm Bureau, June 10.

Constantine, Larry L., and Floyd M. Martinson, eds. 1981. *Children and Sex: New Findings, New Perspectives*. Boston: Little, Brown.

Cooley, Michael. 1982. *Architect or Bee? The Human/Technology Relationship*. Boston: South End.

Cordtz, Dan. 1970. "The Coming Shake-Up in Telecommunications." *Fortune*, Apr., 69ff.

Cowan, Ruth Schwartz. 1983. *More Work for Mother: The Ironies of Household Technology from the Open Hearth to the Microwave*. New York: Basic Books.

Daniels, Arlene Kaplan. 1972. "A Sub-specialty within a Professional Speciality: Military Psychiatry." In *Medical Men and Their Work*, eds. Eliot Freidson and Judith Lorber. Chicago: Aldine-Atherton.

Daufenbach, Robert C. 1984. "Supply Projections of Scientific and Technological Personnel: Dynamic Response to Changing Employment Requirements." Report to the Oklahoma State University and Oak Ridge Associated Universities Labor and Policy Studies Program, May.

Daufenbach, Robert C., and Jack Fiorito. 1983. "Projections of Supply of Scientists and Engineers to Meet Defense and Nondefense Requirements, 1981–87: A Report to the National Science Foundation." Oklahoma State University.

Davis, Chandler. 1980. "Where Did Twentieth-Century Mathematics Go Wrong?" Paper presented at the joint annual meetings of the Society for the History of Technology, History of Science Society, Philosophy of Science Association, and Society for the Social Study of Science, Toronto.

Delacoste, Frederique, and Priscilla Alexander, eds. 1987. *Sex Work: Writings by Women in the Sex Industry*. San Francisco and Pittsburgh: Cleis.

DeMarco, Susan, and Susan Sechler. 1975. "The Green Revolution." In *The Fields Have Turned Brown: Four Essays in World Hunger*. Washington , D.C.: Agribusiness Accountability Project.

Dembart, Lee. 1982. "Computer Era Threatens Pre-eminence of Calculus." *Los Angeles Times*, May 25: Part I, 3, 16.

DeVore, Paul W. 1975. *Review of American Education and Vocationalism: A Documentary History, 1870–1970*. Eds. Marvin Lazerson and W. Norton Grubb. New York: Teachers College Press.

Doigan, Paul. 1979. "Engineering and Technology Degrees, 1978." *Engineering Education*, Apr., 727–38.

Douglas, Susan. 1985. "The Navy Adopts the Radio, 1899–1919." In *Military Enterprise and Technological Change: Perspectives on the American Experience*, ed. Merritt Roe Smith, 117–73. Cambridge: MIT Press.

Dubin, Samuel S. 1977. "The Updating Process." Appendix C in National Science Foundation, Directorate for Science Education, Office of Program Integration, *Continuing Education in Science and Engineering*. Washington, D.C.: Government Printing Office.

Dublin, Thomas. 1975. "Women Work and the Family: Female Operatives in the Lowell Mills, 1830–1860." *Feminist Studies* 3.

DuBois, Ellen Carol, and Linda Gordon. 1984. "Seeking Ecstasy on the Battlefield: Danger and Pleasure in Nineteenth-Century Feminist Sexual Thoughts." In *Pleasure and Danger: Exploring Female Sexuality*, ed. Carole S. Vance, 31–49. Boston: Routledge & Kegan Paul.

Dundes, Alan. 1962. "Earthdriver: Creation of the Mythopoeic Male." *American Anthropologist* 64: 1032–51.

Dworkin, Andrea. 1979. *Pornography: Men Possessing Women*. New York: Perigee.

——. 1983. *Right-Wing Women*. New York: Wideview/Perigee.

Easlea, Brian. 1983. *Fathering the Unthinkable: Masculinity, Scientists and the Nuclear Arms Race*. London: Pluto.

Edwards, Paul N. 1985. "Technologies of the Mind: Computers, Power, Psychology, and World War II" (Working Paper No. 2). Silicon Valley Research Group, University of California, Santa Cruz.

——. 1986. "Artificial Intelligence and High Technology War: The Perspective of the Formal Machine" (Working Paper No. 6). Silicon Valley Research Group, University of California, Santa Cruz.

——. Forthcoming. "The Army and the Microworld: Computers and the Militarized Politics of Gender Identity." *Signs*.

Ehrenreich, Barbara, and Deirdre English. 1973. *Witches, Midwives and Nurses: A History of Women Healers.* Old Westbury, N.Y.: Feminist Press.

Ehrenreich, Barbara, Elizabeth Hess, and Gloria Jacobs. 1986. *Remaking Love: The Feminization of Sex.* Garden City, NY: Anchor.

Engineering Council on Professional Development (ECPD). 1976. *44th Annual Report,* 2 vols.

English, Deirdre, Amber Hollibaugh, and Gayle Rubin. 1982. "Talking Sex: A Conversation on Sexuality and Feminism." *Feminist Review* 11 (Summer): 40–52. (Reprinted from *Socialist Review* 58 [1981], 43–62.)

Enroe, Phillip C. 1981. "Cambridge University and the Adaptation of Analytics in Early 19th Century England." In *Social History of Nineteenth Century Mathematics,* eds. Herbert Mehrtens, Henk Bos, and Ivo Schneider, 135–48. Boston: Birkhauser.

Equal Employment Opportunity Commission (EEOC). 1971. *A Unique Competence: A Study of Equal Employment Opportunity in the Bell System.* Washington, D.C.: Government Printing Office.

Erasmus, Desiderius. 1965. *The Colloquies of Erasmus.* Trans. Craig R. Thompson. Chicago: University of Chicago Press.

Ernest, John. 1976. "Mathematics and Sex." Mathematics Deptartment, University of California, Santa Barbara. Unpublished.

Fazio, Alfred, Robert T. Fazio, and David W. Jacobs. 1978. "Discussion of Unionization of American Engineers." *Issues of Engineering—Journal of Professional Activities,* Apr., 162–63.

Fechter, Alan. 1984. Discussant on panel, "Reassessing Personnel Supply and Demand in Scientific and Technical Occupations." Presented at the annual meetings of the American Association for the Advancement of Science, New York, May.

Feldberg, Roslyn. 1978. "Early Unions Among Clerical Workers." Paper presented at the annual meetings of the Society for the Study of Social Problems, San Francisco.

Feldberg, Roslyn, and Evelyn Nakano Glenn. 1980. "Effects of Technological Change on Clerical Work." Paper presented at annual meetings of the American Sociological Association, New York.

Ferber, Marianne A., and Helen Lowry. 1976. "Women: The New Reserve Labor Army of the Unemployed." *Signs* 1: 213–32.

Ferguson, Ann, Jacquelyn N. Zita, and Kathryn Pyne Addelson. 1981. "On 'Compulsory Heterosexuality and Lesbian Existence': Defining the Issues." *Signs* 7: 158–99.

Ferguson, Eugene. 1977. "The Mind's Eye: Nonverbal Thought in Technology." *Science,* 827–36.

———. 1981. National Endowment for the Humanities Summer Seminar on the History of Engineering, University of Delaware, Newark.

Finch, James Kip. 1948. *Trends in Engineering Education: The Columbia Experience.* New York: Columbia University Press.

Florman, Samuel. 1976. *The Existential Pleasures of Engineering.* New York: St. Martin's Press.

———. 1981. *Blaming Technology: The Irrational Search for Scapegoats.* New York: St. Martin's Press.

Fortune. 1978. "Business Communications: The New Frontier." Oct. 9.

Foucault, Michel. 1978. *The History of Sexuality.* Vol. 1, *An Introduction.* Trans. Robert Hurley. New York: Pantheon.

———. 1979. *Discipline and Punish: The Birth of the Prison.* Trans. Alan Sheridan. New York: Vintage.

Freeman, John Henry. 1973. "Environment, Technology and the Administrative Intensity of Manufacturing Organizations." *American Sociological Review* 38: 750–60.

Galloway, Jonathan. 1972. *The Politics and Technology of Satellite Communications.* Lexington, MA: Leexington.

Garson, Barbara. 1977. *All the Livelong Day: The Meaning and Demeaning of Routine Work.* New York: Penguin.

Gibbs, Jack P., and Harley L. Browning. 1966. "The Division of Labor, Technology and the Organization of Production in Twelve Countries." *American Sociological Review* 31: 81–92.

Gilmore, Daniel F. 1983. "Military Is Also in Education Business." *Los Angeles Times,* May 5: Part I-Q, 7.

Glenn, Evelyn Nakano, and Roslyn L. Feldberg. 1976. "Structural Change and Proletarianization: The Case of Clerical Work." Paper presented at the annual meetings of the Society for the Study of Social Problems, New York.

Goffman, Erving. 1963. *Stigma: Notes on the Management of Spoiled Identity.* Englewood Cliffs, NJ: Prentice-Hall.

Goldman, Paul. 1978. "Technological Displacement in the Retail Industry." Paper presented at the Technology and Jobs Workshop, Oregon State University, August.

Gordon, David M. 1976. "Comment." *Signs* 1: 238–44.

Goulden, Joseph C. 1970. *Monopoly.* New York: Pocketbooks.

———. 1972. "A Peek at the Books." *The Nation,* Jan. 10, 37–41.

Gouldner, Alvin W. 1970. *The Coming Crisis in Western Sociology.* New York: Basic Books.

———. 1976. *The Dialectic of Ideology and Technology: The Origins, Grammar and Future of Ideology.* New York: Seabury.

Grabiner, Judith V. 1981. *The Origins of Cauchy's Rigorous Calculus.* Cambridge: MIT Press.

Greenbaum, Joan. 1976. "Division of Labor in the Computer Field." *Monthly Review* 28: 40–55.

Griffin, Susan. 1981. *Pornography and Silence: Culture's Revolt against Nature.* New York: Harper & Row.

Griffitt, William. 1987. "Females, Males, and Sexual Responses." In *Females, Males, and Sexuality: Theories and Research,* ed. Kathryn Kelley, 141–73. Albany: State University of New York Press.

Grubb, W. Norton, and Marvin Lazerson. 1975. "Rally 'Round the Workplace: Continuities and Fallacies in Career Education." *Harvard Education Review* 45: 451–74.

Hacker, Barton. 1977a. "The Prevalence of War and the Oppression of Women: An Essay on Armies and the Origin of the State." Paper presented at the Conference on Women and Power, University of Maryland.

——. 1977b. "Weapons of the West: Military Technology and Modernization in 19th Century China and Japan." *Technology and Culture* 18: 43–55.

——. 1982. "Imaginations in Thrall: The Social Psychology of Military Mechanization, 1919–1939." *Parameters* 12 (March): 50–61.

——. 1987. "'A Corps of Able Engineers' Military Institutions and Technical Education since the 18th Century." Paper presented at the annual meeting of the Society for the History of Technology, Durham, N.C.

Hacker, Bart, and Sally L. Hacker. 1987. "Military Institutions and the Labor Process: Noneconomic Sources of Technological Change, Women's Subordination, and the Organization of Work." *Technology and Culture* 28: 743–75.

Hacker, Sally L. 1977a. "Farming Out the Home." *Second Wave: A Magazine of the New Feminism* 5 (Winter): 38–49.

——. 1977b. "Man and Humanism: Language, Gender and Power." *Humanity and Society* 2.

——. 1978. "The Impact of Technological Change on Minorities in Industry." Paper presented at the Northwest Regional Racial Minorities Conference, Portland State University, Portland, OR.

——. 1979. "Sex Stratification, Technology and Organizational change: A Longitudinal Case Study of AT&T." *Social Problems* 26: 539–57.

——. 1980. "The Automated and the Automaters: Human and Social Costs of Automation." In *Proceedings of the Third Conference on Systems Approach to Development, International Federation of Automatic Control, Morocco.* New York: Pergamon.

——. 1981. "The Culture of Engineering: Women, Workplace and Machine." *Women's Studies International Quarterly* 4: 341–53.

——. 1983. "The Mathematization of Engineering: Limits on Women and the Field." In *Machine ex Dea: Feminist Perspectives on Technology*, ed. Joan Rothschild, 35–58. New York: Pergamon.

——. 1984. "Engineering the Shape of Work." In *Beyond Whistleblowing: Defining Engineers' Responsibilities*, ed. Vivian Weil, 300–16. Chicago: Illinois Institute of Technology.

——. 1985. "Doing It the Hard Way: Ethnographic Study of Ideology in Agribusiness and Engineering Classes." *Humanity and Society* 9: 123–41.

——. 1989. *Pleasure, Power, and Technology.* Boston: Unwin Hyman.

Hacker, Sally L., Eleen Baumann, Dorice Tentschoff, Jule Wind, and Sutree Irving. 1984. "Some Material and Ideological Bases of the Radical Sex Controversy." Paper presented at the annual meeting of the Society for the Study of Social Problems, San Antonio, Tex.

Hamilton, Martha. 1972. *The Great American Grain Robbery and Other Stories.* Washington, D.C.: Agribusiness Accountability Project.

Haraway, Donna J. 1985. "A Manifesto for Cyborgs: Science, Technology, and Socialist Feminism in the 1980s." *Socialist Review* 80: 65–107.

Harris, Norman C., and John F. Grede. 1977. *Career Education in Colleges.* San Francisco: Jossey-Bass.

Harrison, Bennett, and Barry Bluestone. 1975. Statement, Hearings before the Subcommittee on Equal Opportunities of the Committee on Education and Labor, First session on HR50, Boston, 299–318. Washington, D.C.: Government Printing Office.

Hartmann, Heidi. 1977. "Capitalism, Patriarchy and Job Segregation." In *Woman in a Man-Made World: A Socio-Economic Handbook*, eds. Nona Glazer and Helen Youngelson Wacher, 71–84. Chicago: Rand McNally.

Harvey, Edward. 1968. "Technology and the Structure of Organizations." *American Sociological Review* 33: 247–59.

Hashimoto, David. 1974. "EEOC's Use of Consent Decrees." Draft of thesis, University of Wisconsin. Unpublished.

Hazelrigg, Lawrence E. 1985. "Were It Not for Words." *Social Problems* 32: 234–37.

Helfgott, Roy B. 1966. "EDP and the Office Work Force." *Industrial and Labor Relations Review* 19: 503–16.

Hightower, Jim. 1973. *Hard Tomatoes, Hard Times* (A Report of the Agri-Business Accountability Project). Cambridge, Mass.: Schenckman.

Hochschild, Arlie Russell. 1982. "Emotional Labor in the Friendly Skies." *Psychology Today* 16 (June), 13–15.

Hodgkin, Luke. 1981. "Mathematics and Revolution from Lacroix to Cauchy." In *Social History of Nineteenth Century Mathematics*, eds. Herbert Mehrtens, Henk Bos, and Ivo Schneider, 50–71. Boston: Birkhauser.

Holt, Irvin. 1983. "Electronics Technology at Brigham Young University." *Engineering Education* 73 (May): 784–86.

Hoos, Ida Rossakoff. 1960. "When the Computer Takes Over the Office." *Harvard Business Review* 38: 102–12.

——. 1972. *Systems Analysis in Public Policy: A Critique*. Berkeley: University of California Press.

Hounshell, David A. 1984. *From the American System to Mass Production, 1800–1932: The Development of Manufacturing Technology in the United States*. Baltimore: Johns Hopkins University Press.

Hughes, Thomas Parke, ed. 1966. *Selections from Lives of the Engineers, with an Account of Their Principal Works, by Samuel Smiles*. Cambridge.: MIT Press.

Institute for Electrical and Electronic Engineers (IEEE). 1980. "Engineering Technology Report." *IEEE Transactions on Education* E-23(1): 1–15.

——. 1982. "Engineering Technology Report." *IEEE Transactions on Education*.

Iowa Cattleman's Association. 1973a. Cowbelles Corner." Vol. 3(3).

——. 1973. "Cowbelles Corner." Vol. 3(4).

——. 1973. "Cowbelles Corner." Vol. 3(5).

Iowa Farm Bureau. 1977. *Facts on Iowa Agriculture*. Communications Division, March.

Iowa Security Commission. 1975. *Manpower Information for Affirmative Action Programs*.

Johnson, Ana Gutierrez, and William Foote Whyte. 1977. "The Mondragon System of Worker Production Cooperatives." *Industrial and Labor Relations Review* 31: 18–30.

Jones, Ann Rosalind. 1987. "Nets and Bridles: Early Modern Conduct Books and Sixteenth-Century Women's Lyrics." In *The Ideology of Conflict: Essays on Literature and the History of Sexuality*, eds. Nancy Armstrong and Leonard Tennehouse, 39–71. New York: Methuen.

Joyce, Lynda. 1976. *Annotated Bibliography of Women in Rural America*. University Park: Department of Agricultural Economics and Rural Society, Pennsylvania State University.

Jusenius, Carol L. 1976. "Economics" (review essay). *Signs* 2: 177–89.

Kandiyoti, Deniz. 1984. "Women and Society." Address on women and development presented at Oregon State University, Corvallis.

Kanter, Rosabeth Moss. 1975. "Women and the Structure of Organizations: Explorations in Theory and Behavior." In *Another Voice: Feminist Perspectives on Social Life and Social Science*, eds. Marcia Millman and Rosabeth Moss Kanter, 34–74. Garden City, N.Y.: Anchor.

———. 1977. *Men and Women of the Corporation*. New York: Basic Books.

Kaplan, E. Ann. 1983. "Is the Gaze Male?" In *Powers of Desire: The Politics of Sexuality*, eds. Ann Snitow, Christine Stansell, and Sharon Thompson, 309–27. New York: Monthly Review Press.

Karabel, Jerome. 1972. "Open Admissions: Toward Meritocracy or Democracy?" *Change*, May, 38–43.

Kasarda, John D. 1974. "The Structural Implications of Social System Size: A Three Level Analysis." In *Another Voice: Feminist Perspectives on Social Life and Social Science*, eds. Marcia Millman and Rosabeth Moss Kanter. Garden City, N.Y.: Anchor.

Katz, Israel. 1977. *Continuing Education in Science and Engineering* (National Science Foundation, Directorate for Science Education, Office of Program Integration). Washington, D.C.: Government Printing Office.

Keller, Evelyn Fox. 1980. "Baconian Science: A Hermaphroditic Birth." *Philosophical Forum* 11(3).

———. 1985. *Reflections on Gender and Science*. New Haven, Conn.: Yale University Press.

Kellogg, J. H. 1882. *Ladies' Guide in Health and Disease: Girlhood, Maidenhood, Wifehood, Motherhood*. Battle Creek, MI: Modern Medicine Publishing Co.

Kidder, Tracy. 1981. *The Soul of a New Machine*. New York: Avon.

Killingsworth, Charles C., and Jack Steiber. 1966. "Structural Unemployment in the United States." In *Employment Problems of Automation and Advanced Technology: An International Perspective*, ed. Jack Steiber. New York: Macmillan and St. Martin's Press.

Kimberly, John R. 1976. "Organizational Size and the Structuralist Perspective: A Review, Critique, and Proposal." *Administrative Science Quarterly* 21: 571–97.

Knaak, Nancy, ed. 1977. "Rural Women." *Do It NOW* 10 (April) (special issue).

Kolodny, Annette. 1975. *The Lay of the Land: Metaphor as Experience and History in American Life and Letters*. Chapel Hill: University of North Carolina Press.

Kornegger, Peggy. 1975. "Anarchism—The Feminist Connection." *Second Wave* 4(2): 26–37.

Kraft, Philip. 1977. *Programmers and Managers*. New York: Springer-Verlag.

Kraft, Philip, and Steven Dubroff. 1983. "Software Workers Survey." *Computer World*, Nov., 3, 5, 6, 8–13.

Kramer Associates, Inc. 1978. *Manpower for Energy Research: Design of a Comprehensive Manpower Information System for Energy Research, Development, and Demonstration*. Washington, D.C.: U.S. Department of Energy, Office of Education, Business, and Labor Affairs.

Krantz, Harry. 1977. "The Current Status of Disparate Impact." Paper presented at the third annual meeting of the American Association of Affirmative Action, Washington, D.C.

Kravitz, Linda. 1974. *Who's Minding the Coop? Farmer Control of Farmer Cooperatives*. Washington, D.C.: Agribusiness Accountability Project.

Lakey, George. 1973. *Strategy for a Living Revolution*. New York: Grossman.

———. 1987. *Powerful Peacemaking: A Strategy for a Living Revolution*. Philadelphia: New Society.

Lambeth, Edmund B. 1967. "COMSAT, Ma Bell and ETV." *The Nation*, Jan. 23, 109–12.

Langer, Eleanor. 1970. "The Women of the Telephone Company." *New York Review of Books* 14(5 and 6), Mar. 12 and 26, 14–18.

Laws, Judith Long. 1976. "The Bell Telephone System: A Case Study." In *Equal Employment Opportunity and the AT&T Case*, ed. Phyllis Wallace, 157–78. Cambridge: MIT Press. (Original testimony presented in 1971: "Causes and Effects of Sex Discrimination in the Bell System." Expert witness testimony, EEOC exhibit 4, Docket 19143 filed before the FCC, Washington, D.C.)

Layton, Edwin. 1969. "Science, Business and the American Engineer." In *The Engineers and the Social System*, eds. Robert Petrucci and Joal E. Gerstl. New York: Wiley.

Lazonick, William. 1978. "Subjection of Labor to Capital: The Rise of the Capitalist System." *Review of Radical Political Economy* 10.

Leghorn, Lisa, and Mary Rodkowsky. 1977. *Who Really Starves? Women and World Hunger*. New York: Friendship Press.

LeGuin, Ursula K. 1975. *The Dispossessed*. New York: Avon.

Lehrer, Tom. 1981. *Too Many Songs by Tom Lehrer with Not Enough Drawings by Ronald Searle*. New York: Pantheon.

"Leonardo." 1978. Letters to the editor about the reprinted version of Ferguson, "Nonverbal Thought in Technology." *Science* 11: 348–50.

Levin, Henry M., and R. W. Rumberger. 1983. *The Educational Implications of High Technology* (Report A4). Stanford, Calif.: Institute for Research on Educational Finance and Governance, Center for Educational Research, Stanford University.

Lilienfeld, Robert. 1975. "Systems Theory as an Ideology." *Social Research: An International Quarterly of the Social Sciences* 42(4).

———. 1978. *The Rise of Systems Theory: An Ideological Analysis*. New York: Wiley.

Linden, Robin Ruth, Darlene R. Pagano, Diana E. H. Russell, and Susan Leigh Star, eds. 1982. *Against Sadomasochism: A Radical Feminist Analysis*. East Palo Alto, Calif.: Frog in the Well.

Loewenberg, Joern, J. 1962. "Effects of Change on Employee Relations in the Telephone Industry." Ph.D., Harvard University.

MacCannell, Dean, and Juliet Flower MacCannell. 1987. "The Beauty System." In *The Ideology of Conflict: Essays on Literature and the History of*

Technology, eds. Nancy Armstrong and Leonard Tennenhouse, 206–38. New York: Methuen.

McDaniel, Walter. 1964. "Meaning of the Systems Movement to the Acceleration and Direction of American Economy."

McDermott, Jeanne. 1982. "Technical Education: The Quiet Crises." *High Technology* 2 (November-December): 87–90, 92.

McLeod, Eileen. 1982. *Women Working: Prostitution Now*. London: Croom Helm.

McMillan, Penelope. 1983. "Revolution at Work" (series). *Los Angeles Times*, June 3: Part I, 17.

Mann, Charles R. 1918. *A Study of Engineering Education*. Prepared for the Joint Committee on Engineering Education of the National Engineering Societies. Bulletin No. 11. New York: Carnegie Foundation for the Advancement of Teaching.

Marcuse, Herbert. 1964. *One Dimensional Man*. Boston: Beacon.

Marglin, Stephen. 1974. "What Do Bosses Do? The Origins and Functions of Hierarchy in Capitalist Production." *Review of Radical Political Economy* 6(2): Part I.

Marx, Gary. 1972. "Muckraking Sociology: Research as Social Criticism." *Transactions* 1–30.

Matthiessen, Peter. 1969. *Sal Si Puedes: Cesar Chavez and the New American Revolution*. New York: Dell.

Mehrtens, Herbert, Henk Bos, and Ivo Schneider, eds. 1981. *Social History of Nineteenth Century Mathematics*. Boston: Birkhauser.

Melman, Seymour. 1970. *Pentagon Capitalism*. New York: McGraw-Hill.

Mernissi, Fatima. 1975. *Beyond the Veil: Male-Female Dynamics in a Modern Muslim Society*. Cambridge, Mass.: Schenckman.

Merritt, Raymond H. 1969. *Engineering in American Society, 1850–1875*. Lexington: University Press of Kentucky.

Middleton, William. 1980. "A Thorny Issue." *Professional Engineer* 65 (June): 38–40.

Milkman, Ruth. 1976. "Women's Work and the Economic Crises: Some Lessons from the Great Depression." *Review of Radical Political Economy* (Spring).

Millett, Kate. 1970. *Sexual Politics*. Garden City, N.Y.: Doubleday.

Mingle, J. G. 1979. "Engineering vs. Engineering Technnology." Paper presented at the annual meeting of the West Coast Society of Automotive Engineers, Portland, Oregon.

Misa, Thomas J. (1985). "Military Needs, Commercial Realities, and the Development of the Transistor, 1948–1958." In *Military Enterprise and Technological Change: Perspectives on the American Experience*, ed. Merritt Roe Smith, 253–87. Cambridge: MIT Press.

Money, John. 1985. *The Destroying Angel: Sex, Fitness and Food in the Legacy of Degeneracy Theory, Graham Crackers, Kellogg's Corn Flakes and American Health History*. Buffalo, N.Y.: Prometheus.

Moore, Joseph. H., and Robert K. Will. 1973. "Baccalaureate Programs in Engineering Technology" *Engineering Education* 64 (October): 34–36.

Mumford, Lewis. 1966. "Technics and the Nature of Man." *Technology and Culture* 7: 303–17.

———. 1967. *The Myth of the Machine*. Vol. 1, *Technics and Human Development*. New York: Harcourt Brace Jovanovich.

———. 1970. *The Myth of the Machine: The Pentagon of Power*. New York: Harcourt Brace Jovanovich.

Murphy, Dan. 1973. Editorial. *Iowa Farm Bureau Spokesman* 39: 44.

Muscatine Migrant Committee. 1973. *Muscatine Migrant Committee Annual Report: 1973*. Muscatine, Iowa.

National Center for the Quality of Working Life. 1977. *Productivity and Job Security: Attrition—Benefits and Problems*. Washington, D.C.: Government Printing Office.

Nation's Agriculture. 1972. Vol. 47(1).

Nielson, Joyce. 1978. *Sex in Society: Perspectives on Stratification*. Belmont, Calif.: Wadsworth.

Noble, David F. 1977. *America by Design: Science, Technology and the Rise of Corporate Capitalism*. New York: Alfred A Knopf.

———. 1978. "Before the Fact: Social Choice in Machine Design—The Case of Automatically-Controlled Machine Tools." Paper presented at the meeting of the Organization of American Historians, Session: "Beyond Technological Determinism."

———. 1979. "Social Change in Machine Design: The Case of Automatically Controlled Machine Tools." In *Case Studies on the Labor Process*, ed. Andrew S. Zimbalist, 18–50. New York: Monthly Review Press.

———. 1980. "Technology and the Organization of Work." Guest lecture, Department of Sociology, Oregon State University, Corvallis.

———. 1984. *Forces of Production: A Social History of Industrial Automation*. New York: Alfred A. Knopf.

———. 1985. "Command Performance: A Perspective on Military Enterprise and Technological Change." In *Military Enterprise and Technological Change: Perspectives on the American Experience*, ed. Merritt Roe Smith, 329–46. Cambridge: MIT Press.

Nolan, Michael F., and John Galliher. 1973. "Rural Sociological Research and Policy: Hard Data, Hard Times." *Rural Sociology* 38: 491–99.

Nolan, Michael F., Robert A. Hagan, and Mary S. Hoekstra. 1975. "Rural Sociological Research, 1966–74: Implications for Social Policy." *Rural Sociology* 40: 435–54.

Noll, Roger, ed. 1976. "Information, Decision-Making Procedures, and Energy Policies." *American Behavioral Scientist* 19(3) (special issue).

Northwestern Bell Telephone Company. 1973. *Job Descriptions*. Des Moines, Iowa.

Noun, Louise. 1969. *Strong Minded Women: The Emergence of the Woman-Suffrage Movement in Iowa*. Ames: Iowa State University Press.

Nygaard, Kristen. 1977. "Trade Union Participation." Lecture given at the Norwegian Computing Center and University of Oslo, CREST Conference on Management Information Systems, North Staffordshire Polytechnic, Stafford, England.

O'Connor, James. 1980. "Working Class Struggle for Reproduction and Production." Paper presented at the Conference on the Labor Process, University of California, Santa Cruz.

Office of Technology Assessment. 1966. *Technician Manpower: Requirements, Resources, and Training Needs.* (Bulletin No. 1512). Washington, D.C.: Government Printing Office, June.

————. 1984. *Computerized Manufacturing Automates: Employment, Education, and the Workplace* (OTA-CIT-235). Washington, D.C.: Government Printing Office.

O'Hair, Michael T. 1984. "Trends in Engineering Technology Education." *Engineering Education* 8 (May): 703–7.

Ott, Mary Diederich, and Nancy A. Reese. 1975. *Women in Engineering.* Ithaca, N.Y.: Cornell University Press.

Owen, John P., and L. D. Belzung. 1967. "An Epilogue to Job Displacement: A Case Study of Structural Unemployment." *Southern Economic Journal* 33: 395–408.

Peiss, Kathy. 1983. " 'Charity Girls' and City Pleasures: Historical Notes on Working-Class Sexuality, 1880–1920." In *Powers of Desire: The Politics of Sexuality,* eds. Ann Snitow, Christine Stansell, and Sharon Thompson, 74–87. New York: Monthly Review Press.

Perlman, Michael. 1976. "Efficiency in Agriculture: The Economics of Energy." In *Radical Agriculture,* ed. Richard Merrill. New York: New York University Press.

Perrow, Charles. 1978. "The Society of Organizations." Paper presented at the annual meetings of the American Sociological Association, San Francisco.

Petroski, Henry. 1985. *To Engineer Is Human: The Role of Failure in Successful Design.* New York: St. Martin's Press.

Pfohl, Stephen. 1985. "Toward a Sociological Deconstruction of Social Problems." *Social Problems* 32: 228–32.

Pincus, Fred L. 1980. "The False Promises of Community Colleges: Class Conflict and Vocational Education." *Harvard Educational Review* 50: 332–61.

Pirsig, Robert M. 1975. *Zen and the Art of Motorcycle Maintenance.* New York: Bantam.

Pivar, David J. 1972. *Purity Crusade: Sexual Morality and Social Control, 1868–1900.* Westport, Conn.: Greenwood.

Pondy, Louis R. 1969. "Effects of Size, Complexity and Ownership on Administrative Intensity." *Administrative Science Quarterly* 14: 47–60.

Reed, E. D. 1971. "Lasers in the Bell System." *Bell Labs Record,* Oct., 263–69.

Restivo, Sal P., and Randall Collins. 1980. "Mathematics and Civilization: A Sociological Theory." Paper presented at the meeting of the International Society for the Comparative Study of Civilizations, Syracuse, NY.

Rich, Andrienne. 1980. "Compulsory Heterosexuality and Lesbian Existence." *Signs* 5: 631–60.

Roemer, J. E. 1978. "Differentially Exploited Labor: A Marxian Theory of Exploitation." *Review of Radical Political Economy* 10.

Rony, Vera. 1971. "The Organization of Black and White Farm Workers in the South." In *The Underside of American History: Other Readings 11,* ed. Thomas R. Frazier, 153–74. New York: Harcourt Brace Jovanovich.

Rosenbrock, H. H. 1977. "The Future of Control." *Automatic* 13: 389–92.

Rossi, Alice. 1965. "Barriers to the Career Choice of Engineering, Medicine or Science among American Women." In *MIT Symposium on American Women in Science and Engineering, 1964: Women in the Scientific Professions*, eds. Jacquelyn Van Aken and Carol Van Aken. Cambridge.: MIT Press.

———. 1973a. "Analysis vs. Action." In *The Feminist Papers: From Adams to de Beauvoir*, ed. Alice Rossi. New York: Bantam.

———. 1973b. "Social Roots of the Women's Movement in America." In *The Feminist Papers: From Adams to Beauvoir*, ed. Alice Rossi, 241–82. New York: Bantam.

Rothschild, Joan, ed. 1981. "Women, Technology and Innovation." *Women's Studies International Quarterly* 4: 289–388 (special issue).

Rothschild-Whitt, Joyce. 1974. *China: Science Walks on Two Legs*. New York: Science for the People/Avon.

———. 1979. "The Collectivist Organization: An Alternative to Rational-bureaucratic Models". *American Sociological Review* 44: 509–27.

Rubin, Gayle. 1984. "Thinking Sex: Notes for a Radical Theory of the Politics of Sexuality." In *Pleasure and Danger: Exploring Female Sexuality*, ed. Carole S. Vance, 267–319. Boston: Routledge & Kegan Paul.

———. 1987. "The Leather Menace: Comments on Politics and S/M." In *Coming to Power: Writings and Graphics on Lesbian S/M*, ed. members of Samois, 194–229. Boston: Alyson.

Ruether, Walter P. 1955. Prepared testimony. Pp. 219–43 in U.S. Congress, Subcommittee on Economic Stabilization of the Joint Committee on the Economic Report, *Automation and Technological Change*, Hearings, 84th Cong., 1st Sess., 14–28 October.

Russo, Nancy Felipe. 1981. "Mathematics and Sex: The 19th Century Revisited." *National Forum* 61(4): 19.

Rybczynski, Witold. 1983. *Taming the Tiger: The Struggle to Control Technology*. New York: Viking.

Ryscavage, Paul M. 1967. "Changes in Occupational Employment over the Past Decade." *Monthly Labor Review* 90: 27–30.

Sabagh, Rita. 1983. "Fiscal Relationships in an Urban Strip Club." Paper presented at the annual meeting of the Pacific Sociological Association, San Jose, California.

Safilios-Rothschild, Constantina. 1976. "Dual Linkages between the Occupational and family systems: A Macrosociological Analysis." *Signs* 1: 51–60.

Sagarin, Edward. 1973. "The Research Setting and the Right Not to Be Researched." In "Social Control of Social Research," *Social Problems* 21(1) (special issue), eds. Gideon Sjoberg and W. Boyd Littrell, 52–64.

Samois, Members of, eds. 1987. *Coming to Power: Writings and Graphics in Lesbian S-M*. Boston: Alyson.

Sandkull, Bengt. 1980. Guest lecture, industrial sociology, Oregon State University.

Schneider, Joseph W. 1985. "Defining the Definitional Perspective on Social Problems." *Social Problems* 32: 232–34.

Sells, Lucy. 1978. "Mathematics: A Critical Filter." *Science Teacher* 45(2).

Shepherd, William G. 1971. "The Competitive Margin in Communications." In *Technological Change in Regulated Industries*, ed. William M. Capron. Washington, D.C.: Brookings Institution.

Sheridan, Patrick. 1980. "Engineering and Technology Degrees, 1979." *Engineering Education*, Apr., 756.

Shils, Edward B. 1963. *Automation and Industrial Relations*. New York: Rinehart & Winston.

Signs: A Journal of Women in Culture and Society. 1976. "Women and the Workplace." Vol. 1(3), Part 2.

———. 1977. "Women and Development." Vol. 3(1) (special issue).

Silberman, Charles E. 1967. "The Little Bird That Casts a Big Shadow." *Fortune* 75(2): 108–11, 223–28.

Silverman, William. 1966. "The Economic and Social Effects of Automation in an Organization." *American Behavioral Scientist* 9: 3–8.

Simmel, Georg. 1984. "Flirtation." In *Georg Simmel: On Women, Sexuality, and Love*, trans. Guy Oakes, 133–52. New Haven, Conn.: Yale University Press. (Original work published 1923)

Sjoberg, Gideon, and W. Boyd Littrell, eds. 1973. "Social Control of Social Research." *Social Problems* 21(1) (special issue).

Sjoberg, Gideon, and Paula Jean Miller. 1973. "Social Research on Bureaucracy: Limitations and Opportunities." In "Social Control of Social Research," *Social Problems* 21(1) (special issue), eds. Gideon Sjoberg and W. Boyd Littrell, 129–44.

Smith, Dorothy E. 1987. *The Everyday World as Problematic: A Feminist Sociology*. Boston: Northeastern University Press.

Smith, Margaret, and Barbara Waisburg. 1985. *Pornography: A Feminist Survey*. Toronto: Boudicca.

Smith, Merritt Roe, ed. 1985. *Military Enterprise and Technological Change: Perspectives on the American Experience*. Cambridge: MIT Press.

Smoot, L. Douglas, and Michael R. King. 1981. "Engineering and Technology: Differences and Similarities." *Engineering Education*, May, 757–60.

Smuts, Robert W. 1971. *Women and Work in America*. New York: Schocken.

Snitow, Ann Barr. 1983. "Mass Market Romance: Pornography for Women Is Different." In *Powers of Desire: The Politics of Sexuality*, eds. Ann Snitow, Christine Stansell, and Sharon Thompson. New York: Monthly Review Press.

Snyder, Benson R. 1971. *The Hidden Curriculum*. New York: Alfred A. Knopf.

Sokoloff, Natalie. 1980. *Between Money and Love: The Dialectics of Women's Home and Market Work*. New York: Praeger.

Spencer, Gary. 1973. "Methodological Issues in the Study of Bureaucratic Elites: A Case Study of West Point." In "Social Control of Social Research," *Social Problems* 21(1) (special issue), eds. Gideon Sjoberg and W. Boyd Littrell, 90–102.

Spinrad, Norman. 1972. *The Iron Dream*. New York: Avon.

Stanley, Autumn. 1980. "Daughters of Ceres: Women Inventors in Agriculture." Paper presented at the annual meetings of the National Women's Studies Association, Bloomington, Indiana.

———. 1981. "Daughters of Isis, Daughters of Demeter: When Women Sowed and Reaped." *Women's Studies International Quarterly* 4: 289–304.

——. 1983. "Women Hold Up Two-Thirds of the Sky: Notes for a Revised History of Technology." In *Machina ex Dea: Feminist Perspectives on Technology,* ed. Joan Rothschild, 3–22. New York: Pergamon.

Staudenmaier, John M. 1985. *Technology's Storytellers: Reweaving the Human Fabric.* Cambridge: Society for the History of Technology and MIT Press.

Stimpson, Catharine R., and Ethel Spector Person, eds. 1980. *Women: Sex and Sexuality.* Chicago: University of Chicago Press.

Stine, Jeffrey K. 1980. "Professionalism vs. Special Interest: The Development of Engineering Education in the U.S." Department of History, University of California, Santa Barbara. Unpublished.

Street, John. 1983. "Socialist Arguments for Industrial Democracy." *Economic and Industrial Democracy* 4: 519–39.

Sutton, Edward S. 1977. "Total Human Resources Development System in AT&T." *Training and Development,* Jan.

Technician Education Yearbook. 1963–64. Ann Arbor, Mich.: Prakken.

——. 1978–79. Ann Arbor, Mich.: Prakken.

Tetrault, Jeanne, and Sherry Thomas. 1976. *Country Woman: A Handbook for the New Farmer.* Garden City, NY: Anchor/Doubleday.

Thayer, G. N. 1968. "BIS in the Bell system." *Bell Labs Record* Dec., 355–61.

Theweleit, Klaus. 1987. *Male Fantasies.* Vol. 1, *Women, Floods, Bodies, History.* Trans. Stephen Conway, with Rita Carter and Chris Turner. Minneapolis: University of Minnesota Press.

Thompson, Craig R., trans. 1965. *The Colloquies of Erasmus.* Chicago: University of Chicago Press.

Tirman, John, ed. 1984. *The Militarization of High Technology.* Cambridge, Mass.: Ballinger.

Tobias, Sheila. 1978. *Overcoming Math Anxiety.* New York: Norton.

Treadwell, David, and Tom Redburn. 1983. "Revolution at Work" (series). *Los Angeles Times,* Apr. 24: Part I, 12.

U.S. Bureau of Education. 1911a. *Undergraduate Work in Mathematics in Colleges of Liberal Arts and Universities.* International Commission on the Teaching of Mathematics, the American Report, Committee No. X, Bulletin No. 7. Washington, D.C.: Government Printing Office.

——. 1911b. *Examinations in Mathematics Other Than Those Set by the Teacher for His Own Classes.* International Commission on the Teaching of Mathematics, the American Report, Committee No. VII, Bulletin No. 8. Washington, D.C.: Government Printing Office.

——. 1911c. *Mathematics in the Technological Schools of Collegiate Grade in the United States.* International Commission on the Teaching of Mathematics, the American Report, Committee No. IX, Bulletin No. 9. Washington, D.C.: Government Printing Office.

U.S. Bureau of Labor Statistics. 1966.

U.S. Congress. 1984. *Computerized Manufacturing Automation: Employment, Education, and the Workplace.* OTA-CIT 235. Washington, D.C.: Government Printing Office, April.

U.S. Department of Commerce, Social and Economic Statistics Administration, Bureau of the Census. 1970. "Nativity by Age, Race and Sex, 1970 and 1960," Table 189. In *Detailed Characteristics: U.S. Summary, 1970 Census of Population*. Washington, D.C: Government Printing Office.

U.S. Department of Labor. 1973. *Outlook for Technology and Manpower in Printing and Publishing*. Bulletin 1774. Washington, D.C: Government Printing Office.

———. 1976. "Interarea Pay Comparisons—Relative Pay Levels by Industry Div., 1967–74," Table 87. In *Handbook of Labor Statistics*. Bureau of Labor Statistics Bulletin 1905, 163–76. Washington, D.C: Government Printing Office.

———. 1977. *Technological Change and Its Labor Impact in Five Industries*. Bulletin 1961. Washington, D.C.: Government Printing Office.

Valverde, Mariana. 1987. *Sex, Power and Pleasure*. Toronto: Women's Press.

Vance, Carole S. 1983. "Gender Systems, Ideology, and Sex Research." In *Powers of Desire: The Politics of Sexuality*, eds. Ann Snitow, Christine Stansell, and Sharon Thompson, 371–84. New York: Monthly Review Press.

——— ed. 1984. *Pleasure and Danger: Exploring Female Sexuality*. Boston: Routledge & Kegan Paul.

Vanski, Jean E. 1984. "How Labor Market Analysis Fails the Science and Technology Policy Analyst." Paper presented at the annual meetings of American Association for the Advancement of Science, New York, May.

Walker, Alice. 1982. *The Color Purple*. New York: Harcourt Brace Jovanovich.

Weber, Max. 1968. *Economy and Society: An Outline of Interpretive Sociology*. Trans. Ephraim Fischoff et al.; eds. Guenther Roth and Claus Wittich. New York: Bedminster.

Weinbaum, Batya, and Amy Bridges. 1976. "The Other Side of the Paycheck: Monopoly Capital and the Structure of Consumption." *Monthly Review* 28: 88–103.

Weiss, Robert S., Edwin Harwood, and David Riesman. 1971. "Work and Automation: Problems and Prospects." In *Contemporary Social Problems*, eds. R. K. Merton and R. Nisbet. New York: Harcourt, Brace, Jovanovich.

Weizenbaum, Joseph. 1976. *Computer Power and Human Reason: From Judgement to Calculation*. San Francisco: W. H. Freeman.

Whalley, Peter. 1985. "Deskilling Engineers? The Labor Process, Labor Markets, and Labor Segmentation." *Social Problems* 32(2): 117–32.

Wickenden, William E. 1930–1934. *Report of the Investigation of Engineering Education, 1923–1929, Accompanied by Supplemental Report on Technical Institutes*, 2 vols. Pittsburgh: Society for the Promotion of Engineering Education.

Williams, Ron. 1980/1981. "Where Are We Going?" *Engineering Education* 7 (Dec. 1980): 196; (Jan. 1981): 262.

Winner, Langdon. 1977. *Autonomous Technology: Technics-out-of-Control as a Theme in Political Thought*. Cambridge: MIT Press.

———. 1980. "Do Artifacts Have Politics?" *Daedalus* (Winter): 121–36.

Woloch, Nancy. 1984. *Women and the American Experience*. New York: Alfred A. Knopf.

Woodward, Joan. 1965. *Industrial Organization*. New York: Oxford University Press.

Woolgar, Steve, and Dorothy Pawluch. 1985a. "Ontological Gerry-mandering: The Anatomy of Social Problems Explanations." *Social Problems* 32: 214–27.

——. 1985b. "How Shall We Move Beyond Constructivism?" *Social Problems* 32: 159–62.

Zald, Mayer, and Feather Davis Hair. 1972. "The Social Control of General Hospitals." In *Organization Research on Health Institutions*, ed. Basil S. Georgopoulis, 51–81. Ann Arbor, Mich.: Institute for Social Research.

ABOUT THE AUTHOR

Sally Hacker (1936-1988) was Professor of Sociology at Oregon State University at the time of her death. Long active in the National Organization for Women, she was the author of numerous articles on gender and technology and the book *Pleasure, Power, and Technology* (1989).

ABOUT THE EDITORS

Dorothy E. Smith is Professor of Sociology at the Ontario Institute for Studies in Education. Susan M. Turner is a doctoral candidate in the Department of Sociology in Education at the Ontario Institute for Studies in Education.

Index